lonely planet
NEW
ZEALAND
I0796862
Brett Atkinson, Peter Dragicevich, Elen Turner,
Jacqui Gibson, Craig McLachlan, Tommy de Silva,
Roxanne de Bruyn, Nicole Mudgway

Meet our writers

Brett Atkinson

@travelwriternz

From his Auckland home, Brett is always keen to escape the city and explore the South Island. Highlights include expedition cruising around remote Fiordland, tackling alpine walks in Aoraki/Mt Cook National Park, and enjoying what's new and exciting in ever-evolving Christchurch.

Peter Dragicevich

@peterdragnz

Peter is a New Zealand–based travel writer who has co-authored dozens of Lonely Planet titles and whose work regularly appears in newspapers and magazines.

Elen Turner

@eleninthewilderness

Elen Turner is a writer and editor who grew up in Northland and studied in Dunedin but is now very happy to call Nelson home.

Jacqui Gibson

@jacquigibson_

Based in Wellington, freelancer Jacqui Gibson loves the capital's wild weather, creative food and drink culture and closeness to Kāpiti and Wairarapa.

Picton (3-4hrs)
WELLINGTON
Wellington 142
Martinborough
Nelson & Marlboroug 160
Nelson
Picton
Blenheim
Cape Palliser
Westport
Murchison
St Arnaud
Punakaiki
Reefton
Greymouth
Kaikōura
Tasman Sea
Hokitika
Arthur's Pass
Westland Tai Poutini National Park
Franz Josef Glacier
Pegasus Bay
Fox Glacier
Christchurch
Queenstown (5hrs)
Bunks Peninsula
Lake Tekapo
Haast
Akaroa
Lake Tekapo
Lake Pukaki
Ashburton
Mt Aspiring National Park
Central South Island 176
Timaru
Milford Sound
Lake Wānaka
Milford Sound
Wānaka
Waimate
Ōamaru
SOUTH PACIFIC OCEAN
Lake Te Anau
Queenstown
Alexandra
Te Anau
Palmerston
Lake Manapouri
Manapōuri
Fiordland National Park
Dunedin
The Deep South 208
Foveaux Strait
Bluff
Oban
Ruapuke Island
Stewart Island/ Rakiura

CHAYANIT ITTHIPONGMAETEE/SHUTTERSTOCK

Hike through alpine valleys and around volcanic lakes. Be refreshed with craft beer made with local hops. Enjoy a relaxed long lunch at an island vineyard restaurant. Negotiate quieter coastal roads to remote beaches. Experience the spectacle and energy of a Māori *haka*. Feast on seasonal produce at a farmers market. Fly high above mountains and glaciers. Kayak to forest-clad coves. Challenge yourself on the end of a bungy cord. Explore protected bird and wildlife sanctuaries.

This is New Zealand.

TURN THE PAGE AND START PLANNING YOUR NEXT BEST TRIP →

0 200 km
0 100 miles
Cape Reinga
North Cape
Bay of Islands
Kaitāia
Kerikeri
Russell
Hen & Chicken Islands
SOUTH PACIFIC OCEAN
Opononi
Whangārei
Dargaville
Northland 62
Wellsford
Great Barrier Island
Kaipara Harbour
Hauraki Gulf
Coromandel Town
Whitianga
Auckland Region 38
Auckland
Thames
Christchurch (1hr)
Wellington (¾hr)
Tasman Sea
Huntly
Raglan
Hamilton
Mt Maunganui
Tauranga
Bay of Plenty
Whakatāne
Hicks Bay
Waitomo Caves
Rotorua
Ōpōtiki
Central North Island 84
Taupō
Lake Taupō
Napier (2hrs)
Gisborne
New Plymouth
Whanganui National Park
Tongariro National Park
Wairoa
Stratford
Ōpunake
Hāwera
Napier
Hawke Bay
Lower North Island 122
Hastings
Whanganui
Waipawa
Palmerston North
Marlborough Sounds
Abel Tasman National Park

Craig McLachlan

@yuricraig

Queenstowner Craig loves nothing more than opening the bedroom curtains each morning for views out over Lake Wakatipu and the Remarkables. A rebel at heart, he created his own job description of 'freelance anything' and has been writing guidebooks for Lonely Planet for 25 years.

Tommy de Silva

Tommy's favourite part about exploring Te Tai Tokerau (Northland) is visiting significant historical sites, including Ranghihoua where his earliest Pākehā ancestors in Aotearoa first lived. But as a Māori, he can also bring an indigenous POV to this book.

Roxanne de Bruyn

@faraway_worlds

Originally from South Africa, Roxanne has lived in New Zealand for over 20 years. She has travelled extensively through Europe, the Middle East and the South Pacific. As Roxanne is based in a relatively remote country, she tends to travel for longer periods of time and enjoys travelling slowly whenever possible. Sampling the local food and wine is also a priority for any trip!

Nicole Mudgway

@travelwithsmudge

Nicole loves to cycle the Bridge Pa vineyards in summer. She enjoys not just the wine but the live music, platters and exercise too. The flat roads and well-spaced wineries mean each stop feels especially deserved!

Contents

TRABANTOS/SHUTTERSTOCK

Cable car (p158), Wellington

NZ'S MĀORI POPULATION

In 2024, NZ's Māori population was estimated at 914,400, representing 17% of the country's population.

Regions with the highest percentage of Māori include Tairāwhiti Gisborne (51%), Northland (34%) and the Bay of Plenty (28%).

EXPERIENCING **MĀORI CULTURE**

Informing the increasingly confident heart of New Zealand art, music, sport and government, New Zealand's indigenous Māori culture is both accessible and engaging throughout the country. Watch a performance of *waiata* (traditional songs), enjoy the energetic *haka* (war challenge) or celebrate with a *hāngī* (food cooked underground). Big-city and regional museums and galleries showcase historical and cultural *taonga* (treasures), but this is also a vibrant and contemporary living culture.

→ THE THRILL OF THE ALL BLACKS' HAKA

New Zealand's national rugby team alternates between performing the traditional Ka Mate *haka* and its own Kapa o Pango.

CHRIS HYDE/GETTY IMAGES

Left Māori warriors commemorate Waitangi Day
Right All Blacks perform the *haka*
Below Ngā Wai Hono i te Pō wears a *moko kauae*

LEARNING TE REO MĀORI

Scotty Morrison's bestselling book series *Māori Made Easy* provides an entertaining way to learn the basics of the Māori language (maorilanguage.net).

RIGHT: PHIL WALTER/GETTY IMAGES

↑ MOKO (MĀORI TATTOO)

High-profile wearers of the *moko kauae* (women's chin tattoo) include Ngā Wai Hono i te Pō, New Zealand's new Māori queen crowned in 2024.

Best Māori Cultural Experiences

- **Explore Auckland's Māori history atop its *maunga* (ancestral mountains).** (p49)
- **Learn about ancient Māori history at Hokianga's Manea: The Footprints of Kupe.** (p69)
- **Delve into Aotearoa's shared Māori and colonial history in Waitangi.** (p68)
- **Paddle around Wellington harbour in a traditional Māori *waka* with local *iwi*.** (p108)
- **Rise before dawn for a spiritual experience atop the sacred summit of Mt Hikurangi.** (p133)

EXCELLENCE IN FOOD & WINE

Eating and drinking well is an undoubted highlight of travelling in New Zealand, and chefs, winemakers and artisan producers throughout the country all harness excellent local and seasonal ingredients. *Kai moana* (seafood) befits New Zealand's southern Pacific status as an island nation, vineyards often team with superb on-site restaurants, and local farmers markets make it easy for travellers to self-cater and maximise their on-the-road budget.

→ THINK LOCAL, EAT SEASONAL

Seek out Central Otago stone fruit and cherries from December to March, and Northland mandarins and oranges from May to September.

RYBARMAREKK/SHUTTERSTOCK

Left Vineyard cheese platter
Right Fresh apricots from Central Otago
Below White wine, Marlborough region (p166)

SAVING MONEY WHEN DINING OUT

Based in Queenstown, but operating globally, First Table (firsttable.co.nz) offers discounts of 50% for restaurant meals all around New Zealand.

RIGHT: NCHANT/GETTY IMAGES

↑ ICONIC NEW ZEALAND WINES

Deserved icons of NZ's winemaking scene include Kumeu River's Maté's Vineyard Chardonnay and the Ned Pinot Noir from Marlborough's Marisco Vineyards.

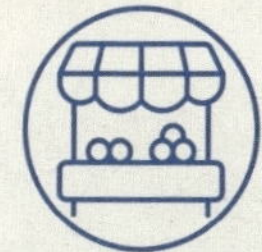

Best Food & Wine Experiences

- **Journey to Waiheke Island to experience Auckland's relaxed vineyard restaurants.** (p44)
- **Stock up on summer surprises and seasonal market bounty in Hawke's Bay.** (p126)
- **Embark on a foodie road trip along Nelson-Tasman's flavour-packed Great Taste Trail.** (p170)
- **Discover there's more to the Marlborough region than world-beating sauvignon blanc.** (p166)
- **Explore the culinary renewal of post-earthquake Christchurch.** (p192)

ACTIVE ADVENTURES

The southern hemisphere's adventure sports capital of Queenstown is a fine place to start – bungy jumping was invented here after all – but it's also easy to get an action sports buzz on in Auckland, Taupō and Rotorua.

Beyond the extreme rush of jetboating, skydiving and canyon swings, kayaking, white-water rafting and canoeing are all (usually...) more gentle alternatives to teaming Aotearoa's distinct scenery with action and adventure.

→ NZ'S BUNGY PIONEERS

Opened in 1998, and still going strong, Queenstown's Kawarau Bridge is the site of the world's first commercial bungy operation.

BENNG/SHUTTERSTOCK

Left Jetboating, Queenstown
Right Bungy jumping from Kawarau Bridge (p234)
Below Sea kayaks, Abel Tasman National Park (p168)

DOLLAR-SAVING THRILLS

When booking adventure activities, especially at Waitomo and Queenstown, check for online booking discounts or combo deals incorporating several different experiences.

RIGHT: PHOTOIMAGESNZ/GETTY IMAGES
LEFT: JUDITH LIENERT/SHUTTERSTOCK

ZIPLINE ADVENTURES

Other zipline adventures include EcoZip's experiences on Waiheke Island and near Kaikōura, and soaring high for southern Pacific views at the Christchurch Adventure Park.

Best Active Adventures

- **Tackle a zipline, abseil or negotiate subterranean rivers and waterfalls in the Waitomo Caves.** (p92)
- **Discover Auckland's urban thrills atop the Sky Tower and Harbour Bridge.** (p52)
- **Canoe down the Whanganui River on a journey combining history and remote scenery.** (p136)
- **Sea kayak amid the quieter bays of the northern part of Abel Tasman National Park.** (p168)
- **Boost your adrenaline levels by diving into Queenstown's exciting array of extreme adventures.** (p218)

HIKING & BIKING

Many New Zealanders love to get active amid their country's stellar scenery, and well-defined hiking and biking trails also make it easy for travellers to experience the best of Aotearoa. Convenient trailhead transport, comprehensive online planning tools and a surprising range of accommodation all maximise the enjoyment of multiday trails, while shorter experiences mean you can be back in town for a great meal at the end of the day.

Ben Lomond

Stellar lake and mountain views

Completing the considerable challenge of walking up Ben Lomond (1748m), looming high above Queenstown, is compensated by superb 360-degree views of Lake Whakatipu. Once you've completed your descent, celebrate with a well-earned treat from the nearby Bespoke Kitchen cafe.

1 day (11km)

▸ p214

Routeburn Track

Just maybe NZ's greatest hike

A contender for the title of 'NZ's best multiday hike' (up there with the Milford Track), the Routeburn begins at Lake Whakatipu's northern end near a spot called Paradise, and continues through equally idyllic landscapes to Mt Aspiring National Park.

3–4 days (33km)

▸ p234

Ōhakune Old Coach Road

Mountain biking through history

One of the country's best half-day rides crosses the historic Hapuawhenua and Taonui viaducts, and also traverses ancient forests that survived the volcanic super-eruption around 1800 years ago that formed Lake Taupō (apparently an event heard around the world).

½ day (15km)

▶ p113

Tongariro Alpine Crossing

A Kiwi classic

Regarded as one of the finest one-day hikes on the planet, this outdoor adventure takes in a diverse alpine landscape of steaming volcanic vents and hot springs, lunar-like terrain and superb views of the iridescent Emerald Lakes.

1 day (19.4km)

▶ p114

West Coast Wilderness Trail

Family-friendly adventure

This four-day cycling adventure incorporating bush tram lines, alpine lakes and a rugged coastline can also be broken down into easily achievable one-day rides. From the coastal town of Greymouth, it ends at the historic gold-mining village of Ross.

4 days (132km)

▶ p202

Otago Central Rail Trail

History and scenery

Beautiful big-sky landscapes and the heritage streetscapes of former gold-mining towns combine on NZ's most popular and well-established cycle trail. En route there's the daily opportunity to enjoy a cold beer or a local pinot noir at historic pubs.

3–5 days (152km)

▶ p230

New Plymouth
Mt Taranaki
Tongariro National Park
Tūrangi
Kaweka Forest Park
Whanganui National Park
Napier
Hastings
Whanganui
Tasman Sea
Marlborough Sounds
Nelson
Karamea Bight
Mt Richmond Forest Park
Wellington
Blenheim
Westport
South Pacific Ocean
Arthur's Pass National Park
Christchurch
Canterbury Bight
0 200 km
0 100 miles

NATIVE BIRDS

Look out for these avian locals:

Kiwi NZ's flightless national icon

Kea The world's only alpine parrot (pictured)

Ruru Small nocturnal owl (also known as a morepork)

▶ Learn about the Birds of Aotearoa on p226

WILDLIFE **WONDERS**

It's a case of the big and the small when considering New Zealand wildlife. Sperm whales and humpbacks swing by the nutrient-rich waters of the Kaikōura Canyon from June to August (other whales are resident year-round), while delicate endemic bird life enlivens protected offshore island reserves. In between, there are plenty of other marine mammals to check out, and larger birds including the spectacular ocean-going royal albatross.

Best Wildlife Experiences

▶ **Experience marine diversity while snorkelling or diving at the Poor Knights Islands Marine Reserve.** (p80)

▶ **Commune with giant cetacean visitors and other marine mammals around Kaikōura.** (p200)

▶ **Spend the night sharing the offshore eco-sanctuary of Kāpiti Island with 1200 little spotted kiwi.** (p156)

▶ **Say kia ora to fur seals, sea lions, penguins and royal albatrosses around the Otago Peninsula.** (p232)

▶ **Explore the stellar bird life of Ulva Island's protected sanctuary.** (p224)

CRAFT-BEER COUNTRY

Independent breweries all around New Zealand craft punchy pale ales, refreshing summer-friendly lagers and interesting Kiwi takes on traditional American, Belgian and German beer styles. Definitely try beers harnessing Tasman's world-famous Riwaka, Nectaron and Nelson Sauvin hop varieties, often tinged with the distinctive flavours of citrus, cut grass or stone fruit.

BRETT ATKINSON/LONELY PLANET

↑ CLASSIC NZ BEERS

Popular beers reflecting the flavours of hops from the Tasman region include 8 Wired's Hopwired NZ IPA and Panhead's Port Road Pilsner.

LAZINGBEE/GETTY IMAGES

Best Craft-Beer Experiences

- **Try beers from around NZ at the Auckland Beer Mile's bars and taprooms.** (p61)
- **Enjoy regional beers from smaller breweries at the Canterbury Brewers Collective in Christchurch.** (p193)
- **Sample always innovative wild-fermented brews from Wellington's Garage Project.** (p151)
- **Join in the hoppy fun at Wellington's annual Beervana festival.** (p150)

★ JUMP ABOARD A BEER TOUR

Combine mountain and lake scenery with excellent food and interesting beers on a guided experience with Queenstown Beer Tours (*queenstownbeertours.co.nz*).

Above Tasting flight, 8 Wired Brewing, Matakana (p61)
Left Hops used in craft-beer brewing

BEYOND BEACHES

Up north, arcing beaches like the Karikari Peninsula's Maitai Bay contrast with the roiling surf of Ahipara, while on the South Island, the Marlborough Sounds' quiet coves and the sheltered bays of the Abel Tasman National Park attract summertime swimmers, kayakers and hikers. Freshwater lake and river destinations are also popular with travelling Kiwi families across warmer months.

STARGRASS/SHUTTERSTOCK

↑ HOT POOLS & THERMAL SPRINGS

Check out NZ Hot Pools (*nzhotpools.co.nz*) for maps and reviews of thermal springs and hot pools around the country.

ROD HILL/GETTY IMAGES

Best Water Experiences

- **Enjoy the sheltered beaches of Northland's east coast and also more rugged western alternatives.** (p66)
- **Explore beyond Coromandel Town to the remote beaches of the peninsula's far north.** (p96)
- **Relax in hot pools and cool lakes around Rotorua and Taupō.** (p106)
- **Secure beachside accommodation to recreate the classic NZ summer holiday experience.** (p110)

★ SWIMMING SAFELY

Water conditions around the Greater Auckland region, including stormwater overflows and surf reports, are monitored on Safeswim's (*safeswim.org.nz*) searchable online map.

Above Lake Tikitapu (p107)
Left River swimming, Rotorua

↘ WORLD FAMOUS IN NZ

Highest mountain Aoraki/Mt Cook (pictured; 3724m). Dubbed 'cloud piercer' by Māori.

Longest glacier The 27km-long and 4km-wide leviathan of the Tasman Glacier.

Biggest lake Lake Taupō, formed by one of history's biggest eruptions.

ALPINE VIEWS

New Zealand is a country defined by spectacular alpine landscapes, which punctuate both the North and South islands (with geothermal activity further enlivening the North Island's Central Plateau) away from the nation's coastline and rolling farmland. Volcanic peaks surge upwards in the North Island, while in the south, glaciers stretch to near the ocean, and Milford Sound/Piopiotahi rises steeply from the 300m depth of Milford Sound.

Best Alpine Experiences

- **Ascend Mt Ruapehu for a view of the mountain's crater lake.** (p113)
- **Cross the mountainous spine of the South Island on the TranzAlpine train.** (p196)
- **Explore Aoraki/Mt Cook National Park on the popular Tasman Glacier and Hooker Valley day walks.** (p184)
- **Splash out on a scenic flight high above the Fox and Franz Josef glaciers.** (p186)
- **Negotiate Milford Rd and Homer Tunnel to Milford Sound.** (p220)

JASON FRIEND PHOTOGRAPHY LTD/GETTY IMAGES

Demand for accommodation peaks after Christmas/New Year and continues throughout January. Book tours and activities in advance at lonelyplanet.com/new-zealand/activities.

Christmas Day, Boxing Day, New Year's Day and 2 January are public holidays. Cities are quiet and Kiwis head to the beach.

← Festival of Lights

New Plymouth's Pukekura Park is enlivened with music and family-friendly performances for six weeks from mid-December.

▶ New Plymouth, p130

▶ festivaloflights.nz

↖ Lupins Season

Wild lupins bloom around Central Otago and the Mackenzie Country, starting in December and continuing colourfully through to February.

DECEMBER

Average daytime max: 21°C
Days of rainfall: 9

JANUARY

New Zealand in SUMMER

FROM LEFT: MB PHOTOGRAPHY/GETTY IMAGES, JAMES SER/SHUTTERSTOCK, KERRY MARSHALL/GETTY IMAGES, BEN LEWIS/ALAMY STOCK PHOTO, CHAMELEONSEYE/SHUTTERSTOCK, BACKGROUND IMAGE: KHOROSHUNOVA OLGA/SHUTTERSTOCK

↘ Marlborough Wine & Food Festival

New Zealand's home of sauvignon blanc celebrates in mid-February with wine, craft beer and plenty of fine food.

▸ Blenheim, p166

▸ marlboroughwinefestival.com

→ Art Deco Festival

Napier's architectural style is celebrated with music, food, wine and heritage fashion across a February long weekend.

▸ Napier, p139

▸ artdecofestival.co.nz

January and February are peak months for Kiwis to enjoy hiking. Book Great Walks huts well ahead of travel (p24).

Average daytime max: 22°C
Days of rainfall: 8

FEBRUARY

Average daytime max: 23°C
Days of rainfall: 7

← Waitangi Day

Commemorating the 1840 signing of the Treaty of Waitangi, New Zealand's national day of 6 February is a public holiday.

Packing Notes

Wear a hat and apply sunscreen to protect against high summertime UV levels.

↓ Pasifika

Across a vibrant March weekend, Auckland's Pacific Island communities celebrate their shared Polynesian culture through food, music and dance.

▶ Auckland, p48

▶ aucklandnz.com/pasifika

← Marchfest

The world-beating hops of the Tasman region are showcased at this popular Nelson craft-beer festival in late March.

▶ Nelson

▶ marchfest.com

↙ Wildfoods Festival

Head to Hokitika in mid-March for this foodie extravaganza, washing down challenging treats like insect larvae with wine and beer.

▶ Hokitika

▶ wildfoods.co.nz

MARCH

Average daytime max: 22°C
Days of rainfall: 7

APRIL

New Zealand in AUTUMN

FROM LEFT: PHIL WALTER/GETTY IMAGES, CORY WOODRUFF/SHUTTERSTOCK, KAI SCHWOERER/GETTY IMAGES, MARTY MELVILLE/STRINGER/GETTY IMAGES, DAVE SIMPSON/WIREIMAGE VIA GETTY IMAGES, JANIS APELS/SHUTTERSTOCK, DIANNE MANSON/GETTY IMAGES, BACKGROUND IMAGE: PATRIKSTEDRAK/GETTY IMAGES

↓ Wairarapa Balloon Festival

At Easter, head north across the Remutaka Range from Wellington for five days of spectacular ballooning.

▶ Wairarapa

▶ nzballoons.co.nz

→ Autumn Colours

Dappled autumn colours are at their best in Central Otago and the historic streets of Arrowtown around April.

▶ Arrowtown, p218

← New Zealand International Comedy Festival

Kiwi comedians combine with international performers to bring plenty of laughs to Auckland, Wellington and regional centres in May.

▶ Mainly Auckland and Wellington

▶ comedyfestival.co.nz

MAY

Average daytime max: 19°C
Days of rainfall: 8

Average daytime max: 17°C
Days of rainfall: 9

Settled weather and lower visitor numbers (excluding Easter) make March and April an ideal time to explore New Zealand.

← Bluff Oyster & Food Festival

Bivalves galore at this shuckingly good May festival at the southern tip of the South Island.

▶ Bluff

▶ bluffoysterfest.co.nz

Packing Notes

Cooler weather makes dressing in layers important, especially when hiking in alpine regions.

Whale Watching

Migrating whales arrive to feed amid the nutrient-rich waters off Kaikōura from June to August.

▶ Kaikōura, p198

→ Matariki

Inaugurated as a public holiday in 2022, June or July's Māori New Year is celebrated nationwide with Māori art, music, culture and cosmology.

← Steampunk NZ Festival

Blending science fiction and Victoriana, Steampunk culture is celebrated in Ōamaru's historic precinct across early June's King's Birthday weekend.

▶ Ōamaru, p228

▶ steampunk.org.nz

JUNE

Average daytime max: 15°C
Days of rainfall: 10

JULY

New Zealand in WINTER

FROM LEFT: BOB HILSCHER/SHUTTERSTOCK, FIONA GOODALL/GETTY IMAGES, LOVE THE WIND/SHUTTERSTOCK, NAZAR_AB/GETTY IMAGES, MASTER1305/SHUTTERSTOCK. BACKGROUND IMAGE: JOSHUA SMALL/GETTY IMAGES

Winter Pride

During August, LGBTIQ+ diversity and inclusion is celebrated with dance parties and snow sports events in Queenstown.

▶ winterpride.co.nz

→ Wellington on a Plate

The country's best burgers and innovative fine dining also attract travelling foodies to the nation's capital in August.

▶ Wellington

▶ visawoap.com

→ Beervana

Kiwi craft-beer drinkers descend on Wellington in August for this annual hop-fuelled celebration at the city's Westpac Stadium.

▶ Wellington, p150

▶ beervana.co.nz

AUGUST

Average daytime max: 14°C
Days of rainfall: 11

Average daytime max: 14°C
Days of rainfall: 11

Book ahead for accommodation in popular snow sports locations including Queenstown, Wānaka and Ohakune, especially during July's school holidays.

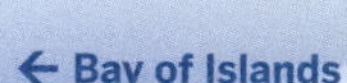

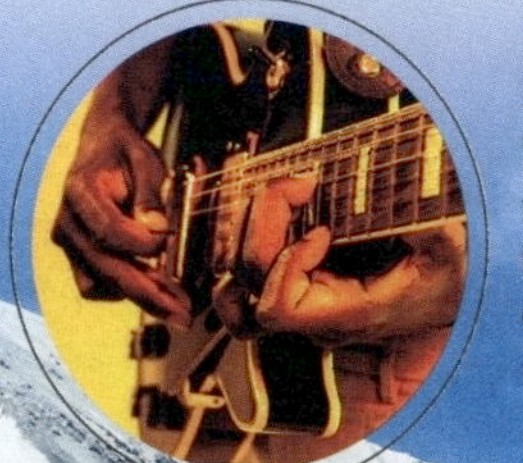

← Bay of Islands Jazz & Blues Festival

Warmer Northland winter weather is the relaxed background to this three-day mid-August festival.

▶ Russell and Paihia

▶ boimusicfestivals.com

Packing Notes

Weather can be very changeable. Be prepared for four seasons in one day.

DOC's Great Walks hiking season spans late October to April. Book ahead for popular experiences including the Kepler, Milford and Routeburn Tracks.

▶ bookings.doc.govt.nz

Spring lambs dot rolling pastures on the South Island. In Auckland, visitors can see them in centrally located Cornwall Park.

▶ Auckland region, p58

↖ Winter Games

In early September, the world's best skiers and snowboarders arrive in Queenstown for a week of high-flying extreme action.

▶ Queenstown

▶ wintergamesnz.kiwi

World of Wearable Art

Also known as WOW, this spectacle of music, theatre and wearable arts spans two weeks from late September.

▶ Wellington, p152

▶ worldofwearableart.com

SEPTEMBER

Average daytime max: 16°C
Days of rainfall: 10

OCTOBER

New Zealand in SPRING

↓ Nelson Arts Festival

Plenty of indoor distractions – including comedy, cabaret, music and dance – for two weeks in October.

▸ Nelson

▸ nelsonartsfestival.nz

↗ Crayfest Kaikōura

In November, Kaikōura cafes and restaurants team New Zealand's favourite crustacean with local beer and wine. Biennial in odd-numbered years.

▸ Kaikōura

▸ facebook.com/crayfestkaikoura

NOVEMBER

Average daytime max: 17°C
Days of rainfall: 9

Average daytime max: 19°C
Days of rainfall: 11

The first two weeks of October are usually school holidays in New Zealand. Book accommodation and activities in advance.

← Ōamaru Victorian Heritage Celebrations

Ōamaru's white-stone heritage precinct hosts November's week-long celebration of the Victorian era. Penny farthing races are a highlight.

▸ Ōamaru

▸ vhc.co.nz

Packing Notes

A spring rain shower is never far away. Pack a lightweight waterproof jacket.

NORTHERN WANDER
Trip Builder

TAKE YOUR PICK OF MUST-SEES AND HIDDEN GEMS

After big-city harbourside adventures around Auckland, head north to explore beaches and Māori and colonial history, or south to the caves and surf of the Waikato region. Gold-mining history and a spectacular coastline are highlights of the Coromandel Peninsula.

Trip Notes

Hub towns Auckland, Paihia, Hamilton

How long Allow around 2 weeks

Getting around Hire a car for off-the-beaten-track exploring at your own pace. Visiting Waiheke Island by passenger ferry and public bus is a recommended option for a short visit.

Tips During summer, leave your vehicle at the car park at the entrance to Hahei, and catch the shuttle bus to Cathedral Cove.

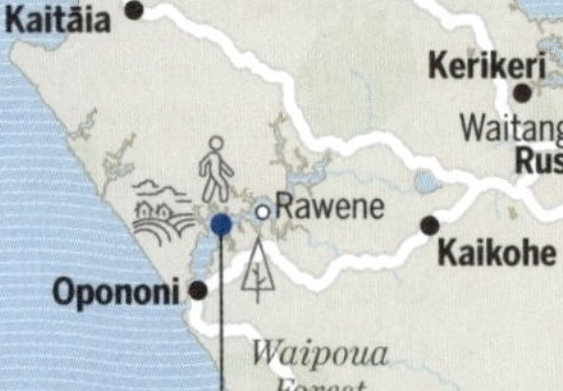

Hokianga Harbour
Browse heritage buildings in sleepy Rawene and stroll on forest boardwalks to Tāne Mahuta, a spiritually and culturally important kauri tree in the Waipoua Forest.
1hr from Paihia

Auckland
Experience the multicultural energy of this harbourside city, combine walking and wine tasting near West Coast surf beaches, and explore Auckland's volcanic *maunga* (ancestral mountains).

Waitomo Caves
Challenge yourself on a subterranean abseiling, ziplining or black-water rafting adventure, or ride a boat leisurely past glowworms on an underground river.
1hr from Hamilton

Bay of Islands

Explore Aotearoa's shared multicultural history at Waitangi, wander the quaint colonial streetscape of Russell, or tackle the challenging but spectacular Cape Brett Walkway.

Russell: 30min from Paihia

Waiheke Island

Journey to Auckland's island of wine for relaxed vineyard restaurants or take in Hauraki Gulf views while ziplining or negotiating clifftop walking trails.

45min from Auckland

Coromandel Town

Stroll through gold-mining history, ride the ziplines and bush railway at Driving Creek, and explore the remote isolation and beaches of Coromandel Peninsula's northern tip.

2½hr from Auckland

Hahei

Wander along the gently rolling coastal trail to Cathedral Cove, kayak the region's stellar coastline, and dig your own natural spa pool at Hot Water Beach.

2½hr from Auckland

Raglan

Combine local arts and crafts with good eating and drinking at New Zealand's favourite surf town. Savvy locals also recommend the area's kayaking and paddle boarding.

40min from Hamilton

NORTH ISLAND EXPLORER
Trip Builder

TAKE YOUR PICK OF MUST-SEES AND HIDDEN GEMS

Mountain landscapes formed by a volcanic past, present and future provide the spectacular background for hiking, biking and canoeing. Explore Māori culture in Rotorua, navigate East Cape to sunny Gisborne and Hawke's Bay, or enjoy Wellington's culinary and cultural highlights.

Trip Notes

Hub towns Taupō, Napier, Gisborne, Wellington

How long Allow 2 to 3 weeks

Getting around Having a rental car or camper van is definitely needed for on-the-road flexibility. For winter travel to Mt Ruapehu's ski fields, tyre chains are essential.

Tips Shuttle operators in National Park village offer trailhead transport and vehicle relocation services for completing the Tongariro Alpine Crossing.

Rotorua
Relax in hot pools warmed by geothermal activity, feast on a *hāngī*, and learn about traditional Māori arts and culture around Rotorua.
1hr from Taupō

Whanganui Journey
Embark on a classic New Zealand outdoor adventure by canoeing or kayaking down the scenic, and historically and culturally important, Whanganui River.
2hr from Taupō

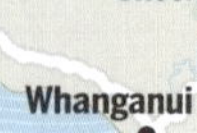

Wellington
Combine craft beer, exciting and spectacular coastal hikes, and learning about some of cinema's biggest movies in New Zealand's cool capital city.

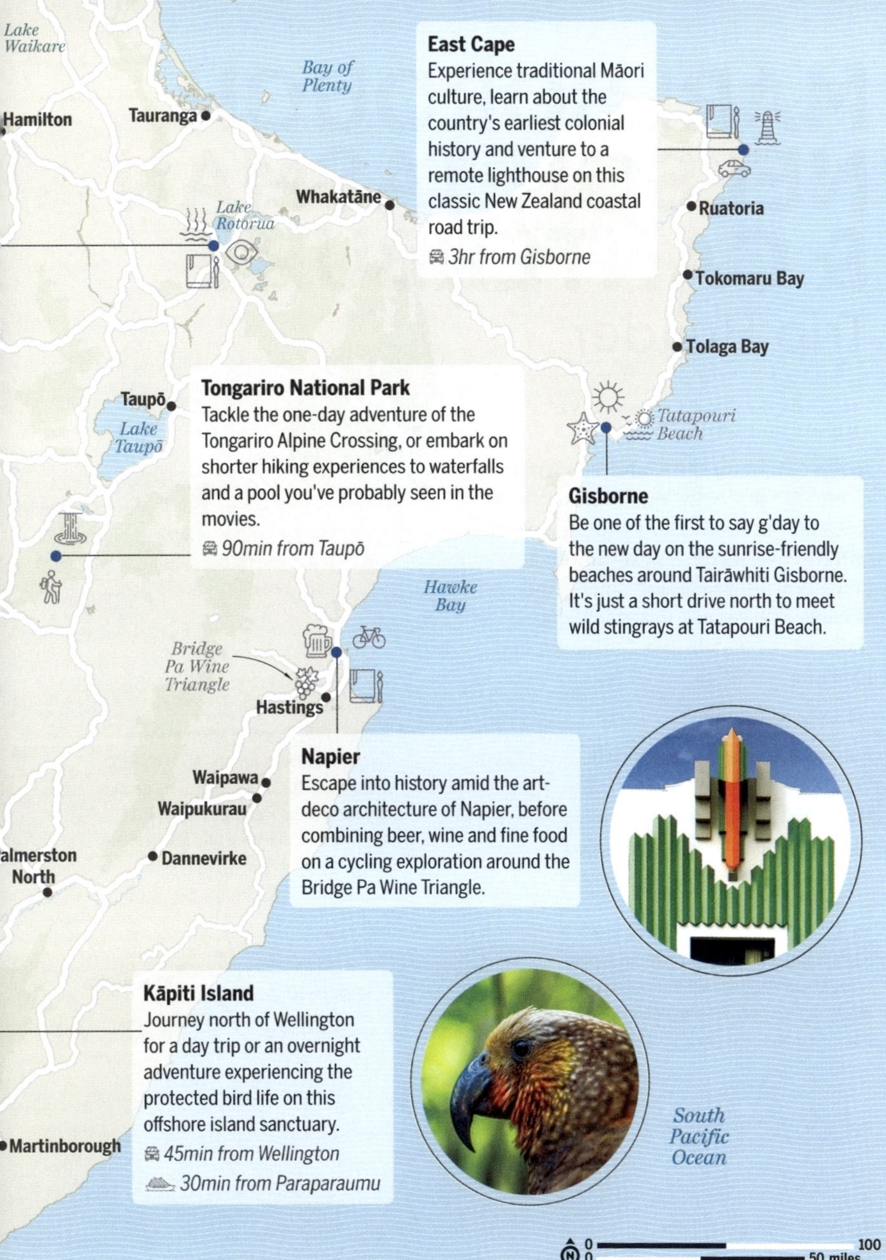

Lake Waikare
Bay of Plenty
Hamilton
Tauranga
Whakatāne
Lake Rotorua
East Cape
Experience traditional Māori culture, learn about the country's earliest colonial history and venture to a remote lighthouse on this classic New Zealand coastal road trip.
3hr from Gisborne
Ruatoria
Tokomaru Bay
Tolaga Bay
Taupō
Lake Taupō
Tongariro National Park
Tackle the one-day adventure of the Tongariro Alpine Crossing, or embark on shorter hiking experiences to waterfalls and a pool you've probably seen in the movies.
90min from Taupō
Tatapouri Beach
Gisborne
Be one of the first to say g'day to the new day on the sunrise-friendly beaches around Tairāwhiti Gisborne. It's just a short drive north to meet wild stingrays at Tatapouri Beach.
Hawke Bay
Bridge Pa Wine Triangle
Hastings
Napier
Escape into history amid the art-deco architecture of Napier, before combining beer, wine and fine food on a cycling exploration around the Bridge Pa Wine Triangle.
Waipawa
Waipukurau
almerston North
Dannevirke
Kāpiti Island
Journey north of Wellington for a day trip or an overnight adventure experiencing the protected bird life on this offshore island sanctuary.
45min from Wellington
30min from Paraparaumu
Martinborough
South Pacific Ocean
0
100 km
0
50 miles
N

MARLBOROUGH, NELSON-TASMAN & CANTERBURY
Trip Builder

TAKE YOUR PICK OF MUST-SEES AND HIDDEN GEMS

Celebrate Christchurch's urban re-emergence, enjoy one of New Zealand's best food and wine regions, and discover diverse destinations for viewing wildlife big and small. And because you're in Aotearoa, of course there are opportunities for hiking and kayaking.

Trip Notes

Hub towns Blenheim, Christchurch, Nelson, Hokitika

How long Allow around 2 weeks

Getting around A good way to discover the Marlborough wine region is on a self-guided e-bike tour.

Tips Booking well ahead for the inter-island ferry linking Wellington to Picton is recommended for school-holiday and public-holiday periods. At other times, booking a few days prior is sufficient.

FROM LEFT: TUPUNGATO/SHUTTERSTOCK, KONRAD MOSTERT/SHUTTERSTOCK

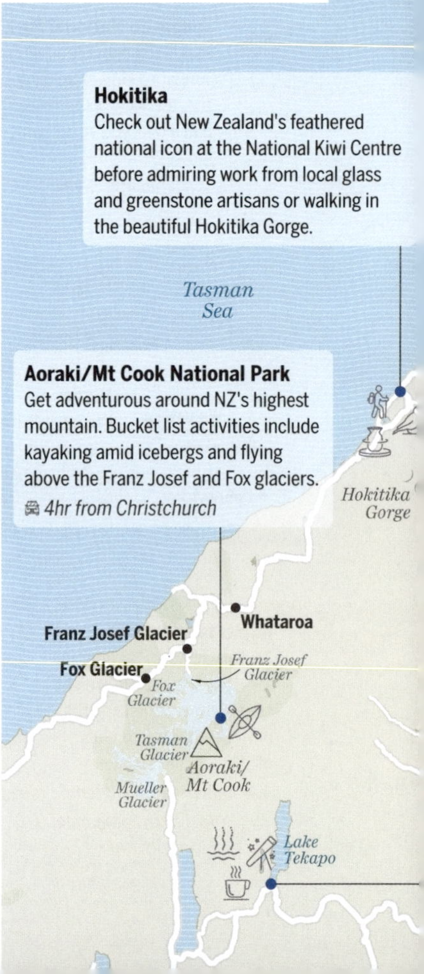

Hokitika
Check out New Zealand's feathered national icon at the National Kiwi Centre before admiring work from local glass and greenstone artisans or walking in the beautiful Hokitika Gorge.

Aoraki/Mt Cook National Park
Get adventurous around NZ's highest mountain. Bucket list activities include kayaking amid icebergs and flying above the Franz Josef and Fox glaciers.
4hr from Christchurch

Abel Tasman National Park

Hike or kayak around the coves and bays of NZ's smallest national park. You'll also hear (and see) the diverse bird life making this region home.

1hr from Nelson

Blenheim

Discover there's more to Marlborough than world-beating sauvignon blanc. Excellent restaurants abound, sometimes also offering family-friendly *pétanque* or croquet.

Arthur's Pass

Journey through this alpine village on the TranzAlpine train or use it as a base for hiking and exploring the nearby natural spectacles of Castle Hill and Cave Stream.

2hr from Christchurch *2½hr from Christchurch*

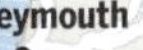

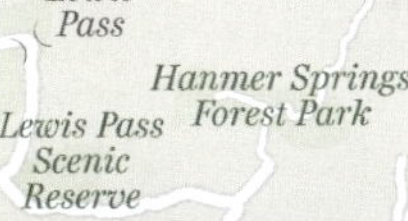

Kaikōura

Experience the natural grandeur of Kaikōura's marine mammal visitors, including leviathan humpback and sperm whales, before dining on local seafood such as ocean-fresh crayfish.

90min from Blenheim

Lake Tekapo

Combine hot-tub bathing with stargazing in the heart of the spectacular Mackenzie Country. An essential detour is coffee, cake and superb views at Mt John's Astro Cafe.

3hr from Christchurch

Christchurch

Enjoy the Garden City's post-earthquake revival by eating and drinking at the Riverside Market, Little High Eatery and along New Regent St. Don't miss Dimitri's souvlaki.

SOUTHERN HIGHLIGHTS
Trip Builder

TAKE YOUR PICK OF MUST-SEES AND HIDDEN GEMS

New Zealand's far south showcases the action sports thrills of Queenstown, heritage highlights around Ōamaru and Arrowtown, and Central Otago's brilliant food and wine scene. Outdoor adventures include NZ's favourite cycle trail and world-renowned Great Walks, while wildlife and bird-watching fans head to the Otago Peninsula and even further south.

Trip Notes

Hub towns Queenstown, Dunedin, Te Anau, Invercargill

How long Allow around 2 weeks

Getting around Exploring this diverse region is best accomplished with a rental car or camper van. The area contains some of New Zealand's most scenic Department of Conservation (DOC) campsites.

Tips DOC hut accommodation on the Milford, Routeburn and Kepler Tracks must be booked in advance during the Great Walks season from December to April.

Queenstown
Climb Ben Lomond before refuelling at the Bespoke Kitchen or enjoying a craft beer by the lake at Altitude Brewing. Exciting adrenaline-fuelled activities also abound around town.

Really Great Walks
Book ahead for experiences on New Zealand's most popular Great Walks, including the Kepler Track (pictured). Both the Milford and Routeburn tracks showcase the rugged best of Te Waipounamu (the South Island).

90min from Te Anau

Arrowtown

Wander the historic gold-rush-era streets of Arrowtown during the day before returning to some of the best bars and restaurants in the southern lakes region after dark.

30min from Queenstown

Milford Road

Spend a day negotiating the road from Te Anau to Milford Sound/Piopiotahi, stopping for forest walks, before being dwarfed by the snow-framed entrance to the Homer Tunnel.

90min from Te Anau

Ōamaru

Experience quirky steampunk culture amid Ōamaru's 19th-century white-stone historic precinct before lining up to see the nightly arrival of the town's *kororā* (little blue penguins).

90min from Dunedin

Central Otago

Savour the best of Central Otago's world-beating wines, including excellent pinot noir from the rocky soils of Bannockburn. Visit during summer for fresh cherries and stone fruit around Cromwell.

45min from Queenstown

Otago Peninsula

Journey to the peninsula's northeastern tip and the world's only mainland breeding colony of the northern royal albatross. Options to see the birds also include boat trips.

45min from Dunedin

Stewart Island/Rakiura

Travel by ferry or plane from Invercargill to Stewart Island/Rakiura, tackling the 32km Rakiura Track before venturing to Ulva Island for an enjoyably noisy symphony of bird life.

1hr from Invercargill (Bluff)

15min from Invercargill (Bluff)

7 Things to Know About NEW ZEALAND

INSIDER TIPS TO HIT THE GROUND RUNNING

1 Four Seasons in One Day

It's not just a song by Kiwi-Australian band Crowded House. New Zealand's weather can be famously fickle, so it's important to dress in layers, and always have suitable apparel for cold and rain in the country's sub-alpine and mountain areas. Courtesy of a hole in the ozone layer, New Zealand's southern hemisphere sun is harsh and strong, so cover up, wear a hat and sunglasses, and apply sunscreen.

▶ See more about weather on p18

2 Be Physically Prepared

If you're planning on hiking, be prepared with a good level of fitness. Some visitors overestimate physical abilities when venturing out in NZ's wilderness.

▶ See more about hiking safety on p244

3 Rush Hour NZ-style

In rural areas, road hazards sometimes include farmers moving cows or sheep. Slow to a crawl, or stop your vehicle altogether, and let the animals move unrestricted around the car.

▶ See more about road conditions on p243

4 Welcome to the Shaky Isles

New Zealand has around 20,000 earthquakes every year. Only 250 or so are actually felt, but significant seismic events have occurred in Christchurch (2011) and Kaikōura (2016). Adhere to local civic defence advice (civil defence.govt.nz).

Note: beaches on the North Island's east coast are sometimes affected by tsunami warnings. Many beaches have signs indicating safe inland areas to shelter.

1 KOTOFFEI/SHUTTERSTOCK, 4 NOTIONPIC/SHUTTERSTOCK, 7 FRANS LEMMENS/GETTY IMAGES

5 Don't Try to See It All

There's a misconception that New Zealand is a 'small island nation', but in surface area it's actually bigger than the United Kingdom. Roads, especially on the South Island, are often more winding than international visitors are used to, and covering the kilometres can take longer than expected. Slow down, enjoy the journey and be realistic in your travel plans.

▶ See more about getting around on p242

6 Local Lingo

Learning a few words of Kiwi vernacular will help you get by and make friends along the way.

tramping The local word for hiking or bush walking.

The Ditch The Tasman Sea separating New Zealand and Australia.

jandals Rubber flip-flops, known as 'thongs' across 'the Ditch' in Australia.

yeah/nah Non-committal way for New Zealanders to say no (or maybe).

chur bro! A way of showing appreciation.

hokey pokey Vanilla ice cream studded with crunchy chunks of butterscotch; reputedly more popular in New Zealand than chocolate ice cream.

L&P (Lemon & Paeroa) A lemon-flavoured soft drink (soda) originally made from natural springs in the Coromandel town of Paeroa. It is now mass-produced by Coca-Cola Amatil, but is still refreshing.

chilly bin A portable drinks cooler, essential at a barbecue or at the beach.

ka pai 'All good' or 'well done' in te reo Māori.

sweet as The everyday Kiwi translation of '*ka pai*'.

7 Respecting Māori Culture

Adhere to Māori protocols when visiting a *marae* (meeting house). A *karakia* (prayer) will be offered to bless the food, and you may be welcomed with a *hongi*, the Māori greeting of pressing together foreheads and noses. The *hongi* represents the mutual sharing of the breath of life.

▶ See more about etiquette on p247

Read, Listen, Watch & Follow

READ

The Bone People (Keri Hulme; 1984) Booker Prize–winning tale intertwining love, violence and Māori spirituality.

Dogside Story (Patricia Grace; 2001) Māori family life in the remote Tairāwhiti region.

A History of New Zealand in 100 Objects (Jock Phillips; 2022) Revelatory and insightful with stories exploring Aotearoa's past.

The Axeman's Carnival (Catherine Chidgey; 2022) Darkly comic satire grounded in rural NZ and tinged with magic realism.

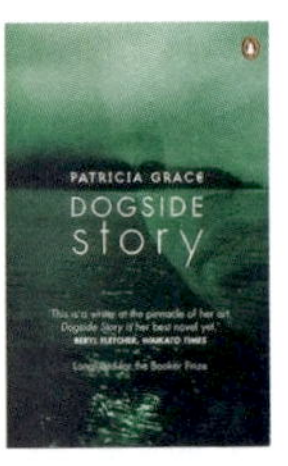

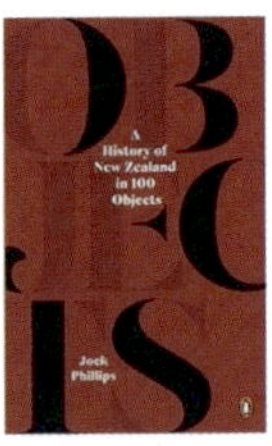

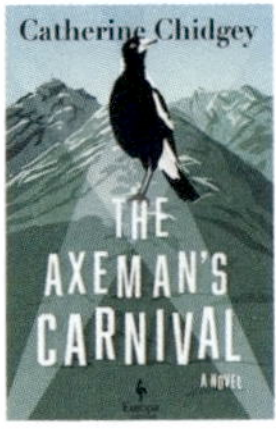

LISTEN

Expert in a Dying Field (The Beths; 2022) Pop-tastic and poignant indie tunes from Auckland rockers making big waves internationally.

Tally Ho! Flying Nun's Greatest Bits (various artists; 2011) Essential 'best of' compilation from Dunedin's seminal Flying Nun label.

Te Whare Tīwekaweka (Marlon Williams; 2025) Folk- and country-influenced songs delivered in te reo Māori by the man with the best voice in the land.

Waiata Anthems (various artists; 2019 & 2021) Top NZ musicians re-record their favourite songs in te reo Māori.

DIMITRIOS KAMBOURIS/GETTY IMAGES

Pure Heroine (Lorde; 2013) Where it all began for New Zealand's most famous 21st-century singer-songwriter.

WATCH

Whale Rider (2002; pictured top right) Magic realism, and Māori myths and spirituality on a remote east coast beach.

Boy (2010) Taika Waititi's gentle coming-of-age drama is set around the isolated East Cape.

Hunt for the Wilderpeople (2016; pictured bottom right) Taika strikes again with a warm-hearted rural comedy-drama.

Whina (2022) The story of land rights campaigner and beloved Māori matriarch Dame Whina Cooper.

Head South (2024) Coming-of-age story set amid the post-punk music scene of late 1970s Christchurch.

MARKA/ALAMY

MOVIESTORE COLLECTION LTD/ALAMY

FOLLOW

The Spinoff (thespinoff.co.nz) News, culture and opinionated podcasts.

100% PURE NEW ZEALAND

@purenewzealand Tourism New Zealand's official Instagram account.

Waiata/Anthems (@waiataanthems on YouTube) Te reo Māori versions of popular NZ songs added on a regular basis.

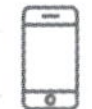

undertheradar.co.nz Music news, gigs and ticket sales.

Lazy Susan (search Facebook) Crowd-sourced recommendations on dining countrywide.

AUCKLAND REGION

ISLANDS | RESTAURANTS | ACTIVITIES

ASIATRAVEL/SHUTTERSTOCK

AUCKLAND
Trip Builder

Framed by two harbours, New Zealand's biggest city is a dynamic and multicultural gateway to a region of rugged surf beaches, urban thrills and island adventures. A sophisticated eating and drinking scene combines surprising wine regions and impressive harbourside dining.

Relax in stylish cafes, restaurants and bars along **Ponsonby Road** (p60)
10min from Auckland's Ferry Building

Negotiate clifftop walking trails high above **West Coast surf beaches** (p50)
1hr from Auckland's Ferry Building

Explore **Auckland's volcanic field** to discover the region's Māori history (p58)
15-30min from Auckland's Ferry Building

Ore
Silverd
Waimauku
Huapai
Kumeū
Muriwai Beach
Waitākere
Waitema
Harbou
Te Henga (Bethells Beach)
Piha
Waitākere Ranges Regional Park
Huia
Manukau Harbour

0 — 20 km
0 — 10 miles

Great Barrier Island (see Inset) (40km)

Inset

Experience pristine southern hemisphere night skies on **Great Barrier Island** (p54)
30min from Auckland Airport

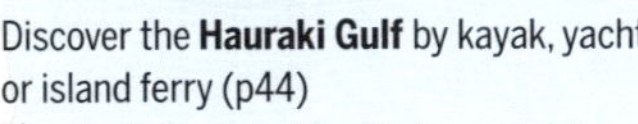

Discover the **Hauraki Gulf** by kayak, yacht or island ferry (p44)
45min from Auckland's Ferry Building

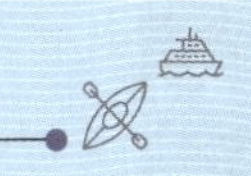

Ascend the **Sky Tower** for isthmus views and action-packed thrills (p52)
10min from Auckland's Ferry Building

Motutapu Island

Rangitoto Island

Combine relaxed dining and maritime history on Auckland's **harbourfront** (p56)
5min from Auckland's Ferry Building

Learn about New Zealand art at the **Auckland Art Gallery** (p61)
15min from Auckland's Ferry Building

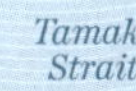

Maraetai

Enjoy the beaches, vineyards and restaurants of **Waiheke Island** (p44)
45min from Auckland's Ferry Building

Whitford

Clevedon

Be immersed in cultural and culinary diversity along **Karangahape Road** (p49)
15min from Auckland's Ferry Building

FROM LEFT: YOSENANG/SHUTTERSTOCK, CHAMELEONSEYE/SHUTTERSTOCK, DENIZUNLUSU/GETTY IMAGES, NATALIACATALINA.COM/SHUTTERSTOCK

Practicalities

CHAMELEONSEYE/SHUTTERSTOCK

ARRIVING

Auckland Airport is 21km south of the city centre, with adjacent international and domestic terminals a 10-minute walk from each other. SkyDrive is a direct bus service between the airport and city centre (adult/child $20/9). SuperShuttle provides shared minibus transfers (price varies depending on group size). Auckland Transport's Airport Link service, combining trains and buses, is the public-transport option. Taxis and ride-share services to the central city cost $60 to $100 depending on traffic.

HOW MUCH FOR A

Coffee
$5

Food truck meal
$15

Craft-beer pint
$13

WHEN TO GO

DEC–FEB
Warm weather and summer music festivals. Much is closed over Christmas/New Year.

MAR–MAY
Starts hot and gradually cools. March's Pasifika festival is a highlight.

JUN–AUG
Winter is cool and often wet but rarely freezing.

SEP–NOV
Changeable spring weather. Wrap up for boat trips and West Coast beaches.

GETTING AROUND

Bus Auckland Transport's Link bus network (incorporating the CityLink, InnerLink, OuterLink and TāmakiLink services) take in most of the city's key sights. Pay with your contactless card or smartphone, or purchase a prepaid AT HOP smart card for up to 25% off standard bus fares. Visit at.govt.nz for information.

Ferry Fullers360 (fullers.co.nz) runs regular passenger services to Waiheke and other Hauraki Gulf islands, and heads across the Waitematā Harbour to Devonport. Sealink (sealink.co.nz) operates vehicular ferries to Waiheke and Aotea/Great Barrier Island. Explore (exploregroup.co.nz) covers some of the smaller islands.

Car It's worth renting a car to explore the beaches, regional parks and vineyards at the city's rural fringes, and to make the most of a stay on Waiheke and Aotea islands.

EATING & DRINKING

Brunch Ease into the day with a flat white coffee, and wild mushrooms and burnt baba ganoush on sourdough at Chur Bae.

Global flavours Auckland's diverse multicultural future is revealed along raffish Karangahape Rd.

Beer Try craft brews with NZ hops along the Auckland Beer Mile as it passes through the central suburbs of Mt Eden, Kingsland and Morningside.

Vineyards Waiheke Island, West Auckland and Matakana all offer essential expressions of the region's coastal terroir.

Must-try dish

Waiheke Island's Te Matuku oysters (p47)

Best one-stop dining destination

The brick-lined laneways of Ponsonby Central (p60)

TOP: MOAIMAGE/GETTY IMAGES BOTTOM: BRETT ATKINSON/LONELY PLANET

CONNECT & FIND YOUR WAY

Wi-fi All Auckland public libraries offer free wi-fi hotspots, conveniently also available outside of opening hours. For on-the-go access, purchase a SIM and travel plan from One NZ or Spark. Both have branches in the arrivals hall of Auckland Airport and around the city.

Navigation Google Maps is well-established. Most Aucklanders will happily offer directions.

WHERE TO STAY

Book accommodation well ahead if a big concert or sports event is planned.

Area	Pros/Cons
City Centre	Good shopping and eating. Well located for Waiheke ferries and buses. Mainly hotels. Lacks charm.
Ponsonby	Bars, cafes, restaurants and shopping. Airbnbs, good hostels. Limited parking.
Parnell & Newmarket	B&Bs, smaller hotels. Good shopping and eating. Near the museum; short bus ride to city centre.
Mt Eden	Good boutique B&Bs, heritage village ambience. Convenient for Maungakiekie/One Tree Hill and Maungawhau/Mt Eden.
Devonport	Historic, quiet neighbourhood linked to downtown by ferry. Good restaurants and heritage B&Bs. Road access can be slow.
Waiheke Island	Holiday rentals, Airbnbs. Good restaurants and vineyards. Summer gets busy.

AUCKLAND'S NIGHT MARKETS

Eating at one of Auckland's eight night markets (aucklandnightmarkets.co.nz) is a good way to dine cheaply on a wide variety of cuisine.

MONEY

Free entertainment From January to April, Auckland Council offers free concerts (musicinparks.co.nz) and free outdoor film screenings (moviesinparks.co.nz).

01 Gourmet WAIHEKE

WINE | FOOD | OUTDOORS

With its winemakers, chefs and craft brewers all inspired by Waiheke's relaxed ambience and sunny microclimate, the Hauraki Gulf's most popular island is an essential destination for travelling foodies. A longer flavour-packed sojourn of a few days is definitely recommended.

NEVILLE MARRINER/ALAMY STOCK PHOTO

How to

Getting here Catch the passenger ferry in downtown or board the car ferry at Half Moon Bay.

When to go Try and visit midweek, and book ahead for accommodation on weekends and during school holidays.

Don't rush back to the mainland Waiheke's beachside villas, apartments and retro cottages are all options for an extended stay (staywaiheke.com).

Get on the bus The 50 bus route conveniently links most of Waiheke's tastiest destinations.

ANASTASIARAS/GETTY IMAGES

Southern Europe or the Southern Hemisphere?

Enlivened by a Mediterranean microclimate, Waiheke's vineyards combine a relaxed New Zealand ambience with some surprising touches from sun-blessed European destinations. **Casita Miro** teams its own albariño with Spanish tapas and a Gaudí-inspired garden, while **Poderi Crisci** channels a distinctly southern hemisphere version of Sicily.

Ascend the long tree-lined entrance to **Tantalus Estate's** elegant tasting room in Onetangi for excellent Bordeaux-style red wines, or pick up a rigger of locally brewed craft beer downstairs in **Alibi Brewing's** brick-lined taproom. Despite the name and rock'n'roll vibe, **Soho Family Vineyard** has strong Croatian connections. Wood-fired

KRUG_100/SHUTTERSTOCK

Island Zipline Thrills

Soar above vineyards with views of downtown Auckland on **EcoZip Adventures' ziplines** (ecozipadventures.co.nz). The popular attraction is a short drive from the vineyards and restaurants of Onetangi, and experiences conclude with a bush walk through regenerating native forest. Packages include transport from Matiatia Wharf's ferry terminal.

Above left Tantalus Estate restaurant
Above Vineyards, Waiheke Island
Left Harbour, Waiheke Island

pizza and top-notch wines are an ideal Mediterranean-style combination at **Man O' War's** secluded bay-front tasting room. Add in a swim off the wharf or a game of beach cricket for a distinctly Kiwi summertime vibe.

Beachfront Dining

Onetangi is Waiheke's best swimming beach, and a trio of waterfront dining and drinking establishments means you need never leave.

Named after the first three digits of Waiheke phone numbers, **Three Seven Two** proudly showcases ingredients from the Auckland region and around New Zealand, with seasonal menus often including local oysters, creamed *paua* (abalone), sustainable line-caught fish, and farmhouse cheeses from prime North Island dairy country. The summer-ready terrace and tropical back garden are ideal for warmer months, and the wine list is a handy primer to the best of the island.

A couple of doors down, on the corner, is **Ki Māha's** (the name broadly translates

Waiheke's Best Beaches

Oneroa Only a 25-minute walk from the ferry (or a short hop by bus), Oneroa is the main 'town' beach, with plenty of good shops and cafes nearby.

Little Oneroa A sheltered scoop with a playground and an excellent food truck.

Palm Beach This pretty horseshoe bay is a real locals' favourite. Discreetly tucked beyond some rocks at its western end is Little Palm Beach, the island's main nudist area.

Onetangi A long stretch of sand at the centre of the island, Onetangi's exposed position makes it the best beach for bodysurfing and boogie-boarding.

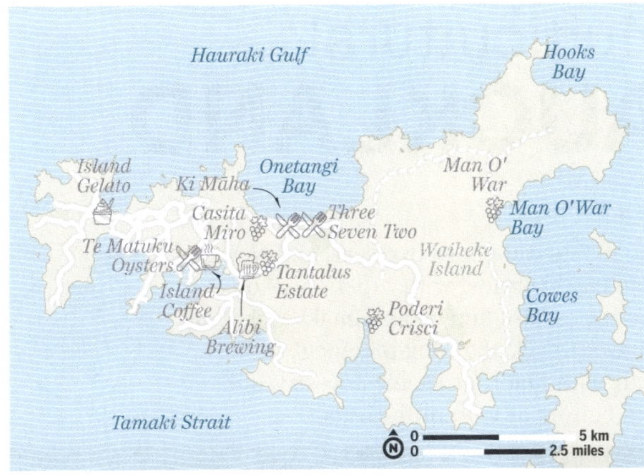

Left Wine tasting, Casita Miro (p45)
Below Te Matuku Oysters

from Māori as 'towards abundance'), where the restaurant's own wines and craft beers partner with Mediterranean-influenced plates of oysters, octopus, scallops and homemade pasta.

The most relaxed option on this strip is **Charlie's**, a longstanding pub with a sunny front deck and a kitchen kicking off with breakfast and staying open right through the day.

Seek Out Local Treats

You'll find Waiheke's treasured **Te Matuku oysters**, farmed within the sheltered waters of the Te Matuku Marine Reserve, on menus all over the island and in many of the country's best restaurants. Try them with a splash of lemon juice and Tabasco sauce.

Tucked away behind the shops in Ostend, **Island Coffee** serves brews from its house-roasted beans alongside homestyle baking from Little Tart Bakery – the cinnamon brioches are especially good.

Waiheke's most refreshing summertime treats are at the Oneroa home base of **Island Gelato Company**, an Auckland mini-chain serving award-winning gelato and sorbet.

02 Multicultural AUCKLAND

CULTURE | FOOD | FESTIVALS

Around 40% of Aucklanders were born overseas, and New Zealand's most cosmopolitan city is packed with experiences uncovering the diversity of the region also known as Tāmaki Makaurau. Go off the beaten track in flavour-packed dining precincts, explore contemporary art from locals with Māori or Pacific ancestry, and discover a world of food and culture at vibrant festivals.

PAUL KENNEDY/ALAMY STOCK PHOTO

How to

Getting here Local buses reach Auckland's multicultural inner suburbs, or it's a quick journey using ride-share services.

When to go Annual festivals include the Lantern Festival (celebrating Lunar New Year; January or February), Pasifika (March), Polyfest (March or April) and Diwali (October or November).

The world comes to town CultureFest (late March or early April) showcases the food, music and dance of more than 70 nationalities that call Auckland home.

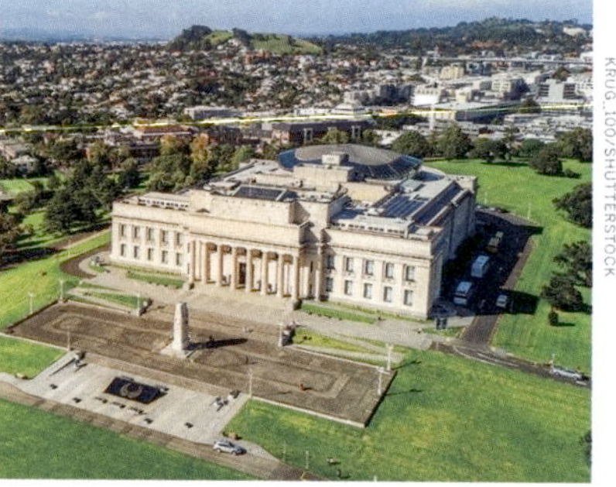

KRUG_100/SHUTTERSTOCK

Left Samoan dancers, Pasifika
Below Auckland Museum

Discovering Diversity

Auckland's volcanic field Ascend Tāmaki Makaurau's volcanic *maunga* (mountains) to discover the region's historic Māori *pā* (fortified settlements), before exploring the world-leading Māori galleries at the **Auckland Museum**, itself crowning the volcanic crater known as Pukekawa in **Auckland Domain**.

Matariki Held throughout the country in June, the annual Māori New Year festival (matarikifestival.org.nz) grows in spectacle and importance each year.

Karangahape Rd Span the globe along Auckland's most multicultural thoroughfare with Spanish tapas (**Candela**), Lebanese family recipes (**Gemmayze Street**), traditional Malaysian fare (**Sri Pinang**), elevated Latin American cuisine (**Tempero**) and Turkish pastries (**Zeki's Mediterranean Bakery & Café**). Contemporary Pacific Islands art is showcased at **Tautai** (tautai.org), while downstairs **Artspace Aotearoa** can be relied on for a diverse selection of temporary installations.

Dominion Rd Embark on a regional Chinese culinary adventure along Dominion Rd, segueing from mouth-numbing Sichuan flavours at **Eden Noodles** to *xiao long bao* (soup dumplings) at **Jolin Shanghai** and Muslim-influenced flatbreads and cumin-laced lamb skewers at **Xi'an Food Bar**. Welcome to one of Auckland's most dynamic dining scenes.

Sandringham Spice up an Auckland sojourn in this Indian and Sri Lankan precinct a few blocks northwest of Dominion Rd. **Paradise** specialises in Mughlai Indian cuisine, with a sit-down restaurant and a separate takeaway outlet.

Best of Multicultural Auckland

Hapunan Auckland's (other) best food truck! Try the Filipino beef 'Kare Kare' in a peanut and annatto sauce. Also has a permanent location in Kumeū.

Tianze Dumpling House Try the sizzling eggplant stuffed with pork or the clam noodle soup. Get adventurous. It's all good!

Avondale Art Park An ever-evolving outdoor gallery exhibition of Auckland's finest graffiti and street artists.

Sacred Tattoo From traditional to classic and modern, the tattoo art created here is world-class.

The Ghost of Freddie Cesar Troy Kingi's 2020 album is influenced by his father's love of 1970s funk and soul.

Recommended by Otis Frizzell *artist and co-owner of The Lucky Taco food truck. @otis.frizzell @theluckytaco_nz*

03 Auckland's WILD WEST

BEACHES | BIRDS | WALKING

Detour on a day trip or an overnight adventure to the surf beaches and bush-clad forests of West Auckland's Waitākere Ranges Regional Park. Piha, Te Henga (Bethells Beach) and Muriwai all offer wild and windswept West Coast grandeur, while the region's gourmet bounty of food, beer and wine provides rewards after negotiating clifftop trails or hiking to a hidden lake.

JUSTIN FOULKES/LONELY PLANET

How to

Getting here Piha is around 40km from central Auckland. North of Piha, Muriwai is a similar distance from downtown.

When to go Visit on a weekday for smaller crowds and easier parking.

You'll need wheels Rent a car, as public transport is limited. Bush and Beach (bushandbeach.co.nz) offers guided tours.

FYI Between Titirangi and Piha, stop at the Arataki Visitor Centre for views, natural history displays and bush-walking information.

STARGRASS/SHUTTERSTOCK

Left Lion Rock, Piha Bay
Below *Tākapu* colony, Muriwai Beach

Beaches, Bird Life & Clifftop Walks

Hike high above the Tasman Sea surf Even on a windy and grey day, Piha's **Lion Rock** is a spectacular sight, crowning the black-sand beach that's one of Auckland's most popular surfing locations. Always swim between the flags under the watchful gaze of surf lifeguards. On a fine, blue-sky day, tackle Piha's **Mercer Bay Loop Walk** for brilliant coastal views high above the beach's southern edges.

Negotiate sand dunes to a hidden lake Framed by towering sand dunes, the walk to **Lake Waimanu** near Te Henga (Bethells Beach) is a classic West Coast experience. At the time of writing, the track was officially closed due to damage caused by the 2023 cyclone, although you could still reach it by wading along the stream. Afterwards, head to the wide open expanses of the wild surf beach.

A surf-side seabird spectacle Perched on the cliffs above Muriwai's arcing surf beach is a large *tākapu* (Australasian gannet) colony which is home to thousands of birds from August onwards. Chicks are usually born from December to January, and by March the fledgling birds have established the confidence and skills to embark on the 2000km journey west to Australia. Build up your own skill base by negotiating a Blokart (land yacht) on Muriwai's surf-lined sandy racetrack (muriwaisurfschool.co.nz).

Best of the West

Between West Coast beach-hopping, check out these eating and drinking favourites.

Crafty Baker Superior pies and pastries in Titirangi village.

Kumeu River World-renowned wines on the outskirts of Kumeū, including superb chardonnay.

Soljans Estate Winery Award-winning sparkling wines, and its bistro is a popular spot for brunch or lunch.

Good! from Scratch Locavore cookery classes in a rural setting near Muriwai.

Hallertau Complete the day with craft beers brewed on-site at this Riverhead beer garden.

Catalina Bay Farmers Market Head to Hobsonville Point on weekend mornings for delicious food stalls.

04 Action-Packed AUCKLAND

ACTION | VIEWS | OUTDOORS

Elsewhere in New Zealand, Queenstown, Rotorua and Taupō are renowned adventure sports hubs, but Auckland also offers spectacular ways to combine adrenaline-fuelled fun with views of the harbour city. After tackling the heights of the Sky Tower and the Auckland Harbour Bridge, embark on outdoor adventures on Hauraki Gulf islands, or negotiate canyons and waterfalls on the rugged West Coast.

CHAMELEONSEYE/SHUTTERSTOCK

How to

Getting here Dominating central Auckland from the corner of Victoria and Hobson Sts, the Sky Tower is impossible to miss.

Stretch your Kiwi budget Discounted combo deals including the SkyWalk, SkyJump and the Auckland Bridge Climb and Bungy are available (bungy.co.nz).

Sporting and movie-making excellence Both adjacent to the Sky Tower, the All Blacks Experience and Wētā Workshop Unleashed offer entertaining insights into New Zealand's rugby and cinematic success.

TRAVELLIGHT/SHUTTERSTOCK

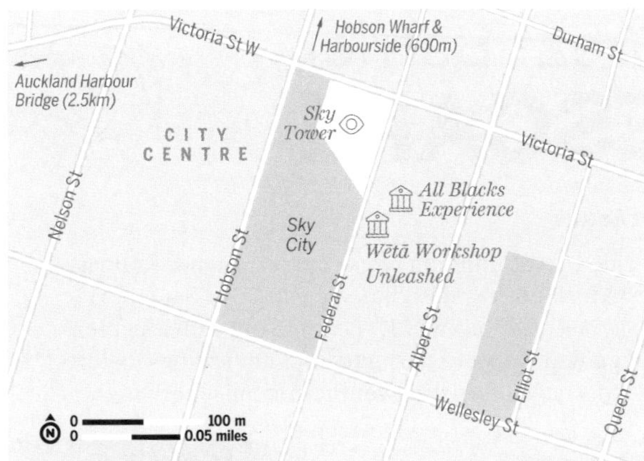

Sky-High Thrills

Are they mad? That could be your reaction as you watch people undertaking Auckland's **SkyWalk**. The 1.2m-wide walking platform encircles the **Sky Tower** at a height of 192m – around the same elevation as Maungawhau/Mt Eden. Participants are secured with a harness, but there are no safety rails or handholds – just a very, very long drop to the streets below. Stellar city and harbour views come as standard. If you're not keen on Auckland's most extreme adventure, ascending the Sky Tower to an enclosed viewing floor is also an option; good luck with those see-through glass floor panels. An alternative way to descend is the **SkyJump**, a controlled 11-second, 85km/h wired descent from the tower's observation deck.

Harbour Bridge adventures Maybe in the future it will be possible to walk or ride a bike across the Auckland Harbour Bridge to the North Shore, but right now the only way to get up close and personal with the span is on a guided bridge climb, or by taking a 40m leap of faith towards the waters of the Waitematā Harbour from a pod attached to the bridge's undercarriage with **Auckland Bridge Bungy** (bungy.co.nz). Both offer unique views of downtown Auckland, although you may be too busy screaming to notice them.

Left Sky Jump, Sky Tower
Below Auckland Harbour Bridge

Adventures Beyond the CBD

Auckland Sea Kayaks Offers kayak tours across the harbour to Rangitoto Island and half-day adventures to the extinct volcano of Motukorea (Browns Island).

AWOL Canyoning Adventures Canyoning and abseiling adventures near Piha Beach and in the forests of the Waitākere Ranges Regional Park.

Explore Hands-on harbour adventures on an authentic America's Cup match-racing yacht. Also offers whale-watching trips and dinner cruises.

Fullers360 Ferries to the islands of the Hauraki Gulf for hiking to the forested summit of Rangitoto or visiting the bird sanctuary of Tiritiri Mātangi. Departures are from downtown Auckland.

05 Great Barrier ESCAPE

STARGAZING | WALKING | BEACHES

Discover a different side to Auckland on Great Barrier Island. Known to Māori as Aotea, the forested island was designated a Dark Sky Sanctuary by the International Dark-Sky Association in 2017. Learn about Aotea's green-tinged sustainable ethos on guided walks to harbours and hot springs, before experiencing the after-dark spectacle of pristine southern hemisphere night skies.

EVGENY GORODETSKY/SHUTTERSTOCK

How to

Getting here Departing from Auckland or North Shore airport, flights to Great Barrier Island take around 30 minutes. The ferry crossing takes 5½ hours and can be rough.

When to go For better weather and to avoid busier weekends and school holiday periods, try to visit the island midweek from February to April.

Making it easy Book packages incorporating car hire, flights and accommodation with Go Great Barrier Island (greatbarrierisland tourism.co.nz).

JULIE MACHADO/SHUTTERSTOCK

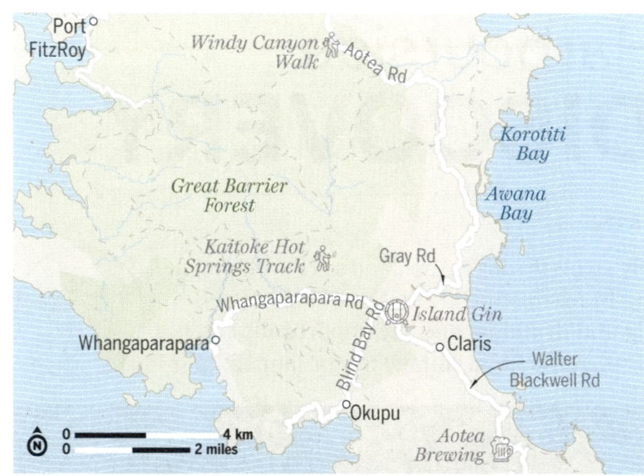

Stargazing & Forest Walks

Night-sky experiences Depending on the progression of the astronomical year, Aotea's celestial highlights could include sightings of Jupiter, Venus and Saturn, and softly glimmering displays of the Magellanic Clouds and the Milky Way. Dark Sky Ambassadors Hilde Hoven and Deborah Kilgallon are superb guides to the pollution-free night skies above their adopted island home, setting up **Good Heavens**' (goodheavens.co.nz) powerful telescope amid the undulating sand dunes along the graceful arc of Medlands Beach. Their authoritative commentary incorporates astronomical observations alongside an understanding of the cosmos from a traditional Māori perspective. Stargazing participants are guaranteed a few wedges of quite possibly New Zealand's best chocolate brownie. Booking ahead with Good Heavens for your first night on the island is recommended to allow for flexibility with weather conditions.

Exploring history and nature Discover the island's heritage, culture and flora while exploring Aotea's more remote west coast on a guided walk. Highlights include a morning boat ride to a historic 19th-century timber mill, and then a forest hike with views of the silvery expanse of Whangaparapara Harbour. Born and bred on Great Barrier Island, chatty walking guide Benny Bellerby from **StarTreks** (startreks.kiwi) also usually comes equipped with a few home-baked organic treats. Other island adventures to check out with Benny or independently include the **Kaitoke Hot Springs Track** and the spectacular **Windy Canyon Walk**.

Left View from Mt Hobson, Great Barrier Island
Below Stargazing, Great Barrier Island

Artisan Endeavours on Aotea

Aotea Brewing Visit its rustic taproom to sample craft beers brewed entirely off the grid, or fill up a recyclable flagon for a takeaway purchase of the hoppy Solar Charged American Pale Ale. Check aoteabrewing.co.nz for occasional weekend live music in summer.

Island Gin Harnessing native bush botanicals and other local ingredients including citrus fruits and wild honey, Andi Ross from Island Gin crafts artisan spirits near Claris in a shiny copper still. The unique bottles are made of recycled glass and shaped to resemble a kina (sea urchin). Tastings are by appointment only.

06 Harbourside DISCOVERY

ART | HISTORY | RESTAURANTS

Embark on a leisurely stroll through Auckland's redeveloped harbourside precinct, taking in interesting art and markets, waterfront destinations for eating and drinking, and the opportunity to get out on the water in a heritage yacht or vintage motor launch.

BRETT ATKINSON/LONELY PLANET

How to

Getting around Start at the Lighthouse, 500m from Auckland's Ferry Building at the end of Queens Wharf.

When to go Try to time your visit for a heritage cruise. Sailings from the Maritime Museum depart at 11.30am and 1.30pm, Friday to Monday.

How long? You're looking at around 2km. How about a leisurely two to three hours?

What to drink Beers from Auckland craft breweries including 8 Wired, McLeod's and Liberty.

A Chef's Choice

Hello Beasty Superb Asian fusion dishes and great music.

Sri Pinang Fabulous Malaysian food as I remember it.

Forest Most innovative vegetarian/vegan dining in Auckland.

Avondale Market Great food stalls and produce from Auckland's wide range of ethnic communities.

Recommended by Peter Gordon, *chef consultant and fusion-cuisine pioneer @chefpetergordon*

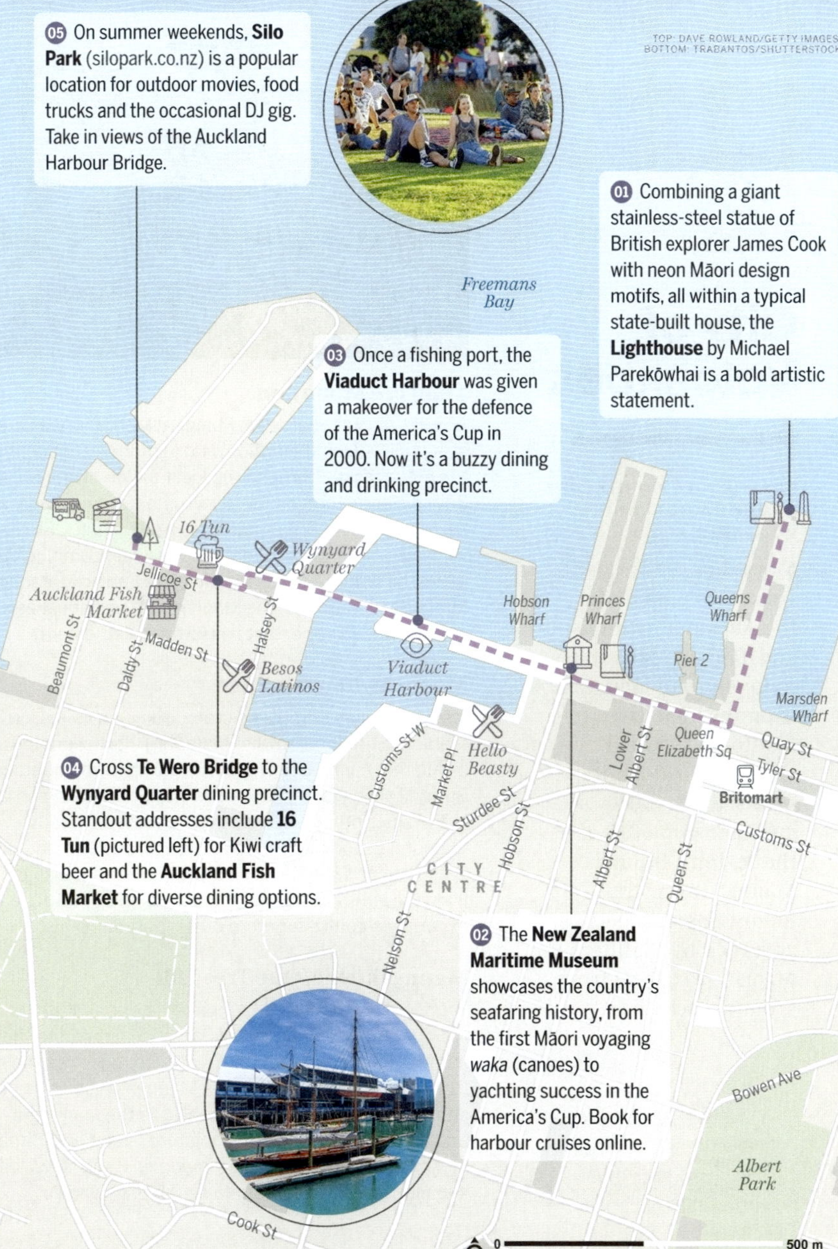

TOP: DAVE ROWLAND/GETTY IMAGES, BOTTOM: TRABANTOS/SHUTTERSTOCK

City of Volcanoes

EXPLORE MĀORI HISTORY AROUND AUCKLAND'S VOLCANIC FIELD

More than 50 dormant volcanoes punctuate the Auckland isthmus, and Tāmaki Makaurau's unique urban landscape is on the Tentative List to be awarded Unesco World Heritage status. Since 2014, guardianship of 13 of the region's Tūpuna Maunga (ancestral mountains) has been governed by 13 different Māori *iwi* (tribes) from around Auckland.

Left Maungakiekie/One Tree Hill, Cornwall Park
Centre Takarunga/Mt Victoria
Right Rangitoto Island

FILIP FUXA/SHUTTERSTOCK

Māngere Mountain

Around 70,000 years ago, Māngere Mountain was created by a huge volcanic eruption, and in more recent centuries the *maunga* was home to the local Te Wai-o-Hua *iwi*. Almost 80 *rua* (food storage pits) punctuate the landscape, while *kai moana* (seafood) bounty was also plentiful. Fertile volcanic soils and easily defended terrain combined to make the landmark also known as Te Pane o Mataoho (the forehead of Mataoho, the Māori god of earthquakes and volcanoes), an important *pā* (fortified settlement).

Maungawhau/Mt Eden

Maungawhau's 50m-deep crater is known as Te Upu Kai a Mataoho (the food bowl of Mataoho). Earthwork terraces frame the *maunga*, now protected by a raised boardwalk. Summit views take in Auckland's two harbours, and many of the city's other volcanoes can also be sighted. Views into Mataoho's food bowl are spectacular, and the Sky Tower, Rangitoto and the Harbour Bridge are standout sights from the isthmus' highest natural point. Call into the visitor experience centre for more on its fascinating history.

Maungakiekie/One Tree Hill

Topped by an obelisk, Maungakiekie dominates the rolling farmland of Cornwall Park. On the road to the summit (closed to traffic), it's easy to make out the *pā tūāpapa* (terraces) that made Maungakiekie an important site. Sweeping summit views include the Manukau and Waitematā harbours, Rangitoto Island and Tāmaki Makaurau's other important *maunga*. Central Auckland's second-highest mountain (after Maungawhau),

LEMBI/SHUTTERSTOCK

CKTRAVELS.COM/SHUTTERSTOCK

Maungakiekie was also a prized defensive location for Māori *iwi*.

Maungauika/North Head

The legendary Polynesia explorer Kupe is said to have landed in nearby Te Haukapua (Torpedo Bay), and Devonport's Maungauika/North Head also features other echoes of history. A navigation station marked the entrance to the Waitematā Harbour from 1836, while the Saluting Battery's impressive 8in gun was installed in 1886 to protect against the (perceived) threat of a Russian invasion. To the west, Takarunga/Mt Victoria was also an important Maori *pā* site.

> Sweeping summit views include the Manukau and Waitematā harbours, Rangitoto Island and Tāmaki Makaurau's other important *maunga*.

Rangitoto Island

Rangitoto was formed around 700 years ago, and its volcanic origin is mentioned in Māori oral histories. Linked by a causeway, neighbouring Motutapu Island is around 178 million years old, and was used by local *iwi* for food cultivation. Footprints of an adult, child and dog have been discovered in a 30cm slab of volcanic ash. You can reach Rangitoto's forested volcanic cone along the **Summit Track**, a one-hour hike beginning at coastal mangroves, continuing through a lava field, and finally ascending through New Zealand's biggest pōhutukawa forest.

Best Ways to Explore Auckland's Volcanoes

Māngere Mountain With a car, take SH20 through the Waterview Tunnel and across Māngere Bridge. Otherwise walk from Onehunga Station (40 minutes).

Maungawhau/Mt Eden Learn about Auckland's volcanic history at Te Ipu Kōrero o Maungawhau Visitor Experience Centre.

Maungakiekie/One Tree Hill Start by calling into the Huia Lodge Discovery Hub before tackling the summit.

Maungauika/North Head Catch the Fullers ferry from downtown Auckland to Devonport and continue east along Torpedo Bay.

Rangitoto Island Journey from downtown Auckland with Fullers. Search 'Rangitoto' on doc.govt.nz for details of other longer walking tracks taking in Motutapu.

Listings

BEST OF THE REST

Auckland's Multicultural Menu

Gemmayze St $$

Modern Lebanese dishes packed with seasonal ingredients are served amid the high-ceilinged art-deco ambience of Karangahape Rd's St Kevins Arcade. 'K Rd's' bohemian vibe extends to many other good cafes and restaurants.

Azabu $$

Japanese-Peruvian Nikkei cuisine featuring the freshest of local seafood shines at Azabu's two locations: one in Ponsonby, the other by the beach at Mission Bay.

Ahi $$$

Ingredients from around Aotearoa are harnessed for fine dining with a relaxed Kiwi vibe. Ahi's takes on *kai moana* (seafood) is uniformly excellent, and ocean views reinforce that you're dining in one of the world's great harbour cities. The Commercial Bay location also includes a multicuisine food court that's ideal for lunch.

Hello Beasty $$

Japanese, Korean and Chinese flavours all blend seamlessly on Hello Beasty's innovative and modern menu. Ask for a table at the front of the restaurant to take in Viaduct Harbour's maritime vibe.

Cassia $$$

Cassia's modern spins on traditional Indian flavours partner with a global selection of artisan gins, a well-curated beer list, and fresh and vibrant wine varietals including New Zealand riesling, pinot gris and sauvignon blanc.

Mr Morris $$$

Founded by top New Zealand chef Michael Meredith, Mr Morris is a standout in downtown's Britomart precinct. Local and sustainable ingredients underpin seasonal menus that often feature Asian and Pacific culinary touches which perfectly reflect the city's emerging cultural diversity.

Giapo $

Inventive dessert treats are crafted at this artisan ice-cream shop in central Auckland. Follow co-owner Giapo Grazioli on Instagram (@giapokitchen) to see what intensely creative surprises he's currently dreaming up.

Ponsonby Central $$

From Venezuelan and Turkish to Chinese and Korean, global flavours abound at this essential destination along Ponsonby's eating and drinking strip. Highlights include the tiki bar meets Shanghai ambience of the Blue Breeze Inn and terrific coffee and artisan doughnuts at Foxtrot Parlour.

SARAWOOTP/SHUTTERSTOCK

Ice cream, Giapo

Craft Beer & Cocktails

Galbraith's Alehouse $$

A sunny beer garden, excellent food – including Auckland's best Sunday roasts – and a stellar selection of Kiwi beers make Mt Eden's Galbraith's a perennial contender for the city's best pub. During cooler months, secure a spot inside around the cosy fire.

Auckland Beer Mile $$

Nine different bars, brewpubs and taprooms feature along this 4km route *(facebook.com/aucklandbeermile)* showcasing a hoppy celebration of Auckland's craft-beer scene. Highlights include Churly's for robust IPAs and house-made charcuterie, and 40 taps and visiting food trucks at the Beer Spot.

Freida Margolis $$

Freida's corner location in Grey Lynn is a top spot to combine cocktails, craft beer and diverse sounds from the owner's expansive collection of vintage vinyl. Formerly a butcher's – look for the West Lynn Organic Meats sign.

Churchill $$$

Head up to this sophisticated bar on the 20th floor of the Four Points hotel in the city centre for extraordinary views, pricy-but-worth-it cocktails and a vast array of gins.

Caretaker $$$

Descend to this stylish cellar bar in central Auckland's Britomart Precinct and let the savvy bartenders magic up a bespoke cocktail based on your preferences.

Walk Across the Country

Coast to Coast Walkway

Catch public transport to Onehunga and embark on this 16km urban stroll across Auckland's narrow isthmus to link the Manukau and Waitematā harbours, where you can refuel at the restaurants and bars of Viaduct Harbour.

Walk Across the Country

Coast to Coast Walkway

Catch public transport to Onehunga and embark on this 16km urban stroll across Auckland's narrow isthmus from the Manukau to the Waitematā Harbour. At journey's end, refuel amid the restaurants and bars of Viaduct Harbour.

The Best of New Zealand Art

Auckland Art Gallery Toi o Tāmaki

Emerging Māori and Pacific artists combine with works from iconic New Zealand painters including Ralph Hotere, Colin McCahon and Frances Hodgkins in this elegant French Renaissance–style building on the edge of central Auckland's Albert Park.

Day Trips

Matakana

Journey one hour north of Auckland for Matakana's popular Saturday morning farmers market, barrel-aged beers from 8 Wired Brewing, and the vineyards of the emerging Matakana wine region. (matakanawine.co.nz)

Tiritiri Mātangi

Take an 80-minute ferry ride to this predator-free island that's a sanctuary for some of the world's rarest birds, reptiles and invertebrates.

Family Favourite

Sea Life Kelly Tarlton's Aquarium

Be surrounded by sharks and stingrays as you walk through transparent tunnels, or get up close to king and gentoo penguins in the Antarctic Ice Adventure.

NORTHLAND

BEACHES | CULTURE | HISTORY

WAITANGI TREATY GROUNDS IMAGE LIBRARY

NORTHLAND

Trip Builder

Tiki tour New Zealand's subtropical, northernmost region, nicknamed the Winterless North. Te Tai Tokerau (Northland), a stronghold of te ao Māori (indigenous culture) and Aotearoa (NZ) history, also hosts beautiful beaches, ancient forests, and stunning indigenous and Western art.

Dive at the marine reserve of the **Poor Knights Islands** (p80)
Whangārei

Hike the **Cape Brett Track** in the Bay of Islands (p75)
1¾hr from Whangārei

Find out about Māori and colonial history at **Waitangi** and **Russell** (p68)
1hr from Whangārei

Learn from Māori tour guides in **Hokianga** (p69)
1¾hr from Whangārei

Be dazzled by all things Hundertwasser in **Whangārei**, **Kaurinui** and **Kawakawa** (p72)
2½-3hr from Auckland

Practicalities

ARRIVING

While Whangārei and the Bay of Islands host several regular daily buses and flights from Auckland, most people arrive in Northland by car, providing the most accessibility and flexibility.

MONEY

Northland isn't a low-budget destination. Save money by staying at campsites.

FIND YOUR WAY

The Whangārei and Paihia i-Site visitor information centres have helpful information on attractions around Northland.

WHERE TO STAY

Town	Pro/Con
Whangārei	A small city with great art and dining. Not so near the beach.
Paihia	Plenty of accommodation but very busy in summer.
Russell	More peaceful than Paihia. Take the ferry or drive the long way around.
Rawene	Sleepy and historic but without the tourist crowds or amenities of the east coast.

GETTING AROUND

Car You'll need your own wheels beyond the major hubs.

Ferry Ferries run between Paihia and Russell, and Rawene and Kohukohu.

Bus Long-distance buses travel from Auckland up the east coast and through Whangārei and the Bay of Islands. Local buses are limited to Whangārei.

TOP: OLGA YATSENKO/SHUTTERSTOCK

EATING & DRINKING

With plentiful coastline and a fertile subtropical climate filled with farms and orchards, fresh dairy, *kai moana* (seafood) and produce abound across Northland. While all cuisines can be found locally, eateries of particular note include stylish waterfront restaurants in Whangārei and the Bay of Islands.

Must-try ice cream
NZ Fudge Farm (p82)

Best subtropical wine
Marsden Estate (p83)

DEC–FEB
Hot and humid days, balmy nights; tourist crowds in the summer school holidays.

MAR–MAY
Warm air and sea, uncrowded beaches, decreasing daylight hours.

JUN–AUG
Rainy and humid, with cool nights.

OCT–NOV
Diminishing rain, warmer days but still a bit chilly.

Beaches FOR DAYS

SEA | RELAXATION | NATURE

With a subtropical climate and long eastern and western coastlines, Northland's beaches are numerous and nothing short of spectacular. Whether you're looking for a small shady bay for a swim and a snooze on the sand, somewhere more expansive for a long walk, or an epic surf break, you can find it in Te Tai Tokerau.

How to

Getting here Follow SH1 up the east coast (and north to Cape Reinga) or SH12 down the west coast to find your own beach paradise.

When to go December to March has the warmest sea and air temperatures. Outside busy high summer you might even have the beach to yourself. Winter beach walks are also lovely.

Summer slang Jandals = flip flops/thongs. Togs = bathing suit/swimming costume. Bach = holiday home.

Life's a Northland Beach

A tale of two coasts Like much of New Zealand, the beaches on the east and west coasts of Northland are dramatically different from each other. The east coast is more developed – Bream Bay, the Tutukaka Coast, the Bay of Islands and the Karikari Peninsula are tourist hotspots – and its beaches have picture-perfect white-sand. But don't dismiss the rugged west coast's black-sand beaches either. The currents are stronger and the surf is rougher, so extra caution is needed and swimming is not recommended outside of lifeguard-patrolled spots like **Baylys Beach**. **Ninety Mile Beach** is an invigorating 88km-long stretch of sand for a walk, surfcasting, dune activities or a 4WD tour. At its southern exodus at Shipwreck Bay sits a world-class surf break. Alternatives

CRISTINA R./SHUTTERSTOCK

to Ninety Mile Beach include the 107km-long **Ripiro Beach** on the Kauri Coast, perfect for surfcasting, 4WD adventures (if your rental car insurance allows for it) and long walks on the beach.

Island-hop There's more to the Bay of Islands than Paihia and Russell – don't forget the 144 islands themselves. Island-hopping tours visit island beaches that would be hard to access any other way. Some are reserves with restricted access but many are not. Tours offer a range of activity levels so you can opt to kayak or paddle board, or just relax on the sand.

Birds of the Beaches

When you're on Northland's beaches, keep an eye out for conservation projects aimed at protecting and growing populations of local and migratory seabirds. Sand dunes and estuaries in particular are rich habitats for coastal birds, so heed any warnings to keep out of certain areas. Keen bird-watchers and wildlife enthusiasts can look out for oystercatchers, New Zealand dotterels, Caspian terns, fairy terns and little penguins. Bar-tailed godwits also spend time in Northland's Parengarenga Harbour, Whangārei area and Kaipara Harbour during their annual 10,000km migration.

Above Ninety Mile Beach

08 Meet the Māori of TE TAI TOKERAU

CULTURE | HISTORY | LANDMARKS

Pre-colonisation, Te Tai Tokerau was the most populous and powerful place across all of Aotearoa. Consequently, Northland was the most influential region in the early colonial period. Nowadays, Māori still make up one-third of the region's population, a higher percentage than that of most other places.

UWE MOSER/GETTY IMAGES

How to

When to go Any time is good, but Waitangi is abuzz on Waitangi Day (6 February), the national holiday commemorating the founding of modern NZ.

Should you attend a cultural show? While exploring Northland it is worthwhile to bask in te ao Māori by attending a cultural performance. Perhaps the best opportunities to do so in Te Tai Tokerau are the half-hour shows at the Waitangi Treaty Grounds' Te Whare Rūnanga building, scheduled right after your one-hour guided tour finishes.

WAITANGI TREATY GROUNDS IMAGE LIBRARY

Northland is often called the cradle of New Zealand because it is here that many significant events have happened: Polynesian explorer Kupe is said to have landed in the **Hokianga Harbour** around 1000 years ago; the founding document of modern New Zealand, the Treaty of Waitangi, was first signed in the Bay of Islands in 1840; and the first large-scale battles of the New Zealand Land Wars occurred in Northland in the mid-1840s.

Treaty The **Treaty of Waitangi/Te Tiriti o Waitangi** continues to loom large in modern-day politics and interactions between Māori and Pākehā (Europeans). The treaty which founded the British colony of New Zealand was signed between representatives of the British Crown and northern Rangatira Māori (indigenous leaders) on 6 February 1840 at

RITA BAKER/GETTY IMAGES

A Great Migration

Many tribal stories credit Kupe with being the first Polynesian to arrive in Aotearoa when he landed in the Hokianga Harbour around 1000 years ago. Travellers can learn more about this migration and the narratives surrounding it at the **Manea: The Footprints of Kupe** experience in Opononi and the **Footprints Waipoua** tours through kauri forest.

Above left Waitangi Day
Above Waitangi Treaty Grounds (p70)
Left Hokianga Harbour

what is now the **Waitangi Treaty Grounds**. To learn more about New Zealand history, if you go nowhere else in the country, make sure to spend at least half a day (preferably longer) at Waitangi. The extensive grounds include interactive museums, a carving studio, **ceremonial *waka*** (canoe), a small beach, the British-style **Treaty House**, the incredible carved meeting house **Te Whare Rūnanga**, a **cafe**, and great views across the Bay of Islands from around the 34m **Flagstaff**.

The Hellhole of the Pacific In the 21st century, pretty **Russell** is about as far from its historic moniker of 'Hellhole of the Pacific' as it's possible to be. But a stroll around the village will reveal why the town was so named in the 1830s. There's also plenty of evidence of how Europeans tried to colonise local Māori through Christianity. Check out the **Russell Museum**, the **Pompallier Mission and Printery**, and the **Christ Church**, still displaying bullet holes from a Northern War shoot-out in 1845.

How to Recognise a Pā Site

A *pā* was a fortified Māori settlement, usually upon a hill but sometimes in other locations like riverbanks. Hilltop *pā* sites are common around Northland and road journeys are all the more interesting if you learn to distinguish a pā from, well, just a regular old hill. The slopes were terraced, and that's the giveaway sign that a hill was once a *pā*. One of the most extensive and significant you can visit is Ruapekapeka Pā southeast of Kawakawa, the site of the final battle in the Northern War in 1846 – the first large-scale conflict in the New Zealand Land Wars.

PHOTOGRAPHY BY ULRICH HOLLMANN/GETTY IMAGES

Far left Rangikapiti Pā (p82)
Left Christ Church Cathedral, Russell
Below Ceremonial *waka*, Waitangi Treaty Grounds

While away an hour or two A road trip through Northland reveals many small-town museums providing intimate, hyper-local insights into the region's history and long-standing interactions between Māori and settlers. Some little museums worth a visit include the **Mangawhai Museum**, the **Kauri Museum** in Matakohe, the **Dargaville Museum**, **Clendon House** in Rawene, **Museum @ Te Ahu** in Kaitāia, **Hokianga Museum** and **Archives Centre** in Omapere, and the **Waipu Museum**.

On a mission Learn how European missionaries lived, attempted to convert local Māori to Christianity, and to control what they considered the unsavoury influences of certain settlers (the type giving Russell its hellhole nickname!) on the new colony of New Zealand at mission sites throughout Northland. The **Kerikeri Mission Station**, the **Waimate Mission**, and Russell's **Pompallier Mission and Printery** display exhibits in renovated 19th-century buildings. While no buildings still stand at the very first mission station at **Rangihoua**, its heritage park is still worth a visit.

FAR LEFT: MARK MEREDITH/GETTY IMAGES, LEFT: WAITANGI TREATY GROUNDS IMAGE LIBRARY

A Meeting of Cultures

LOCAL AND INTERNATIONAL ART BLOSSOM IN NORTHLAND

Northland was home to one of the 20th-century's greatest European avant-garde artists in the twilight of his life. More than two decades after his death, Friedensreich Hundertwasser has played a role in uniting diverse artistic traditions in the city of Whangārei and keeping the town of Kawakawa afloat.

Left Hundertwasser Art Centre, Whāngarei
Centre Friedensreich Hundertwasser
Right Hundertwasser Toilets, Kawakawa

FIONA GOODALL/GETTY IMAGES

Austrian-born artist Friedensreich Hundertwasser settled near Kawakawa, Bay of Islands, in the 1970s, turning a patch of Kaurinui farmland into forest and blending in with the rural locals. The avant-garde artist who is known for Central European architectural masterpieces such as the Hundertwasserhaus, an apartment block in central Vienna, was asked to draw up plans for an art centre in Whangārei in the 1990s. But his aesthetic – all wavy lines, colourful tiles and gold domes – was a little too avant-garde for the conservative Whangārei of three decades ago, and his art centre wasn't built during his lifetime.

In the years after Hundertwasser's death in 2000, committed art enthusiasts refused to let his ambitious architectural plans die with him. It took a couple more decades, pandemic-related delays, a bitter public campaign, a referendum and the support of former Prime Minister John Key, but in February 2022, the Hundertwasser Art Centre and Wairau Māori Art Gallery opened in Whangārei's Town Basin.

The incredible gold-domed building is chequered with black-and-white tiles, undulating pathways, and a carpet of 'tree tenants' – Hundertwasser's term for plants integrated into architectural designs – on the roof. That's just the outside, which would be marvellous enough regardless of what lay inside. Inside are two separate galleries, one displaying a collection of 80 original Hundertwasser works (the only permanent display outside Austria) and the other a Māori-curated collection of Māori art. The latter is the first public gallery dedicated solely to displaying the finest contemporary Māori art, and represents a pivotal moment in curatorial practices

STEPHEN JAMES LUNAM/FAIRFAX MEDIA

FQROY/SHUTTERSTOCK

in Aotearoa. Hundertwasser's original plans for the art centre in Whangārei included space for the display of Māori art and that has been honoured in the posthumous incarnation.

The long-overdue project has breathed fresh life into the contemporary arts scene in Whangārei, or at least given it its rightful visibility. The Town Basin and Hatea River areas now boast artistic and architectural attractions that move Whangārei from a 'drive-by' pit stop en route to the Bay of Islands to a stand-alone destination in its own right.

> The incredible gold-domed building is chequered with black-and-white tiles, undulating pathways and a carpet of 'tree tenants' on the roof.

The Hātea Loop walkway connects the Hundertwasser Museum and the Town Basin with other areas of the city along the shores of the Hātea River and the end of Whangārei Harbour. Along the way is a sculpture walk, dotted with sculptural artworks that celebrate the people, history and environment of Whangārei. The Hihiaua Cultural Centre preserves, creates, displays and promotes Māori arts and culture in a purpose-built glass-and-wood building. The laser-cut weathered-steel whorl of the Camera Obscura on the east bank of the river takes an ancient photographic technique and imbues it with place-based significance. And the striking Te Matau ā Pohe bridge, which opens periodically to let boat traffic pass beneath, resembles the traditional Māori fish hook of Pohe, the local chief who first welcomed colonial settlers to Whangārei.

Whangārei may not have been ready for Hundertwasser in the 1990s, but his legacy, and that of the indigenous New Zealand artists he shared this land with, is proudly on display in the 21st century.

Kawakawa: More Than a Loo Stop

Whangārei doesn't get all the Hunderwasser fun. The Bay of Islands town of Kawakawa, close to where Hundertwasser spent the last two decades of his life in his Kaurinui 'Bottlehouse', has been graced with the presence of the Hundertwasser Toilets since 1999, a project the artist saw to fruition in his lifetime. They're probably the only public loos you'll ever want to linger in, as you sit (or stand) and admire the colourful tilework, repurposed glass bottles embedded in the walls and other quirky details. Across the square, Te Hononga Hundertwasser Memorial Park provides a reason to linger in Kawakawa a little longer.

09 A Coastal RAMBLE

OUTDOORS | NATURE | EXERCISE

Getting active and enjoying the views in Northland can be as simple as following a coastal trail. Whether you're looking for a quick walk to stretch the legs or a multiday hike while camping or staying in huts along the way, Northland's long coastline offers plenty of options. Pack those hiking shoes but don't forget the togs, either.

TRISTANBALME/SHUTTERSTOCK

How to

Getting here Many walks around Northland don't require meticulous end-to-end planning of transport transfers. Shuttles can be arranged for the longer routes that do.

When to go Northland's subtropical climate makes walking in the summer rather hot, whereas winter brings rain. Walk in spring and autumn for optimum conditions.

City strolling No time for a longer walk? Whangārei's scenic Hātea Loop connects the Town Basin marina with the Te Matau ā Pohe bridge at the end of Whangārei Harbour.

TILL KLIMA/GETTY IMAGES

Left Waipu Cove to Mangawhai Heads coastal track
Below Cape Brett Lighthouse

Island walks Walking around some of the islands in the Bay of Islands is a great way to enjoy sweeping views of the picturesque bay. The day walks on Moturoa Island and Urupukapuka Island are administered by DOC. There are many archaeological sites on pest-free Urupukapuka.

Headland views Walks around headlands offer panoramas from multiple angles. The Tutukaka Headland Walk to the lighthouse takes around one hour return, while various tracks around the Whangārei Heads offer views of the ocean, Mt Manaia and Whangārei Harbour.

Clifftop trails If you can arrange a drop-off or pick-up at either end (or can commit to the three- to four-hour return walk), the Waipu Cove to Mangawhai Heads coastal track is worthwhile. Follow the cliffs along the coast, stopping at points of interest such as shady pōhutukawa groves and Waipu's own pancake rocks.

Coastal and marine parks Walking through protected land or past marine areas provides extra wildlife-spotting opportunities. The Mimiwhangata Coastal Park north of Tutukaka offers various short walks and the chance of spotting wood pigeons, Australian eastern rosellas, kākā (parrots), and even brown kiwi at night.

Dune bashing The large sand dunes of the west coast offer a different kind of walking experience. Walk across the dunes to the Pouto Point Lighthouse at the entrance to the Kaipara Harbour, or up and across the dunes along the long stretch of Ninety Mile Beach (and then slide down again!).

Bag a Hut

An alternative way of seeing the famous Hole in the Rock, other than the standard boat trip, is to take the **Cape Brett Track**.

This is a rugged, challenging 16-km track from Rāwhiti to the Cape Brett Lighthouse at the end of the Cape Brett Peninsula. It's an eight-hour walk and is usually done over two days, as it can be quite tiring to do in one.

Spend the night at the serviced Cape Brett Hut, which has bunks, toilets and cooking facilities.

It's a good introduction to hiking huts if you're travelling further south in New Zealand on longer multiday hikes.

10 Western Northland ROAD TRIP

NATURE | OUTDOORS | CULTURE

Take the road less travelled on a road trip between Dargaville and Kaikohe that takes in the ancient kauri trees of the Waipoua Forest, the sparkling Kai Iwi Lakes, the grand Hokianga Harbour and low-key hot springs at Ngawha.

RAIMUND LINKE/GETTY IMAGES

Trip Notes

Getting here From Whangārei, head southwest towards Dargaville, from where SH12 winds through the Waipoua Forest (pictured above) and out to the Hokianga Harbour, before continuing inland to Kaikohe.

When to go In summer the fresh waters of the Kai Iwi Lakes beckon, but in the cooler months the hot thermal baths at Ngawha Springs are inviting.

Refuelling Fill up at a petrol station in Dargaville before heading north. There are some stations along SH12 but having a full tank will let you take relaxed detours.

Lakes, Forests & Hot Springs

Give the busy east coast SH1 a miss and instead take your roadie (road trip) along the quieter, arguably even more scenic SH12 (pictured above) between Dargaville and Kaikohe over two to three days.

At Kaikohe, the road forks northeast to the Bay of Islands or northwest to Kaitāia and Cape Reinga beyond.

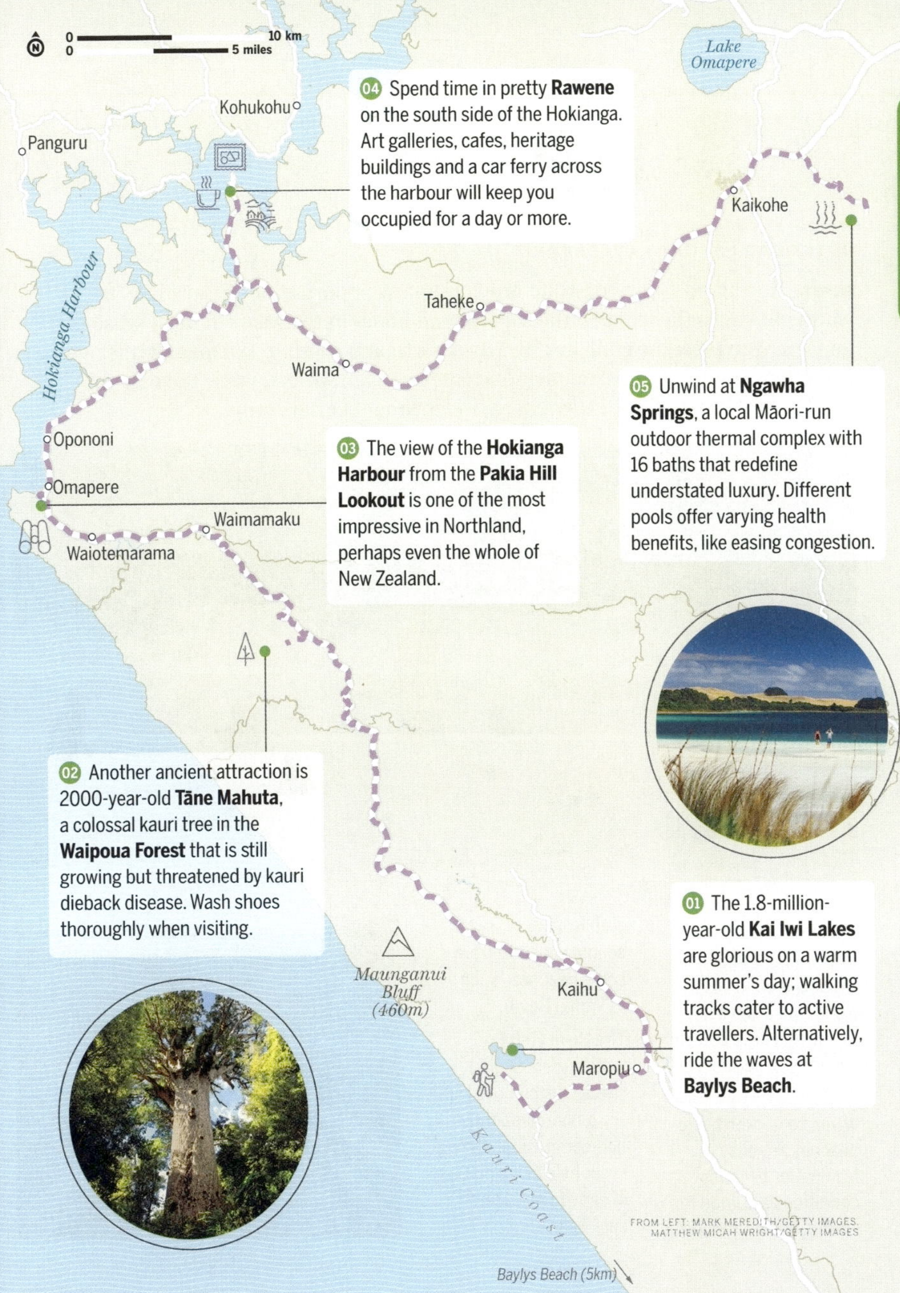

0 10 km
0 5 miles
Lake Omapere
04 Spend time in pretty **Rawene** on the south side of the Hokianga. Art galleries, cafes, heritage buildings and a car ferry across the harbour will keep you occupied for a day or more.
Kohukohu
Panguru
Kaikohe
Hokianga Harbour
Taheke
Waima
05 Unwind at **Ngawha Springs**, a local Māori-run outdoor thermal complex with 16 baths that redefine understated luxury. Different pools offer varying health benefits, like easing congestion.
Opononi
Omapere
03 The view of the **Hokianga Harbour** from the **Pakia Hill Lookout** is one of the most impressive in Northland, perhaps even the whole of New Zealand.
Waimamaku
Waiotemarama
02 Another ancient attraction is 2000-year-old **Tāne Mahuta**, a colossal kauri tree in the **Waipoua Forest** that is still growing but threatened by kauri dieback disease. Wash shoes thoroughly when visiting.
01 The 1.8-million-year-old **Kai Iwi Lakes** are glorious on a warm summer's day; walking tracks cater to active travellers. Alternatively, ride the waves at **Baylys Beach**.
Maunganui Bluff (460m)
Kaihu
Maropiu
Kauri Coast
FROM LEFT: MARK MEREDITH/GETTY IMAGES, MATTHEW MICAH WRIGHT/GETTY IMAGES
Baylys Beach (5km)

11 Surf's UP

OUTDOORS | SPORT | ADVENTURE

Northland's long coastline provides many opportunities to surf but the warm climate is the icing on the cake: spend hours in the water in most seasons and you won't feel the chill. Surf beaches north and south of Whangārei offer consistent conditions for beginner and intermediate surfers, while the east coast is best reserved for experienced, independent surfers only.

GRANT ROONEY PREMIUM/ALAMY

How to

Getting here Road-tripping around coastal Northland is the best way to find both popular and remote beaches for a surf.

When to go Northland beaches are busy in summer because conditions are good for surfing and swimming. Mobile, temporary surf schools operate from some beaches (such as Waipu Cove).

The Cove Fish Fry Keen surfers should check out the Cove Fish Fry, a non-competitive, non-commercial surfing event held at Waipu Cove in early to mid-March each year.

STACEY KAMMERER/SHUTTERSTOCK

Left Children's surf lesson, Waipu Cove
Below Ruakākā Beach

Advanced surfers If you well and truly know your way around a wave, head to **Pataua** (Ngunguru Bay), **Ocean Beach** (Whangārei Heads) or **Baylys Beach** (west coast). The surf at these beaches isn't for the faint of heart and you've got to know how to get on your feet. Some experienced surfers consider the left-hand breaks in New Zealand, specifically parts of Northland, to be among the best in the world.

Body boarding If you're travelling with kids or would rather not surf proper, body boarding is a great alternative. Body boards are lighter and more portable than surfboards, and great for general splashy play. Beaches with smaller waves ideal for body boarding fun: **Matapouri**, **Woolleys Bay**, **Waipu Cove** and **Ruakākā Beach**. For safety's sake, don't skip the flippers.

Best of both worlds While some surf spots are reliably better for beginners or advanced surfers, others cater to differing levels depending on the conditions. Tutukaka's **Sandy Bay** gets big waves when there's a northerly or northeast swell and **Shipwreck Bay** at Ahipara offers 5m waves for experienced surfers, but both places host surf schools catering to beginners.

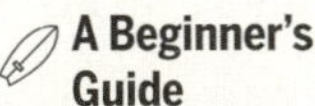

A Beginner's Guide

The east coast of Northland is ideal for beginners, both north and south of Whangārei. Sandy Bay, north of Tutukaka, gets a big swell, but when it's on the lower end it's good for beginners.

Best, though, is Waipu Cove, because the sand banks there make the swell more gentle. The surf schools at Tutukaka and Waipu Cove make these the best places for beginners because not only will you learn surfing skills, you'll learn safety tips and the etiquette of surfing, too.

Nothing annoys an experienced surfer more than a beginner getting in the way because they don't know the etiquette. Surf schools will teach you how to avoid difficult situations.

Recommended by Simon Egginton *surfing instructor at Tutukaka Surf School. @tutukakasurf*

12 Under THE SEA

OUTDOORS | WILDLIFE | ADVENTURE

Warm waters, offshore islands, marine reserves and some incredible wrecks make Northland an unmissable destination for keen divers. It's often said that the Poor Knights Islands, off the east coast of Whangārei, are the best subtropical diving destination in the world. Take a refresher course or rent some gear and find out for yourself.

How to

Getting here The east coast, between Whangārei and the Far North, is the best base for diving. Outfitters operate largely out of Tutukaka and Paihia.

When to go Summer and early autumn provide warm water (relatively speaking!) and good visibility.

Open-water courses Northland is an ideal place to get PADI certified and dive schools offer everything from entry-level courses to instructor courses.

Snorkellers tag along Boat trips out to ocean diving spots often offer snorkelling, too.

It's Better Down Where It's Wetter

It's a wreck Learn about the dramatic history of Greenpeace's *Rainbow Warrior* protest ship before diving to see it at its final resting place in Matauri Bay. Open-water divers (or those who'd like to learn) can check out the intact wreck of the HMNZS *Canterbury* at Deep Water Cove. The *Tui*, off Tutukaka, was sunk deliberately to create a reef.

Those Poor Knights Twenty-two kilometres northeast off the coast of Whangārei, and sometimes visible from shore, are the Poor Knights Islands. They're surrounded by the Poor Knights Islands Marine Reserve. Fishing or disturbing the marine life or land is strictly verboten, but swimming and diving is A-OK and highly recommended.

Hen & Chicks The islands east of Bream Bay are a

fixture on the ocean-scape but they don't just make a pretty scene: you can dive there, too. Trips to the Hen & Chicks are less commercialised than other dive spots along the coast so may be appealing to independent, fully trained divers.

Coastal snorkelling If full-on scuba diving isn't for you, snorkelling from the beach is possible in many places. Choose a sheltered spot without waves, near rock pools. Whale Bay, Whangaumu Bay and Matapouri Bay on the Tutukaka Coast are good spots.

Only Fearless Divers Need Apply

Experienced divers with an appetite for unusual, dramatic and even kind of creepy dive spots aren't short of options in Northland.

Beneath the surface at the Poor Knights Islands are a huge range of dramatic underwater landscapes to explore, from kelp forests and sponge fields to a tumbling staircase and sheer cliffs plunging 100m to the sea floor.

If the name 'Sonic Boom Cave' doesn't send shivers down your spine (or perhaps even if it does), this spot in the Bay of Islands lets you feel the force of the ocean through your whole body. The cave is named after the sound created when waves hit the top.

Above Scorpion fish, Poor Knights Islands Marine Reserve

Listings

BEST OF THE REST

From on High

Mt Manaia

The strenuous climb to the top of 420m Mt Manaia, at the Whangārei Heads, passes through regenerating native forest. Stay a while at the top to enjoy views of Whangārei Harbour, Bream Head and the Hen & Chicken Islands.

Cape Reinga

The journey to the northernmost tip of the North Island is nothing less than a pilgrimage. See and feel the meeting of oceans from Cape Reinga Lighthouse.

Kairara Rock (Duke's Nose)

Look out over Whangaroa Harbour after the short but steep climb up Kairara Rock. Sections of rock scrambling and ropes make this a better option for travellers without small children.

Rangikapiti Pā

Work off those fish and chips from the Mangōnui Fish Shop with a hike up Rangikapiti Pā. Enjoy views over Mangōnui Harbour, Coopers Beach, Doubtless Bay and the Karikari Peninsula.

Maunganuitapu

Not only is this mountain sacred to local Māori, but it also provides visitors with a wonderful walking track through endemic bush with plenty of places to stop for a pristine vista.

Ruapekapeka Pā

From this massively imposing *pā,* one of the most grand earthwork fortresses ever built in Aotearoa, one gains a deep appreciation for Northland's rolling green hills.

Flagstaff Hill

Historically, the flagstaff on this hill was a site of Māori resistance to colonisation, as legendary chief Hone Heke cut it down four times, but today it provides the Bay of Islands' most expansive vantage.

Sweet Treats

Bennetts of Mangawhai $$

Shop for handmade chocolates at this boutique chocolatier before dropping into the connected cafe for a very special hot chocolate or mochaccino drink.

NZ Fudge Farm $

With a wide range of creative fudge flavours and ice creams that are definitely in the running for the title of New Zealand's best, this Town Basin Whangārei establishment will satisfy any sweet tooth.

Craft Shops

Burning Issues Gallery

This gallery at Whangārei's Town Basin sells and displays contemporary handmade glass, ceramics and sculpture, as well as jewellery. Watch glass being blown and fired in the workshop at the back.

NICRAM SABOD/SHUTTERSTOCK

Lighthouse, Cape Reinga

Pipi Gallery Mangawhai

Browse or buy local pottery, ceramics, glass, garden art, jewellery, gifts and flower bouquets in Mangawhai Town, not far from Bennetts chocolate shop.

Quarry Craft Shop and Gallery

The cooperative shop at the Quarry Arts Centre in Whangārei displays the work of more than 30 artists and is an ideal one-stop shop for local arts and crafts. You can also take a workshop at this arts institution.

Waterside Pubs

Duke of Marlborough Hotel — $$

The wrought-iron patios and balconies of the Duke have been sheltering patrons in Russell since 1827. In fact, this place held the first liquor licence in New Zealand, back when Russell was nicknamed the 'Hellhole of the Pacific'.

Parua Bay Tavern — $$

With views of the Whangārei Heads and plenty of outdoor space for the kids to play, the Parua Bay Tavern is a local favourite, especially in the summer.

The Quay — $$$

Pick an outdoor table for the best views of the international yachts at Whangārei Marina as you drink and dine.

Shop Local

Whangārei Growers Market

Give the impersonal supermarkets a wide berth and instead buy fresh local produce from one of the oldest farmers markets in New Zealand. It's held on Saturday mornings in the Water St car park, and more than 100 stallholders set up shop here.

MICHAEL WILLIAMS/ALAMY

Duke of Marlborough Hotel

Old Packhorse Market

This indoor market in Kerikeri sells fresh and artisanal food and a wide range of delicious breads and pastries from Northland producers on Saturdays. Sunday markets sell a wider range of bric-a-brac, clothing and jewellery.

Subtropical Wineries

Marsden Estate

Sample award-winning wines in Kerikeri's oldest winery. Marsden Estate is named after Reverend Samuel Marsden, who planted the first vines in the Bay of Islands in 1819, long before NZ's viticulture boom of the 1990s.

Karikari Estate

Located on the Karikari Peninsula in the Far North, Karikari Estate is NZ's northernmost winery, with subtropical conditions far removed from those of temperate Hawke's Bay or Marlborough. The cellar door is open for tastings year-round.

Okahu Estate

Outside of Kaitāia, Okahu Estate was influential in NZ's wine renaissance of the 1990s. Sample award-winning syrah and chardonnay here.

CENTRAL NORTH ISLAND

VOLCANOES | NATURE | CULTURE

CENTRAL NORTH ISLAND
Trip Builder

The central North Island is a geology textbook written large. Here you'll find New Zealand's mightiest river, largest lake, loftiest volcanoes, most extensive cave systems and most active geothermal areas. In a landscape steeped in sacred sites, Māori culture takes a prominent role.

Auckland

Discover contemporary Māori art and design in **Raglan** (p90)
40min from Hamilton

Kāwhia

Tasman Sea

Float on a subterranean river in **Waitomo** (p92)
1hr from Hamilton

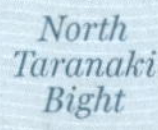

North Taranaki Bight

Trek among volcanic peaks on the **Tongariro Alpine Crossing** (p114)
3hr from Hamilton

New Plymouth

Mt Taranaki (Mt Egmont)

Stratford

Cycle along old cobblestones on the Ōhakune **Old Coach Road** (p113)
3hr from Hamilton

Hāwera

CLOCKWISE FROM LEFT: MATTEO COLOMBO/GETTY IMAGES, SHAUN JEFFERS/SHUTTERSTOCK, CHAMELEONSEYE/SHUTTERSTOCK, WEATHER500/SHUTTERSTOCK

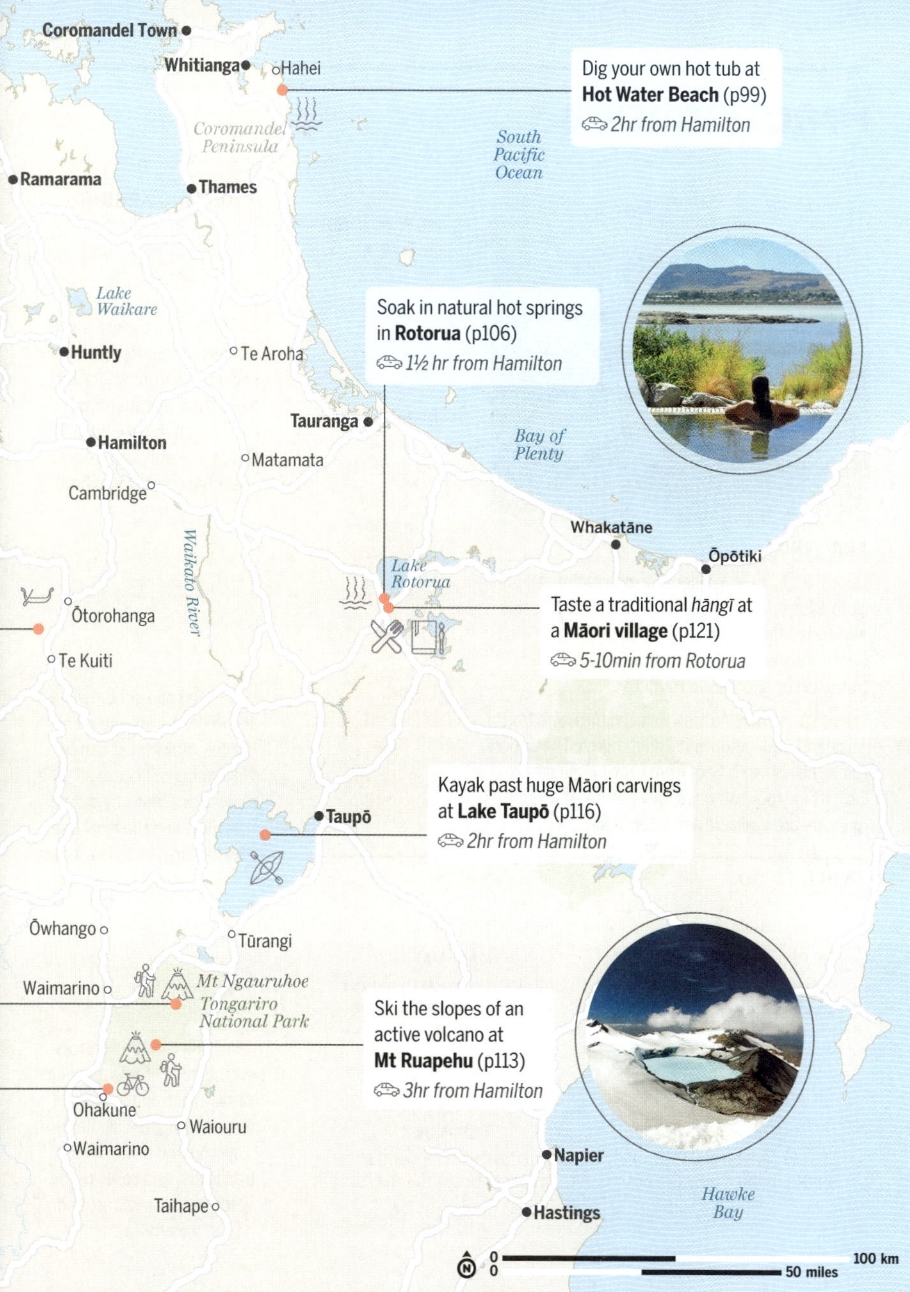

Coromandel Town
Whitianga
Hahei
Dig your own hot tub at **Hot Water Beach** (p99)
2hr from Hamilton
Coromandel Peninsula
South Pacific Ocean
Ramarama
Thames
Lake Waikare
Soak in natural hot springs in **Rotorua** (p106)
1½ hr from Hamilton
Huntly
Te Aroha
Tauranga
Hamilton
Matamata
Bay of Plenty
Cambridge
Waikato River
Whakatāne
Ōpōtiki
Lake Rotorua
Ōtorohanga
Taste a traditional *hāngī* at a **Māori village** (p121)
5-10min from Rotorua
Te Kuiti
Kayak past huge Māori carvings at **Lake Taupō** (p116)
Taupō
2hr from Hamilton
Ōwhango
Tūrangi
Waimarino
Mt Ngauruhoe
Tongariro National Park
Ski the slopes of an active volcano at **Mt Ruapehu** (p113)
3hr from Hamilton
Ohakune
Waiouru
Waimarino
Napier
Taihape
Hastings
Hawke Bay
0
100 km
0
50 miles

Practicalities

BRIAN SCANTLEBURY/ALAMY

ARRIVING

Hamilton Airport Welcoming international flights from Sydney and the Gold Coast from 2025, this airport is 14km south of NZ's fourth-biggest city. Car rentals are available but there's no public transport or shuttles to Hamilton.

Tauranga Airport Air New Zealand flies here from Auckland, Wellington and Christchurch. The airport (pictured above) is 6km from central Tauranga and 5km from Mount Maunganui. Shuttles, taxis and hire cars are available at the terminal.

HOW MUCH FOR A

Hot-springs visit $24-99

Fish & chips $15

***Hāngī* buffet $57-95**

WHEN TO GO

DEC–FEB
Hot. The beach and lake towns swell with domestic holidaymakers.

MAR–MAY
Still warm but getting cooler, making it a great time for hiking.

JUN–AUG
The ski season starts in July on Ruapehu. Enjoy the hot springs.

SEP–NOV
Warm days with rain and snow melts to boost the rivers.

GETTING AROUND

Car Renting a car gives you access to remote springs, secluded nature walks and more rural destinations. To visit attractions like Waitomo Caves or Hobbiton, a car is essential (unless you book a tour).

Buses You can get between the major towns and cities by bus. However, it can be challenging to access all the major attractions by public transport and the local bus networks are limited in some places.

Shuttles Shuttle services take the form of private buses or minivans and are useful for accessing the ski fields, cycling and hiking track trailheads, and some of the geothermal areas around Rotorua.

EATING & DRINKING

This volcanic region is the only place in the country where you can try a *hāngī* cooked in thermal steam. Visit one of Rotorua's Māori cultural attractions and enjoy a meal of steam-cooked meat and vegetables while learning about the local traditions. Or head to the coast for fish and chips on the beach. The central North Island is also the heart of dairy farming in New Zealand, so try the local ice cream and cheese.

Must-try ice cream
Duck Island, Hamilton (p118)

Best creamed paua
Eze Feedz, Mt Maunganui (p119)

CONNECT & FIND YOUR WAY

Wi-fi Local cafes sometimes have free wi-fi, but, it's best to buy a local SIM card at the airport for data. There is good data connection in towns, but be prepared to lose signal when driving on remote roads.

Navigation Routes are well-signposted and easy to follow, with good signage for major attractions.

DESERT ROAD

Check that the Desert Road is open before heading south from Taupō in winter. It's often closed due to ice and snow.

WHERE TO STAY

The central North Island is predominantly farmland and forests, with a few small cities and towns, each with their own personality. Use a couple of these as a base to explore the region.

Place	Pros/Cons
Rotorua	Best place to see geothermal sites. Can be very touristy. Strong sulphur smell.
Mt Maunganui	Seaside town. Can be expensive and is a popular stop for cruise ships.
Raglan	Bohemian surf town with a variety of accommodation options. Remote.
Hahei	Pretty beachside village. Gets very busy during the summer.
Taupō	Central hub for the major attractions in the region.
Ōhakune	Ski town with good access to Tongariro National Park. Quiet outside of the ski season.

MONEY

Sights, activities and top restaurants are expensive. Fish and chips, and baked goods from bakeries are good options for cheaper meals. There are several places where you can soak in hot springs for free, notably Hot Water Beach.

13 Art & Creativity IN RAGLAN

ART | BEACHES | ACTIVITIES

Raglan's easy-going surf-town vibe and excellent cafe and bar scene is backed up with a diverse and vibrant community of artists, designers and craftspeople. After delving into the town's creative side, set out on relaxed walks through native bush to waterfalls, or get active on a kayak, paddle board or surfboard around the region's spectacular coastline.

PETER UNGER/GETTY IMAGES

How to

Getting here Raglan is 45km west of Hamilton. Busit's route 23 (one hour) departs from Hamilton's Transport Centre.

When to go For the best weather and to avoid holidays and busy weekends, visit Raglan midweek from February to April.

Essential purchase Super-comfortable handmade shoes or sandals from Soul Shoes.

Swim safely Ngarunui Beach is the only one to have lifeguards in the warmer months.

MARTIN VLNAS/GETTY IMAGES

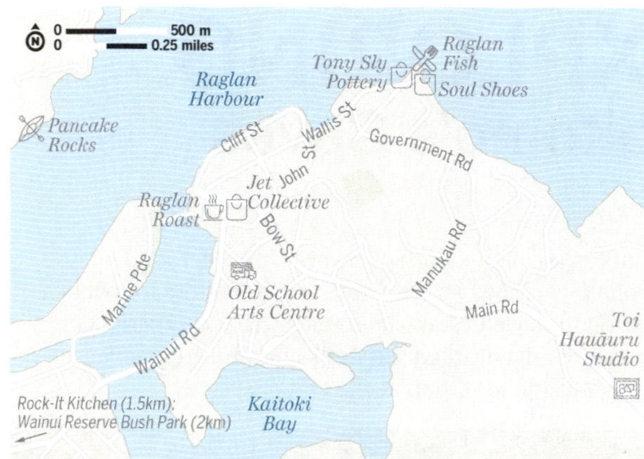

Left Bow St, Raglan
Below Wairēinga/Bridal Veil Falls

Welcome to Arty Whāingaroa

Discover local art An interesting hybrid of gallery and retail store, **Jet Collective** showcases ceramics, painting, textiles and mixed-media works produced by six of Raglan's diverse band of artists and craftspeople, all of whom have been inspired by living around the spectacular harbour known to Māori as Whāingaroa. It's just a short walk to the best coffee in town at **Raglan Roast's** hole-in-the-wall laneway location.

Raglan Creative Market On the second Sunday morning of each month, the **Old School Arts Centre** hosts this excellent event. Look forward to a relaxed vibe, with food stalls selling organic and vegan treats, and plenty of local arts and crafts. A few food trucks usually make the short journey from the nearby Big Smoke of Hamilton.

Contemporary Māori design Meet local Māori artist Simon Te Wheoro at his **Toi Hauāuru Studio**. His work includes stone sculptures and paintings in various media. If you're keen on the ultimate reminder of a visit to Aotearoa, Simon is also skilled at the art of *tā moko* (Māori tattoo). Contact him in advance via his website (simontewheoro.com).

Raglan's historic wharf Browse for both rustic and modern designs at **Tony Sly Pottery**, and stylish leather goods including footwear, bags and satchels at **Soul Shoes**. Also essential is a harbourfront feast of seafood and chips at **Raglan Fish**.

Best Outdoor Experiences

Wainui Reserve Bush Park Cared for by local volunteers, experience peaceful nature walks through this bush reserve with birdsong all around you.

Wairēinga/Bridal Veil Falls A popular proposal spot. Go on a short meandering walk and be greeted at the end by a beautiful plunge waterfall.

Surf Breaks This is what Raglan is known for – amazing surf! Catch the legendary lefthand break at Manu Bay, beginner waves at the beach, or challenge yourself on a big swell day at Whale Bay.

Water Sports Hire a kayak to explore Pancake Rocks, or a stand-up paddle board, and make your way down to Rock-It for lunch.

Recommended by Latesha Hearth *co-founder of Raglan Food Co @raglanfoodco @lateshahearth*

14

EXPLORING Waitomo's Caves

CAVES | ACTION | SCENERY

Waitomo's singular subterranean network of caverns, underground streams and soaring limestone formations has been attracting visitors for over a century. Complementing the region's well-established underground experiences is an exciting and diverse range of adventurous activities guaranteed to give you bragging rights over a cold beer at the local pub at the end of the day.

LUKAS BISCHOFF PHOTOGRAPH/SHUTTERSTOCK

How to

Getting here Waitomo is 70km south of Hamilton. **Great Sights** (greatsights.co.nz) offers combined day trips including Hobbiton, departing Auckland and Rotorua.

When to go With most attractions underground, visiting the caves is possible year-round. Book accommodation in advance for Christmas/New Year and Easter.

Waitomo's quirkiest accommodation Formerly an advertising sign – no, really – the cosy HuHu Chalet is ideal for couples, and Waitomo's best restaurant (of the same name) is right next door. Search on Airbnb.

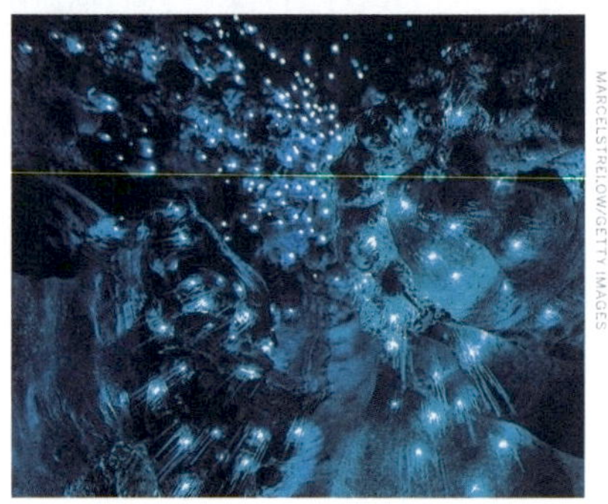

MARCELSTRELOW/GETTY IMAGES

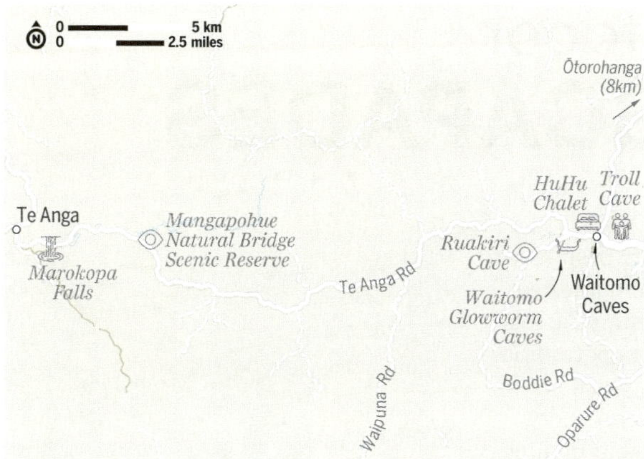

Left Ruakuri Cave
Below Glowworm Cave

Waitomo Three Ways

The big player Waitomo's signature experience is boarding a boat to ride on an underground river to the galaxy-like spectacle of the **Waitomo Glowworm Caves**. This is operated by **Discover Waitomo**, which also offers tours of two other caves (Ruakuri and Aranui) and runs the Legendary Black Water Rafting Company. Combo deals are available for the various experiences.

Sacred space Entered via an innovative 15m-high spiral ramp – allowing full access for wheelchairs – exploration of Waitomo's **Ruakiri Cave** takes in around 1.5km of the cave's entire 7.5km-long system. Underwater streams and waterfalls weave in and out of crystalline banks of limestone. The cave is regarded as an intensely spiritual place by local Māori.

Adrenaline-fuelled action File under 'Only in New Zealand'. From rock climbing, abseiling and underground ziplines to the extreme fun of 'black-water rafting' – floating on a subterranean river on an inner tube while wearing a wetsuit – Waitomo's innovative tourism entrepreneurs offer plenty of ways to combine Aotearoa's adventure sports DNA with the region's natural beauty. **Waitomo Adventures**, **Down to Earth** and the **Legendary Black Water Rafting Company** all offer diverse underground thrills, and booking ahead online often secures a good discount. Good luck with jumping off those underground waterfalls. For younger travellers, Waitomo Adventures' **Troll Cave** is a fun blend of adventure and problem-solving.

Best Scenic Detours

Mangapohue Natural Bridge Scenic Reserve
Kick on 26km west of Waitomo to this duo of natural limestone arches created over millennia by the waters of the Mangapohue Stream. On a wheelchair-accessible pathway, it's a five-minute walk from the road through a narrow gorge shrouded with moss and ferns. Glowworms shimmer and shine after dark, but you'll need a torch to safely make the walk.

Marokopa Falls
Continue for another 6km to the Marokopa Falls, always spectacular in spring after the winter rains. The 30m-high cascade is reached by a 15-minute return track from the roadside car park.

15

Outdoor ESCAPADES

HIKING | BIKING | SCENERY

From the rolling dairy pastures of the Waikato to the craggy and forested spine of the Coromandel Peninsula, this varied area offers plenty of opportunities to get active. Along the way you'll be able to take in bush and river scenery, learn about New Zealand's gold-mining past, and explore a mountain sanctuary focused on protecting the country's endangered native wildlife.

How to

Getting around Renting a car is the most efficient and enjoyable option. Hire bikes in Paeroa or Waihi.

When to go November to April offers the warmest weather and driest trails.

Walk across Coromandel's northern tip Coastal and farmland views are highlights of the 3½-hour 10km hike between Fletcher Bay and Stony Bay on the Coromandel Coastal Walkway. Arrange shuttles in Coromandel Town with Hike & Bike.

Mountain Adventures & Riverside Biking

On two legs Best accessed from the Waikato towns of Cambridge or Te Awamutu, **Sanctuary Mountain Maungatautari** (sanctuarymountain.co.nz) is a superb example of New Zealand's efforts to protect its native species. Not all of 797m triple-peaked Maungatautari is enclosed, but the birdlife spills over into the rest of the public reserve, as you'll see if you hike the five-hour Wairere Traverse (Over The Mountain) Track. It's difficult, muddy and steep – best suited to experienced hikers. There are shorter tracks within the sanctuary itself.

Northeast of Thames, the **Kauaeranga Kauri Trail** (Pinnacles Walk) winds through the Coromandel Forest Park to reach the summit of the Pinnacles (759m) after around four hours. Be immersed in spectacular views of the Coromandel Peninsula before returning, or book ahead to stay overnight in the Department of Conservation (DOC) Pinnacles Hut (doc.govt.nz).

Best Pre- & Post-Action Cafes

The Refinery Fire up the turntable with a record from the overflowing bins of vintage vinyl and team Paeroa's best coffee with a gourmet sandwich. The overflowing Cubano should see you through the best of the Hauraki Rail Trail.

Cafe Melbourne Located in a restored brick-lined bus depot in Thames' historic Grahamstown precinct. Check out the various food stores in the adjacent Depot development for artisan bread and picnic fixings.

Onyx Cambridge cafe which kicks things off with brunch on the weekend and continues into the evening with wood-fired pizza.

On two wheels New Zealand has gone cycle-trail-crazy. The **Hauraki Rail Trail** (haurakirailtrail.co.nz) stretches from Thames all the way south to Matamata, but the most scenic section is the eastern bush-clad spur along the Ohinemuri River through the former gold-mining area of the Karangahake Gorge.

New Zealand's longest river is the interesting backdrop to the **Waikato River Trails** (waikatorivertrails.co.nz). Meandering along tree-lined Lake Karapiro, the 11.5km section linking the Pokaiwhenua Bridge to the rural hamlet of Arapuni is a popular option along the trails' full extent of 104km.

Above Kaka, Sanctuary Mountain Maungatautari

16 Discovering COROMANDEL

BEACHES | HISTORY | ROAD TRIP

The Coromandel Peninsula is criss-crossed by hilly highways and framed by meandering coastal roads. Explore the region's marine landscapes from low-key resort towns; combine gold-mining history and ziplining action around Coromandel Town; or embark on a DIY adventure exploring the peninsula's more remote northern tip.

NAZAR_AB/GETTY IMAGES

How to

Getting here It takes around 2½ hours to drive to Coromandel Town from either Auckland or Hamilton. Self-driving a rental car is the best way to explore the peninsula.

When to go Summer weekends and school holidays (especially) get very busy. Try and visit midweek.

Best bi-valves En route to Coromandel Town, stop at the Coromandel Oyster Company, or enjoy platters of smoked and chilli mussels at the Coromandel Mussel Kitchen.

MATTHEW MICAH WRIGHT/GETTY IMAGES

History & Adventure

Lined with heritage buildings dating from the region's 19th-century gold-mining era, charming **Coromandel Town** is the ideal base for exploring the more remote and rugged northern parts of the Coromandel Peninsula. Cafes and a smattering of design stores and galleries hint at the various arty types living in the surrounding hinterland.

The legacy of pioneering conservationist and potter, the late Barry Brickell, is showcased on the outskirts of town at **Driving Creek**, where gold was first discovered in 1852. Put aside at least half a day to explore the pottery workshops and to partake in the two main attractions that delve through the regenerating native forest here. **Driving Creek Railway** offers one-hour rides on a quirky narrow-gauge train, taking

DAVID WALL/ALAMY

Coromandel by Ferry

Fullers360 usually runs scenic day-trip ferry sailings from downtown Auckland across the Firth of Thames to the Coromandel Peninsula, with free shuttles transporting passengers the final 10km to historic Coromandel Town. The service was on hold at the time of writing; check fullers.co.nz for its current status.

Above left Cathedral Cove (p98)
Above Kayaking to Cathedral Cove (p98)
Left Driving Creek Railway

in spirals, tunnels and switchbacks to end at the 'Eye-full Tower' and views across the Firth of Thames towards Auckland. Also here, **Coromandel Zipline Tours** negotiates an exciting downhill route through the forest on eight separate ziplines, with stops along the way to learn a bit about the site's history.

Coastal Walking & Natural Spa Pools

From the coastal town of **Hahei**, tackle the rolling 45-minute walk to nearby **Cathedral Cove**. The iconic stone arch, often enlivened with a natural waterfall shower, is at its best early or late in the day – avoiding the inevitable crowds for such a popular destination. During summer, **Cathedral Cove Water Taxi** operates a 10-minute shuttle along the coast from Hahei beach to Cathedral Cove that's both scenic and convenient. Cathedral Cove can also be seen on the Hahei Explorer, a fun hour's cruise up and down the coast taking in various sea caves and offshore rock tunnels.

Best Marine Adventures

Explore the coastal caves and rock arches of the **Te Whanganui A Hei Marine Reserve** with Hahei-based **Cathedral Cove Kayak Tours**.

Zip around the marine reserve and check out **Cathedral Cove** from the water on an exciting boat trip from Whitianga with **Ocean Leopard**, **Sea Cave Adventures** or **Cave Cruzer**.

Sail from Whitianga to Cathedral Cove on **Boom Sailing's** catamaran.

Learn to surf with the Kiwi-Brazilian team at **Surf n Stay** at Whangamatā. There's good self-contained accommodation, too.

Join a guided tour or hire a kayak or paddle board from **Surfsup** in Whangamatā to circumnavigate the wildlife sanctuary of **Whenuakura/ Donut Island**.

Left Catamaran, Boom Sailing
Below Spades to dig a natural hot tub, Hot Water Beach

After exploring the cove, journey 10km south to **Hot Water Beach** and dig your own natural Jacuzzi near the rocky outcrop in the middle of the beach. Two hours either side of low tide is recommended to experience the beach's thermal springs, and tide times are listed online (thecoromandel.com). Hire a spade at the nearby **Hot Waves** cafe after digging into its legendary Big Breakfast.

Remote Road-Tripping

For an intrepid adventure, take a loop around the mainly unsealed roads at the far northern end of the peninsula.

From Coromandel Town, head north past **Ōamaru Bay** and **Amodeo Bay** to sleepy **Colville**, a rural village with a hippyish vibe. After **Whangaahei Bay**, cut across the peninsula and continue down the east coast via **Waikawau** and **Kennedy Bay**, before negotiating **Tokatea Hill** back to Coromandel Town. It's only 70km, but count on around two hours' driving time.

Optional extensions include detouring north from Whangaahei Bay along the east coast to remote **Fletcher Bay**, a real end-of-the-road destination at the very north of the peninsula. Alternatively, branch off the inland road and head north via the unsealed northern spur to **Port Charles** and on to **Stony Bay**.

TOMAS PAVELKA/SHUTTERSTOCK

Coromandel's Gold-Mining Heritage

GOLD-INFUSED HISTORY AMID STELLAR FOREST SCENERY

Explore the historic 19th-century shopfronts and streetscapes of Thames and Coromandel Town before learning about the past, present and future of Coromandel gold-mining amid the scenic Karangahake Gorge and in the interesting town of Waihi. The award-winning Waihi Gold Discovery Centre is one of New Zealand's best regional museums.

Left Martha Mine, Waihi
Centre Karangahake Gorge Windows Walk
Right Cornish pumphouse, Martha Goldmine, Waihi

The Attraction of £500

Back in 1852, £500 was a substantial amount of money (equivalent to around $74,000 in contemporary terms), enough of a reward to attract prospectors from around New Zealand hoping to be the first to discover gold in the Hauraki region. Scores of wannabe miners, especially from the then-capital of Auckland (Wellington only became the nation's capital in 1867), descended on the remote rivers of the Coromandel Peninsula in a concerted effort to win the reward and become the luckiest and richest bloke in town.

NZ's First Gold Discovery

Leading the charge was Charles Ring, recently returned from the California goldfields with his brother Frederick. In October 1852, after negotiating access with local Māori, they found gold flakes on the banks of Driving Creek, now just a short distance from Coromandel Town. Alluvial gold deposits in the river ran out after a month – foreshadowing the future emergence of a different kind of gold-mining around the Coromandel – and the discovery of gold in Central Otago in 1861 saw gold fever take hold around Queenstown and Arrrowtown on the South Island.

A Golden Era for Thames

After gold was again discovered nearby in 1867, Thames became the centre for Coromandel gold-mining, but now using a more mechanised and industrial process to extract gold from the region's quartz-laden rock faces. With a population of 15,000 in 1870, Thames was one of New Zealand's most important towns. Banks and a stock exchange lined the main street, and the value of

JEF WODNIACK/SHUTTERSTOCK

MICHAEL YOUNG/GETTY IMAGES

annual gold production surged to more than £1 million by 1871. Mining schools opened in Thames, Coromandel Town and Waihi, and over 100 pubs and three theatres ensured Thames' hard-working residents enjoyed their downtime.

Martha's Time to Shine

In 1878, gold was discovered in Pukewa Hill near Waihi, and from 1878 to 1911, the town's Martha Mine was one of the world's most important gold mines. More than 170km of tunnels criss-crossed inside the hill, employing more than 600 men, and ore from the mine was transported by train to nearby Waikino, where the Victoria Battery was Australasia's largest quartz-crushing plant. Further along the Ohinemuri River rail line linking Waihi to Paeroa, other mining batteries were in the hills lining the rugged Karangahake Gorge, but Waihi's Martha Mine was always the biggest game in town.

> The value of annual gold production surged to more than £1 million by 1871.

Martha's Possible Future

Martha survived a six-month miners' strike in 1912 but, after a downturn in global gold prices, the massive 600m-deep mine was closed in 1952. Following a revival in gold prices, Martha was reopened in the 1980s as an opencast pit mine measuring 1km by 700m, and this style of mining continued until a major landslide in 2015. Underground mining continues at Martha and, at the time of writing, proposals to restart open-pit mining were being considered by the district council. It's thought that there are still many millions of dollars worth of silver and gold in the ground here.

Unearthing Coromandel's Gold-Flecked History

Gold Discovery Centre Learn about Waihi's gold-mining journey at the interactive Waihi Gold Experience.

Waihi Gold Mine Tour Get 'inside the fence' and get the lowdown on a modern-day working gold mine.

Martha Open Pit Walkway Look down into this massive open-pit gold mine right in the middle of Waihi township.

Victoria Battery & Tramway Explore this heritage site in Waikino where ore from Martha Mine was processed from 1897 to 1952.

Karangahake Gorge Windows Walk Negotiate this historic gold-mining area high above the Onhinemuri and Waitawheta Rivers.

Recommended by Eddie Morrow
General Manager, Waihi Gold Discovery Centre

Culture & History in HAMILTON

GARDENS | ART | HISTORY

Often overlooked as a tourist destination, New Zealand's fourth-largest city offers a trio of standout museums and cultural experiences, and there's also an excellent restaurant scene. Before heading west to the arty surf town of Raglan, east to Hobbiton, or south to the Waitomo Caves, spend at least a day experiencing the rural heartland city also known as Kirikiriroa.

NATALIACATALINA.COM/SHUTTERSTOCK

How to

Getting here Hamilton is an easy 90-minute drive south of Auckland.

When to go Hamilton is not a key destination for travellers, so visiting year-round is fine. July and August can be colder and more rainy.

Cross the river Check out the emerging dining scene in Hamilton East – standouts are Hayes Common and GG's Cafe.

TRABANTOS/SHUTTERSTOCK

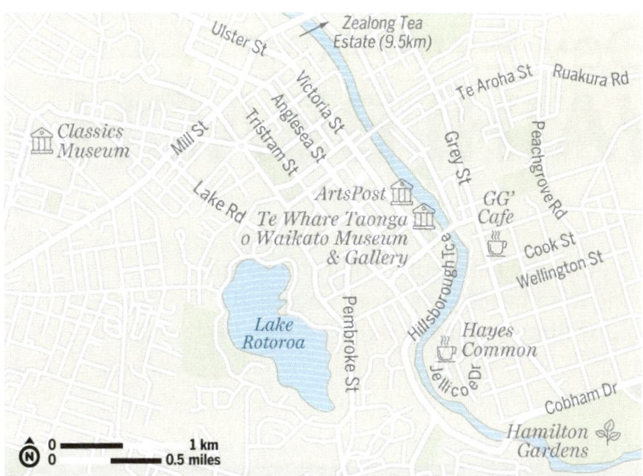

World-class gardens A brilliant destination for all travellers, but especially enjoyable for families, the **Hamilton Gardens** (hamiltongardens.co.nz) are spread over 50 spectacular hectares southeast of the city centre. At its core are 18 magical walled gardens devoted to various themes, including Ancient Egyptian, Italian, Japanese and Chinese gardens. The surprising Surrealist garden is an intriguing and thoroughly entertaining experience inspired by dreams, magic realism and the subconscious. In Te Parapara, the focus is on traditional crops grown for food and medicine by local Māori.

Superb Māori galleries With a riverside location in the city centre, the highlight of **Te Whare Taonga o Waikato Museum & Gallery** (tewharetaonga.nz) is the gallery showcasing *taonga* (treasures) from the Tainui *iwi* who call the broader Waikato region home. Its centrepiece is the magnificent *waka taua* (war canoe), Te Winika. Check online for a rotating schedule of special exhibitions. Adjacent to the museum, **ArtsPost** is a gallery and retail space focused on work from local artists.

A surprising transport museum Just off SH1C on the north-western edge of the city (look for the giant jukebox facade), the **Classics Museum** (classicsmuseum.co.nz) is a treasure trove of more than 100 vintage cars. Seriously cool vehicles include retro Corvette and Maserati sports cars, and the so-crazy-this-might-just-work amphibious Amphicar from the 1960s. There's also a nostalgia-inducing collection of toys, pedal cars and petrol-pump memorabilia.

Left Italian Renaissance Garden, Hamilton Gardens
Below Zealong Tea Estate

Treat Yourself to High Tea

Surrounded by dairy farms 12km northeast of Hamilton, the tea bushes framing the entrance to the **Zealong Tea Estate** (zealong.com) come as a real surprise. Tea plantations usually feature at higher elevations in warmer countries, and Zealong is unique as both New Zealand's only tea estate and the world's largest organic tea-growing enterprise.

The beautiful 48-hectare estate features gardens, a shop with tea tastings, and tours with tea ceremonies. Otherwise you can enjoy estate views over high tea at its elegant teahouse, or venture upstairs for a fine-dining experience at Camellia Restaurant.

18 A Day Exploring WAIHI BEACH

BEACHES | WALKING | EATING

At the base of the Coromandel Peninsula, 11km from Waihi itself, Waihi Beach is a classic Kiwi beach village set on a 9km stretch of gorgeous sand and rolling surf. Easy walks provide stellar views along the coast.

STARGRASS/SHUTTERSTOCK

Trip Notes

Getting here By car, Waihi Beach is 90 minutes from Hamilton, and two hours from Auckland.

When to go Spring and summer are the best times, but try and visit on a quieter weekday during school holidays and at Easter.

Refuel Grab a garden seat at Surf Shack Eatery (surfshackeatery.co.nz), on the road to Athenree, and tuck into delicious burgers and salads.

Waihi's Summer Vibe

The garden bar at the **Waihi Beach Hotel** (waihibeachhotel.co.nz) is a popular summertime destination, with New Zealand bands taking to the little outdoor stage throughout the warmer months. Call in for a craft beer after a hard day's beaching. As the pub's own website says, 'Kiwi as, bro!'

01 At the northern end of Waihi beach, walk up and over the headland on the Orokawa Scenic Reserve Walkway. The cliff-top walk to isolated Orokawa Bay takes around 45 minutes.
02 Browse the shops and galleries along Wilson Road, Waihi Beach's sleepy main drag. Essential stops are authentic Swiss chocolate at Chez Moi and contemporary art at the Waihi Beach Gallery.
03 Combine lunch and views of Mayor Island/Tūhua from Flatwhite cafe's beachfront location. It's the kind of easy-going place where staff and diners both like to wear colourful Hawaiian shirts.
04 Continue to Bowentown at the southern end of Waihi Beach, and negotiate walking tracks around an ancient Māori pā site for views of Matakana Island and Anzac Bay.
05 Top off the day by relaxing in the hot pools at the nearby Athenree Hot Springs. If you're travelling by campervan, there's a good holiday park here, too.
Golden Valley Rd
Ngatitangata Rd
Golden Valley
Mayor Island/ Tuhua (22km)
Orokawa Bay
Beach Rd
Waihi Beach
Waihi Beach Hotel
Emerton Rd
Seaforth Rd
Steele Rd
Athenree
Bay of Plenty
Athenree Rd
Shelly Bay
0 2 km
0 1 mile

19 Hot Springs & COOL LAKES

THERMAL SPRINGS | LAKES | OUTDOORS

Somewhat ironically, the central North Island's explosive past has gifted it with dozens of tranquil lakes and mineral-infused hot springs. Nowhere is this more evident than Rotorua where there are 18 lakes scattered around the steamy city. It's a popular summertime destination for swimming and boating, while the warm thermal waters are a major drawcard all year round.

How to

Getting here Driving is the easiest way to access the more remote lakes, hot springs and geothermal attractions.

When to go The best time for swimming in the lakes is from December through to March, but it gets busy from Christmas to the end of January when the schools are on holiday.

Unique experiences Rotorua is one of the best places to see a Māori cultural performance.

Bubbles and steam Witness New Zealand's volcanic nature bursting to life in the bubbling mud pools, boiling lakes and spurting geysers of Rotorua's ticketed geothermal attractions. **Te Puia** and **Whakarewarewa** are right on the edge of the city, and come with a hefty serving of Māori culture. Further out, **Hell's Gate** (p121), **Wai-O-Tapu Thermal Wonderland**, **Waimangu Volcanic Valley** and **Ōrākei** Kōrako all have meandering tracks past colourful mineral deposits, sulphur pools and even a hot-water waterfall and mud volcano.

Submerge yourself in thermal springs While seeing the boiling lakes and rivers is an amazing experience, soak in a hot spring to truly immerse yourself in volcanic New Zealand. In Rotorua, the classic option is the lakefront **Polynesian Spa**. A cheaper more family-friendly option is **Waikite Valley Thermal Pools** (p121), about 25

DMITRY PICHUGIN/SHUTTERSTOCK

minutes' drive from central Rotorua.

Explore the volcanic lakes
While **Lake Rotorua** is right on the city's doorstep, it's worth taking a 15-minute drive to the picturesque pair known as the 'Blue and Green Lakes'. Spend a few hours boating, swimming or fishing on the azure waters of **Lake Tikitapu** and marvel at the contrast of colours with the emerald **Lake Rotokākahi** next to it; just keep in mind that Rotokākahi is *tapu* (sacred) and off limits. Other options include **Lakes Rotoiti**, **Ōkāreka** and **Tarawera**.

Free Geothermal Experiences

For a free peek at Rotorua's geothermal wonders, head to Kuirau Park or Government Gardens, both of which are just a few minutes' walk from the city centre. In Kuirau Park, paths lead past steaming lakes and boiling mud pools just a few metres away from cars and houses. Finish your walk by soaking your feet in the free public foot bath. After viewing the fenced-off hot springs of Government Gardens, continue on the boardwalk along the lakefront to Sulphur Point where birds roost as the steam wreathes around them.

Above Pōhutu Geyser, Te Puia

20 Food from the Forest & THE SEA

FOOD | FISHING | CULTURE

Discover the traditional flavours of New Zealand while feasting on authentic Māori *kai* (food). The Bay of Plenty is a great place to try *kai moana* (seafood), while Rotorua offers ample opportunities to combine cultural experiences with the rich flavours of roast meats and vegetables slow-cooked in the warm earth of a *hāngī*.

NAURIS KRESLINS/SHUTTERSTOCK

How to

When to go Whitebait is generally available between September and November while *kōura* (crayfish) is served year-round.

Costs *Hāngī* costs from $15 at a food truck to over $50 at a buffet restaurant. Pies can be cheaper.

Top tip It can be challenging to find Māori flavours at restaurants. Instead, head to festivals and events, where there are often food trucks offering a range of traditional Māori foods.

KIM HOWELL/SHUTTERSTOCK

BRIANSCANTLEBURY/GETTY IMAGES

Left Preparing a *hāngī*
Far left *Hāngī*
Bottom left *Kina*

Underground feasts Preparing a *hāngī* is both a labour and a ritual. Food is wrapped in leaves or placed in woven baskets and lowered into a pit lined with super-heated stones. The pit is covered and the meat and vegetables cook slowly, gently flavoured by the smoke from the fire. In areas with geothermal activity like Rotorua, geothermal steam is sometimes used to cook the meat.

Kai moana – the food of the sea, lakes and rivers As an island country, New Zealand has an abundance of *kai moana*. Crayfish is very popular, but it's an expensive treat. Other delicious, more affordable options include large, green-lipped mussels and plump scallops. Paua, a black abalone, and whitebait (tiny juvenile fish) are usually served in fritters; food trucks at markets and festivals are great ways to try these local treats. Kina (sea urchin) is usually eaten raw and is best suited to more adventurous eaters. Try kina shots at festivals and events for a small taste of this local delicacy.

Catch your dinner Reward your fishing efforts by cooking your catch. Common ocean species include snapper, gurnard and tarakihi. It's sometimes possible to have your catch filleted and smoked or cooked by a chef at a local restaurant. Ask your charter operator or hosts for their recommendations before you go fishing so you can arrange with restaurants in advance.

Haka & Hāngī in Rotorua

Steamy **Te Puia** has an inhouse restaurant, **Pātaka Kai**, which serves lunch and dinner buffets featuring *hāngī*-cooked meats and vegetables. Evening visits to the geothermal complex combine the buffet with a cultural performance in a magnificent carved meeting house.

Te Pā Tū is the one for foodies. The four-hour experience starts with transport from town to a recreated pre-colonial *pā* (fortified village) sitting within native bush. A traditional welcome and performances follow, combined with contemporary takes on Māori cuisine, including a *hāngī*.

Longstanding, family-run **Mitai Māori Village** also offers a recreated *pā*, a show and a genuine earth-cooked *hāngī*.

21 A Traditional KIWI SUMMER

BEACHES | CAMPING | FAMILY-FRIENDLY

Experience summer like the locals do – by heading to the beach. The Bay of Plenty is a popular destination, with hot spots around Tauranga and Whakatāne swelling substantially from Christmas to March. Camp near the water and wake up to incredible views. Barbecue your dinners or opt for the Kiwi classic: fish and chips on the beach.

PHOTOS BRIANSCANTLEBURY/SHUTTERSTOCK

How to

Expect to pay Around \$18 per night for a standard DOC campsite and up to \$90 for a powered campervan site at peak season in a holiday park.

Weather The average daily high in the Bay of Plenty is above 20°C from November right through to April, peaking above 24°C in January and February.

Essential supplies Sunscreen and insect repellent. Mosquitos can be a nuisance in the evenings.

JOSHUADANIEL/SHUTTERSTOCK

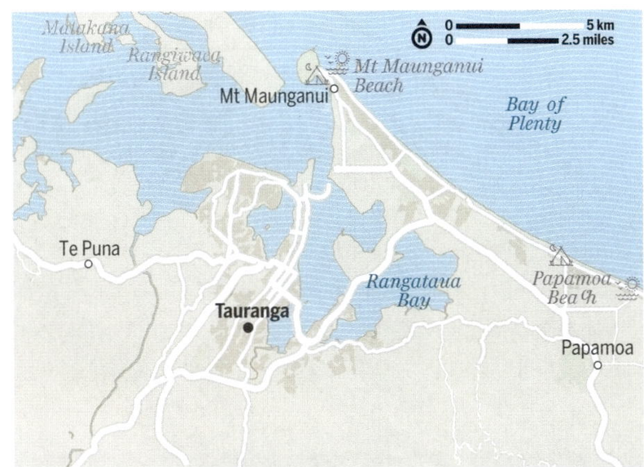

Left Holiday park, Mt Maunganui
Below Mt Maunganui

Camping by the sea Spending a week or more camping at the beach is a Kiwi favourite during the summer. Some favourite locations include **Mt Maunganui**, **Papamoa** and **Ōhope**, where you can wake up with the long, sandy beach on your doorstep. Holiday parks with good facilities abound, or, if you want something a bit more simple in a beautiful location, pick a DOC campsite. Break up your days with ice cream from the local dairy (convenience store) and watch the sunset with fish and chips and beer on the beach.

A home away from home The Kiwi bach (pronounced 'batch') was traditionally a small, simple house near the beach with basic facilities. Nowadays, the name is used for any holiday home, including some which are surprisingly luxurious. Search popular sites bookabach.co.nz or bachcare.co.nz to find your summer home by the sea. Spend your days at the beach and cook your dinner on the barbecue in the evenings.

A holiday highlight Spend at least a day (or more) exploring Mt Maunganui, a seaside suburb just outside of Tauranga city centre. Walk around the volcanic *maunga* (mountain) or hike to the top for extraordinary coastal views. Afterwards, walk down the main street and relax in one of the many local cafes and bars, or prepare a picnic and enjoy it on the sandy beach.

Things to Do in Tauranga

Tauranga is New Zealand's fifth-biggest city, a harbour town that has stretched out to include the surf suburbs of Mt Maunganui and Papamoa. It's worth taking a stroll along the central-city waterfront and on to **The Elms**, a heritage homestead with gardens and daily tours.

For freshwater family fun, head to Waimarino Adventure Park on the Wairoa River where there are waterslides, Tarzan swings and a human catapult into the water. Further upriver, McClaren Falls Park has some good swimming spots, including the pools that make up the falls themselves.

22 Adventures Among VOLCANOES

HIKING | SKIING | CYCLING

Explore the rugged volcanic landscape of Ruapehu and Tongariro. Challenge yourself on strenuous hikes among craters and lake, cycle through forests, and snowboard down volcanoes. Seek out waterfalls and savour the bits of luxury hidden in unexpected places.

MATTEO COLOMBO/GETTY IMAGES

How to

Getting here By car, Tongariro National Park is around four hours from Auckland and 2½ hours from Hamilton. InterCity buses and Northern Explorer trains stop at Waimarino (National Park) and Ohakune.

When to go December to April for hiking and July to October for skiing and snowboarding.

Getting around Private shuttles head to the ski fields and track trailheads from Whakapapa, Waimarino and Ohakune.

JUSTIN PAGET/GETTY IMAGES

Take to the Slopes

Experience skiing or snowboarding on an active volcano. With three ski areas to choose between, **Mt Ruapehu** has well-maintained trails, snowy basins and spectacular views. **Whakapapa** is New Zealand's largest ski field and its Happy Valley ski area is great for kids. **Tūroa** boasts the country's longest vertical descent (722m) and **Tūkino**, a club-operated field, is a low-frills option for avoiding the queues.

IV4NGRIGORYEV/SHUTTERSTOCK

Cycle the Old Coach Road

A fascinating day ride, the **Ōhakune Old Coach Road** connects Ohakune and Horopito. Originally used by horse-drawn coaches, the route is steeped in history, passing through farmland and forest in Tongariro National Park.

Whakapapa Village

This small alpine village on the northern slopes of Ruapehu is home to the excellent **Tongariro National Park Visitor Centre**. More than just a source of tourist information, the centre is like a mini museum, with a 3D model of the park and fascinating displays.

Above left Tongariro Alpine Crossing
Above Cycling, Tongariro National Park
Left Snowboarder, Mt Ruapehu

Find old railway tunnels and bush camps, marvel at the views of Mt Ruapehu and see the remnants of the original cobblestone road as you ride. The bumpy trail also passes two historic railway viaducts including the **Hapuawhenua** viaduct at 45m high and 245m long. This route is suitable for families and is easiest to cycle from Horopito to Ohakune.

Trek Through Volcanic Peaks & Dramatic Landscapes

The **Tongariro Alpine Crossing** is widely regarded as the top single-day hike in New Zealand. The 'crossing' part refers to the route it takes over the saddle between Ngauruhoe and Tongariro, reaching a peak of 1886m above sea level as it traverses the lip of Tongariro's Red Crater before descending past emerald lakes and tussock-covered slopes to shady, green forest.

This reasonably arduous six- to eight-hour (20.2km) hike is best avoided from May to late October when route-finding is difficult and many of the highlights are hidden by snow. You'll need to arrange shuttles to

Après Ski in Ohakune

Sitting immediately below Mt Ruapehu, right on the doorstep of Tongariro National Park, Ohakune is a true outdoors town. In winter it pumps with snow enthusiasts. They melt away in summer, only to be replaced with hikers and mountain bikers. Yet it still feels like a lived-in town, making it the buzziest base for exploring the national park.

The vibe is best when snow drifts down on Ruapehu and people defrost together over a drink back in town after spending the day on the slopes at Tūroa. Despite the chill outside, the après-ski culture comes in hot every season.

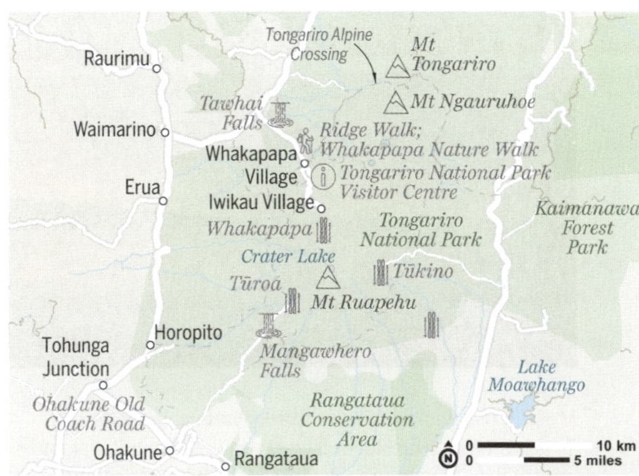

Left Mt Ruapehu
Below Tawhai Falls/Gollum's pool

and from the trailheads, and book your walk through DOC.

Easy Short Walks

You don't have to be geared up for a major expedition to get a taste of what Ruapehu has to offer. The wheelchair-accessible **Whakapapa Nature Walk** is a 15-minute loop through beech trees bearded with moss, in constant earshot of a gurgling stream, starting around 250m above the visitor centre. Nearby is the **Ridge Walk**, a 30-minute, 1.2km return track that starts in beech forest and climbs through tussock and low scrub to a lookout. If you're visiting around sunset, this is the place to be.

Discover Alpine Waterfalls... & Gollum's Pool

Majestic waterfalls are sometimes just a short walk from the road. Follow the sign on Ohakune Mountain Rd and take a 10-minute stroll from the car park to the **Mangawhero Falls**, surrounded by beech forest. In winter, icicles form around the edge.

On the approach to Whakapapa you'll find **Tawhai Falls**, which drop 13m over the edge of an ancient lava flow. It was in the pool at the bottom that Gollum found the ring in the *Lord of the Rings* movies.

STEWART WATSON/GETTY IMAGES

Stories of the Earth

THE PEOPLE AND THE LAND ARE ONE

In Māori tradition, places and the stories about them are inextricably intertwined. Many natural features are considered *tapu* (sacred), and some are even regarded as ancestral figures. The stories of the mountains, rivers and lakes that dominate the North Island illustrate the rich heritage and power of this fiery land.

Left Lake Taupō
Centre Boiling Lake, Kuirau Park
Below Ngātoro-i-rangi carvings, Mine Bay

Most of the geological landmarks within the centre of Te Ika-a-Māui (the North Island) have deep cultural and spiritual significance to local Māori. There are many stories about how that landscape formed, some of which are told differently by different *iwi* (tribes). Here are some stories from just a few of the region's landmarks.

Filling Taupō with Water

One of the largest crater lakes in the world, **Lake Taupō** was formed by a series of huge volcanic eruptions which started around 300,000 years ago. The effects of the last major cataclysm, which took place around 181 CE, were seen as far away as Rome and China.

One of the Māori legends of Lake Taupō tells how the crater filled with water. When the early Polynesian explorer and priest Ngātoro-i-rangi first saw Taupō, it was a huge bowl in the earth. In an effort to promote growth, he uprooted a totara tree and threw it into the dirt. The wind caused him to miss his mark and, after striking a hard bank, the tree landed upside down, its branches piercing the earth.

Fresh water welled up, forming Taupō Moana – 'The sea of Taupō'. This tree is said to still be visible under the water about 70m off the shore at Wharewaka Point. After giving thanks, Ngātoro-i-rangi threw feathers from his cloak into the water where they became the native fish of the lake.

Tongariro's Victory

Tongariro, the great warrior, was one of seven mountains surrounding Lake Taupō. Pihanga was the only female

NATALIACATALINA.COM/SHUTTERSTOCK

NATALIACATALINA.COM/SHUTTERSTOCK

mountain in the range, and she was exceptionally beautiful. The other mountains were all in love with her and fought each other for her favour. As they battled, the land beneath them erupted with fire, smoke and hot rocks, and the ground shuddered beneath them.

Eventually, Tongariro was victorious, winning Pihanga's devotion and the right to stand next to her. The defeated mountains had a single night to move away from the couple and at dawn remained fixed in their new locations forever.

Kuirau Park's Boiling Lake

With its boiling mud pools and steaming rivers, it's not surprising that many local legends take place in Rotorua. In the centre of town is **Kuirau Park**, named after a woman from a tragic tale. The park is known for its boiling lake; however, according to this story, the lake was cool in the past.

> Lake Taupō is so large that when you stand on one side, you cannot see across to the far shore.

The first people to live on its shores were a couple, Tamahika and Kuirau. One day when Kuirau was bathing in the lake, a *taniwha* (sea monster) grabbed her and dragged her down into the depths of the lake.

The gods saw this and were angry, so they made the waters of the lake boil. The *taniwha* was destroyed but Kuirau was also killed, and since that time the lake and the park around it have taken her name.

Stories in Stone

The journeys of the explorer Ngātoro-i-rangi took him through the Bay of Plenty, past Lake Tarawera, past Lake Taupō and to the peaks of Tongariro National Park. His magic also brought cold and frost to the mountain tops and fire to the volcanoes.

In Mine Bay on Lake Taupō you can see a series of carvings, including the stylised 14m-high face of Ngātoro-i-rangi, etched into the cliffs in the late 1970s by master carver Matahi Whakataka-Brightwell and his students. The carvings are also only visible from the water, so book a boat tour or hire a kayak.

Listings

BEST OF THE REST

Favourite Feeds

Rock-It Bar & Eatery, Raglan $$

Have breakfast or lunch in an old woolshed nestled among native plants. It's an unpretentious spot that embodies Raglan's laid-back atmosphere.

ULO's Kitchen, Raglan $$

Noodle- and rice-based dishes influenced by Japan and flavours from around the world. A relaxed vibe with friendly staff and indoor and outdoor seating. Try the cocktails (or mocktails) when you visit.

Huhu Café, Waitomo Caves $$

Modern Kiwi cuisine, wine and craft beer served on a terrace overlooking a verdant valley. It's the standout choice in Waitomo Caves village.

Duck Island Ice Cream, Hamilton East $

High-quality artisan ice cream made locally with a wide range of flavours. Available by the tub from retail stores, but having scoops from the signature store is better. Offers a good range of vegan options.

Gothenburg, Hamilton $$$

Enjoy tapas with a river view in Hamilton. The wide selection of food caters to diverse groups, and vegetarians are catered for. A great spot for a drink and a bite with friends.

Luke's Kitchen, Kūaotunu $$

The go-to for traditional, wood-fire pizza and fresh, organic coffee. There's also a good selection of seafood, salads and cabinet food. Relax with live music and views during the summer.

Blue Ginger, Whitianga $$

Asian fusion at its best with dumplings, stir-fries and fresh salads on the menu. Blue Ginger takes pride in using local seafood and produce, and be sure to try its special seasonal dishes.

Port Road Project, Whangamatā $$

Scandi style and sunny shared tables make this main-street cafe a standout. If paua fritters are on the menu, be sure to try them.

Falls Retreat, Karangahake Gorge $$$

Slow food made with seasonal, organic produce in a picturesque setting. The menu changes frequently, but is always delicious, and the location feels like you're miles away from the world.

Surf Shack, Waihi Beach $$

A family favourite with a kids' play area and child-friendly options. Head there for brunch or try the burgers if you're there later in the day.

Eze Feedz, Mt Maunganui $

Taste authentic Māori and Pasifika food you can usually only get at someone's house (and

SKYIMAGES/GETTY IMAGES

Gothenburg, Hamilton

CENTRAL NORTH ISLAND REVIEWS

then only for a celebration). Try creamed paua on chips, fry bread and even *hāngī*.

Rotorua Night Market $

Thursday nights see Tutanekai St transformed into a lively microcosm of global street food – Māori, Mexican, Malaysian… you name it. Local musicians provide the entertainment.

Atticus Finch, Rotorua $$$

A modern bistro with seats spilling onto the pavement. Food is designed to be shared so go with a group, order some wine and take your time lingering over your meal.

Master of India, Taupō $$

Generous portions of Indian-style curries served with fluffy naan bread. Flavours are authentic and the service is warm, friendly and helpful. Try the banquet if you're in a group and hungry.

Pauly's Diner, Taupō $

On those hungry days head to Pauly's for a burger and chips (or potato and gravy if you prefer). Portions are large, the meals are satisfying and the milkshakes are a must.

Local Watering Holes

Merchant of Matamata, Matamata $$

Have a pint (or two) of locally produced craft beer with some snacks to share. Sample some of the beer on tap and enjoy the friendly, relaxing atmosphere. Stay for a meal if you're hungry – the portions are generous.

Star & Garter, Coromandel Town $$

Sip your drink and soak up your surroundings in this historic building. Choose from a range of local beer and wine. Head outside to the garden bar if it gets hot inside.

Pour House, Hahei $$

Relax with a drink in the peaceful gardens of this small brewery. Taste the craft beers

WALTER BIBIKOW/GETTY IMAGES

Star & Garter, Coromandel Town

or sip a glass of wine in the picturesque surroundings. There are also light meals on offer.

Hop House, Tauranga $$

Spend a leisurely afternoon drinking boutique wine or craft beer in this historic pub in central Tauranga. In summer sit outside in the beer garden. The Sunday lunch is a local favourite.

Powderkeg, Ōhakune $$$

Drop in for a mulled wine or beer after a day out on the slopes. Enjoy the cosy ambience and warm fires, and grab a pub-style meal. There's also live music from time to time.

Adventure Activities

Canyonz, Thames

Abseil down canyons deep in the Coromandel, with waterfalls thundering nearby. Cool off by leaping into deep pools and slipping down waterslides. An exhilarating outdoor adventure.

Redwoods Treewalk, Rotorua

Explore a redwood forest on walkways suspended high in the branches of 125-year-old trees. For extra magic, visit at night when it's illuminated by lanterns. Alternatively, pump up the adrenaline on the three Redwoods Altitude ziplines.

Kaituna Cascades Rafting, Rotorua

Discover the thrill of white-water rafting on the Kaituna River, surrounded by native bush. Float through deep-water canyons and raft over rapids, including what's said to be the world's highest commercially rafted waterfall.

Zorb Rotorua

Careen down a grassy hillside in a big plastic bubble, with or without water inside. There are four tracks to choose between: short and sharp, or zigzagging.

Family-Friendly Fun

Hobbiton Movie Set

Step into Middle Earth and experience life in the Shire for yourself. Take a guided tour through the movie set and finish with a drink at the Green Dragon Inn.

Julians Berry Farm & Café, Whakātane

Spend a morning picking your own berries, then head to the cafe overlooking the berry fields. Children love the berry ice creams and the on-site petting farm, playground and mini golf course.

Skyline Rotorua

Catch the 900m cable-drawn gondola up the slopes of Mt Ngongotahā. At the top, let the kids whizz around on the luge while the grownups enjoy a tasting at Volcanic Hills Winery.

aMAZEme, Rotorua

Get lost in a hedge maze with your family and friends. Race the kids to the middle, get stuck in the dead end and play the other games and activities on site when you finish.

Agrodome, Rotorua

Meet Shaun the Sheep, catch a farm show and ride in a tractor-drawn trailer in this working demonstration farm near Rotorua. The National Kiwi Hatchery is also on site.

Wingspan National Bird of Prey Centre, Rotorua

Time your visit for the 'Flight of the Falcon' at this centre in Ngongotahā (10 minutes from central Rotorua) dedicated to conserving threatened NZ raptors.

Paradise Valley Springs Wildlife Park, Rotorua

The lions (fed at 2.30pm) are the big draw, but there are also native birds, streams full of trout, alpacas and a treetop walkway.

3D Trick Art Gallery, Rotorua

Fill your Instagram feed with optical-illusion snaps in this kooky gallery attached to a heritage farm in Fairy Springs, a 10-minute drive from central Rotorua.

Unique Art & Designs

Puawai Jade, Rotorua

Discover the beauty of New Zealand *pounamu* (jade) and watch as it's carved into intricate patterns. Learn the meanings behind the Māori symbols and consider sharing this traditional gift with a loved one.

Ahu Boutique, Rotorua

For a hint of local flair, check out the Māori-inspired fashion in this small boutique. Admire the colourful prints, artistic fabrics and sophisticated classics. There is also intricate jewellery on display.

Ticketed Geothermal Attractions

Wai-O-Tapu Thermal Wonderland

Wander through a surreal landscape of geothermal wonders, past colourful pools of bubbling water, exploding geysers and the largest mud pool in New Zealand. Allow a couple of hours.

Waimangu Volcanic Valley

Wander down a lush valley lined with native bush passing colourful hot lakes and cascades to Lake Rotomahana, where there's the option to take a cruise.

Hell's Gate

View dramatic geothermal sights then relax in a mud pool, sulphur bath or hot spring. Take the opportunity to learn about the healing properties of the geothermal mud and waters.

Waikite Valley Thermal Pools

Submerge yourself in thermal waters in hot pools filled from a boiling spring. The water is cooled to varying temperatures, so pick the one that relaxes you the most. It's bliss on a cold winter's day.

Free Geothermal Experiences

Kuirau Park

Follow walkways over boiling mud pools and steaming streams in the centre of Rotorua. Marvel at the bubbling lakes and soak your feet in the free foot bath at the end of the path.

Kerosene Creek, near Rotorua

You don't have to pay a thing for a mineral soak in this natural hot stream set in the forest, a 25-minute drive south of Rotorua.

Spa Thermal Park, Taupō

The thermal waters of the Otumuheke Stream meet the bracing Waikato River in this public park, creating a free spa bath within natural nooks.

Waikato River Rapids

Huka Falls, Taupō

When New Zealand's longest river emerges from its largest lake and is slammed through a narrow channel, it creates a mesmerising maelstrom in shades of icy blue. Hike or mountain-bike here along the Huka Trails.

BOB HILSCHER/SHUTTERSTOCK

Te Puia, Rotorua

Aratiatia Rapids, Taupō

Further downriver, watch thousands of litres of water flow from the Aratiatia Dam through a narrow gorge when the floodgates are opened at scheduled times each day.

Māori Culture & Heritage

Mataatua: The House That Came Home, Whakātane

Discover ancient Māori rituals and traditions in the restored Mataatua Wharenui (meeting house). The fully carved house is precious to the Ngāti Awa people, and provides a fascinating setting to hear their stories.

Te Puia, Rotorua

Discover Māori culture, art and food surrounded by geothermal activity. Take the tour to learn about Te Puia's history and lineage and take a peek into how Māori people lived before European settlement.

Whakarewarewa: The Living Māori Village, Rotorua

Have a rare glimpse of traditional Māori life in a fully functional village surrounded by geothermal sights. Experience a Māori cultural performance and try a *hāngī* pie at the on-site cafe.

LOWER NORTH ISLAND

RURAL | CULTURAL | SCENERY

LOWER NORTH ISLAND
Trip Builder

The Lower North Island is a prime example of the unique concentration of diverse landscapes for which New Zealand is famed: rolling farmland, snow-capped mountain chains, surf-battered beaches and wild river gorges all sit within short driving distance.

COUPEK MARTIN/SHUTTERSTOCK

Practicalities

ARRIVING

Hawke's Bay Airport Only 6km from central Napier; taxis and shuttles available.

New Plymouth Airport The airport is 11km east of the city centre, a 15-minute ride by taxi or shuttle.

MONEY

The great outdoors takes top billing here, and most of the main attractions are free.

CONNECT

Don't rely on a phone signal when exploring remote areas such as Whanganui National Park.

WHERE TO STAY

Place	Pros/Cons
New Plymouth	Convenient for hiking, restaurants, beaches and galleries. Plenty of camping options.
Napier	Best nightlife in Hawke's Bay. Art-deco capital and close to airport.
Havelock North	Plentiful boutique options. Excellent cafes and restaurants, plus wineries.
Gisborne	Relaxed coastal vibe with lots of affordable options. Ideal base for surfers.
Whanganui	Voted NZ's most beautiful small city.

GETTING AROUND

Car Necessary for remote areas and those that wish to be time-flexible.

Bus Daily connections available between the main regional centres, with stops at most rural towns.

Bicycle Ideal within the cities, or cycling around the Hawke's Bay wineries.

TOP: DOUGHOUGHTON/ALAMY
BOTTOM: PHAUSTOV/SHUTTERSTOCK

EATING & DRINKING

Fresh produce abounds in Hawke's Bay, with numerous farmers markets and opportunities to pick your own. Wineries in Gisborne and Hawke's Bay are also highly regarded, especially for their chardonnay and Bordeaux-style red blends.

Best coffee Hawthorne Coffee Roasters in Havelock North (p141)

Must-try sparkling wine Organic Hawke's Bay vintages Alpha Domus (p141)

JAN–MAR
Surf's up on both sides of the country; busiest time for festivals.

APR–JUN
Shoulder season brings fewer crowds but still relatively mild temperatures.

JUL–SEP
Watch coastal storms and visit the blooming rhododendrons in New Plymouth.

OCT–DEC
Prime time for spotting lambs and daffodils as temperatures climb.

23 FORAGE in Havelock North

PRODUCE | MARKET | ARTISAN

Hawke's Bay is known for its wine, but the clement climate earns the region another title: the Fruit Bowl of New Zealand. The fertile Heretaunga plains are a patchwork of orchards, vineyards and vegetable farms, and there's no better place to sample the local fare than the quietly prosperous village of Havelock North, nestled under Te Mata Peak.

How to

Getting around The village is compact, but wider exploration requires private transport. Cycling is a popular activity on the Bay's flat roads.

When to go Summer harvest begins in December with asparagus, strawberries and artichokes, while the Bay's famed apples are autumn staples.

Love figs? Te Mata Figs has a dedicated cafe paying homage to its main crop.

Got kids? Arataki Honey provides an educational, interactive and tasty experience.

Local fare Start your Sunday morning as the locals do: stocking up on fresh produce at the **Black Barn Growers' Market** in neighbouring Hastings. Even if your shopping list is blank, the market's rustic stalls, set under a leafy canopy, make an ideal backdrop for browsing and people-watching. You're bound to have a locally roasted coffee or freshly baked goodie in your hands before long.

Strawberry fields Continue your day of foraging at the **Strawberry Patch**, a summertime institution where hand-picking your own berries is the order of the day. Pick-your-own is not the only drawcard here: the long queues – often visible from the road on a hot day – are testament to the popularity

Above Picking strawberries
Right Waimārama Beach

NATMINT/GETTY IMAGES

CAVAN IMAGES/GETTY IMAGES

Favourite Outdoor Picnic Spots

Take some yummy, locally sourced goodies out to **Ocean Beach**, where a picnic can be paired with a swim and a stroll. Or trade the homemade picnic on the beach with some much loved fish and chips from the **Waimārama Beach store**.

Alternatively, grab your bike and stock up on baked treats from **Ya Bon French Baker**, before heading out to the freshwater favourite, **Maraetotara Falls**, for a picnic and swim followed by a coffee or ice cream at **Red Bridge** before cycling back to town.

Recommended by Liv Glazebrook
local foodie
@kitchenoftreats

of the homemade Real Fruit Ice Cream, a delightfully fresh take on the frozen treat that has long been a Kiwi classic.

Treat yourself If you're not too sweeted out, a visit to the quaint oasis at **Birdwoods** is sure to please the whole family. The sprawling lawn will keep kids occupied with space to play, while parents can enjoy the peace of the sculpture garden. The old-style sweet shop stocks every kind of lolly in traditional glass jars, while the cafe offers a basic but delicious menu. After your meal, check out the gallery – a carefully curated gift shop in a beautifully restored church hall.

24 Go Sea to Sky in NEW PLYMOUTH

HIKES | PARKS | MOUNTAINS

With an assortment of outdoor pursuits on its doorstep, New Plymouth offers an enviable balance between urban life and nature. Region-defining Taranaki Maunga invites inspection from all angles, but the plethora of world-class beaches, parks and gardens shouldn't be overlooked.

SIMONE BETZ/GETTY IMAGES

How to

Getting around New Plymouth offers a variety of urban trails and parks, easily walkable from the town centre. The national park is 30 minutes' drive from downtown.

When to go Temperatures are highest between December and March, making it a popular festival period, including the TSB Festival of Lights and WOMAD.

Hike carefully Check online for track conditions. Mountain weather changes notoriously quickly, so be prepared. Tell someone your plans.

WESTEND61/GETTY IMAGES

The Coastal Walkway

Frequented by pedestrians and cyclists, this popular coastal path hugs the foreshore for 13 uninterrupted kilometres, with ample access points and sites of interest. New Zealand artist Len Lye's iconic **Wind Wand** towers over the city waterfront, and stunning **Te Rewa Rewa bridge** mimics the shape of a breaking wave, framing Taranaki Maunga perfectly on a clear day.

MARTIN VLNAS/SHUTTERSTOCK

Pukekura Park

New Plymouth's famed gardens strike a perfect balance between hive of activity and peaceful sanctuary. The idyllic **sports ground** was a key filming location in Tom Cruise's *The Last Samurai*, as well as being voted one of the most beautiful cricket ovals in the world. Continue past ponds and waterfalls, crossing the picturesque **Poet's Bridge** (whose

A Local Favourite

The riverside **Te Henui Walkway** runs perpendicular to the more famous **Coastal Walkway**, linking Fitzroy Beach to the leafy suburb of Welbourn. A preferred refuge for locals from the masses of beachfront tourists, the numerous reserves, gardens, and even two *pā* sites along the way make for a fascinating stroll.

Above left Taranaki Maunga (p130)
Left Poet's Bridge, Pukekura Park
Above Dawson Falls (p131), Te Papa-Kura-o-Taranaki (Egmont National Park)

namesake is in fact a racehorse) to visit the lakefront teahouse. The **Bowl of Brooklands** is surely one of the world's most beautiful concert venues (just ask Elton John), and adjacent **Brooklands Zoo** exhibits meerkats, monkeys and alpaca, among others.

Pukeiti Gardens

The expansive Pukeiti Gardens in the Maunga's western foothills showcase a surprising collection of exotic rhododendrons among thriving native bush. Visit between July and March to see more than 1250 species take turns to explode in colourful bloom.

Taranaki Maunga

With more than 300km of trail, there is something for hikers of all ages and skill levels in the near-perfectly circular boundaries of **Te Papakura o Taranaki** (Egmont National Park).

Dawson Falls Visitor Centre on the *maunga's* southeast slopes is a versatile starting point. Prepare to be enchanted as you make your way through 'goblin' forests,

The Festival of Lights

In the summer months, New Plymouth's Pukekura Park plays host to one of the most visually striking events in the New Zealand calendar: the TSB Festival of Lights. For five weeks from just before Christmas, the picturesque gardens hum with crowds seeking family-friendly fun and live performances. The true magic is revealed as night falls, with the park's trails, lakes and clearings transformed into an LED wonderland that must be seen to be believed. Replete with acres of illuminated sculptures, interactive installations, rainbow waterfalls and futuristic tunnels, the festival gets bigger each year. Best of all – it's entirely free.

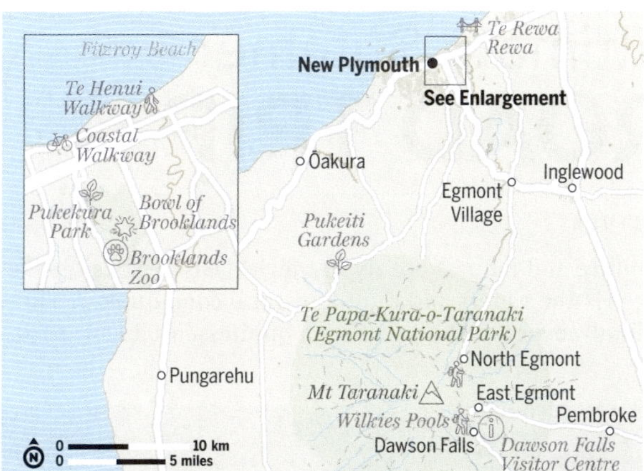

Left Pukekura Park (p129)
Below Te Rewa Rewa Bridge (p129)

twisted labyrinths of young trees covered in ferns and mosses of every conceivable shade of green. Even the access road is magical, with voracious forest threatening to re-swallow the narrow strip of pavement. Notable short hikes beginning from the visitor centre include the family-friendly **Wilkies Pools** and the **Kapuni Loop Track** to the eponymous waterfall, **Dawson Falls**.

While the forested lower slopes provide shelter from inclement weather, the dramatic upper slopes are best visited in clear, calm conditions. Climbing to the summit should only be attempted in summer by fit and experienced hikers, due to its steep approach and volatile weather conditions. On a clear day, the summit offers unmatched 270-degree views of the coast and countryside.

For those not afflicted by summit fever, the multiday **Pouakai Circuit** takes hikers past the active erosion scar of Boomerang Slip, the towering Dieffenbach Cliffs and the ochre waters of the Kokowai Stream. For the time-poor, the **Pouakai Crossing** is a 19km subsection that can be walked in a single day and includes the Circuit's crown jewel: the reflective **Pouakai Tarn**.

25 Ultimate Summer ROAD TRIP

ROAD TRIP | BEACHES | CULTURE

Steeped in Māori culture and natural beauty, Tairāwhiti Gisborne is replete with golden sand beaches, pristine waters and tight-knit rural communities. The coastal highway beyond sun-drenched Gisborne offers a quintessential Kiwi road trip.

DAVID WALL/ALAMY

Trip Notes

Getting around The driving time from Gisborne to the East Cape Lighthouse is three hours, meaning you could theoretically drive there and back in a day. Alternatively, continue around the cape to Ōpōtiki (three hours) and either continue through the Bay of Plenty or loop back on SH2 (another two hours).

When to go Summer guarantees higher temperatures.

Learn some te reo Māori The local *iwi* will appreciate it.

Tatapouri Bay Stingrays

Our guests love the interaction with the stingrays. 'Our girls' – all the stingrays in the bay are female – are friendly and have their own names, distinguishing marks and personalities. Tour times are based around low tide, so our tours run at a different time each day.

Recommended by Christine Savage
Owner, Wild Stingray Tours @divetatapouri

FROM LEFT: C LEVERS/SHUTTERSTOCK, HENRYK SADURA/GETTY IMAGES.

26 Life on the Surf HIGHWAY

BEACHES | HISTORY | VOLCANO

Named for the generations of surfers who have combed this coast for the best breaks, the 109km Surf Highway 45 between New Plymouth and Hāwera offers more than just swells and black sand. A pair of beach towns provides excellent pit stops, while a museum at each end positions the landscape within its historical context, all while Taranaki Maunga watches on.

How to

How long? The total driving time is 90 minutes. From Hāwera you can loop back to New Plymouth on SH3 in an hour.

When to go December to March offers the best swimming temperatures. Taranaki Maunga is frequently shrouded in cloud, any time of the year – take any opportunity you get for a clear photo.

Hungry? Stop for fish and chips in Ōpunake; they're a classic Kiwi beachside delicacy.

Local learnings Surf Highway 45 is bookended by the excellent free **Puke Ariki museum** (p140) in New Plymouth and the exuberant dioramas of the privately owned **Tawhiti Museum** (p140) in Hāwera. The former includes an illuminating display about the nonviolent Māori movement resisting land alienation that arose at Parihaka (near the highway) in the 1860s, and its brutal suppression by government troops.

Landmarks While the volcano views out of the passenger-side windows (heading south) are constant, keep an eye out for a scattering of landmarks set against the coast. At New Plymouth's western edge, a short, steep climb up **Paritutu Rock** provides sweeping views of the city and the nearby **Sugar Loaf Islands** (all remnants of an ancient volcano). Halfway along the drive, at Pungarehu, take a short detour to the photogenic **Cape Egmont Lighthouse**.

WALTER BIBIKOW/GETTY IMAGES

Local Surf Spots

Taranaki's semi-circular coastline exposes it to 180 degrees of swell and wind directions – so on any given day you're bound to find a wave somewhere.

Around New Plymouth, Fitzroy and Ōakura are quality beach breaks suitable for beginners and experts alike. Banks are constantly changing but look for the peaks around the river-mouths. To the south, Ōpunake beach is a friendly beginner's wave that works best on a northerly wind.

Alternatively, search and you will be rewarded – numerous roads radiate from the Surf Highway to the coast, though many of these [breaks] are rocky and for experienced surfers only.

Recommended by Magnus Holding *an enthusiastic surfer and photographer @_mags.nz*

Surf Towns Just 15 minutes west of central New Plymouth, **Ōakura** is an affluent little enclave set against the most beautiful beach on this route. Lifeguards patrol in summer, but New Plymouth locals head here throughout the year for a bite to eat and to catch a gig at the Butler's Reef pub. Closer to Hāwera, **Ōpunake** is an artsy town with good eating options, some interesting shops, a restored community cinema and a little lake. The main attractions are its two beaches, each set in its own little bay.

Above Cape Egmont Lighthouse

Journey Along the WHANGANUI

SCENERY | ADVENTURE | HISTORY

A once critical transport route for Māori and early European settlers, the Whanganui River is now a beautiful backwater traversing some of the North Island's most remote reaches. Be transported through this culturally and spiritually significant waterway by canoe, jetboat or historic paddle steamer – or stay on solid ground and drive or cycle the Whanganui River Rd.

How to

Getting here The main canoe/kayak launch points are Taumarunui (an hour north of Ohakune) and Pipiriki (50 minutes west of Ohakune). Boat cruises leave from Whanganui.

When to go The warmer months (November to April) are the best time to undertake a canoeing or kayaking trip. It's not recommended in winter due to dangerous river conditions.

Hut bookings The three 'Great Walks' huts need to be booked in advance (doc.govt.nz).

Not just any river Springing from the volcanic slopes of **Tongariro National Park**, the 290km Whanganui River snakes its way through untamed New Zealand wilderness before reaching the sea at its namesake city. Due to its huge significance to local Māori it was officially recognised in 2017 as a legal entity: in essence a separate being with its own rights and responsibilities. Te Awa Tupua is the term used to refer to it, which incorporates the entire river system (including its tributaries).

Back to the past **Whanganui National Park** protects the river's upper reaches, an area so remote and rugged that all attempts to settle and cultivate it were abandoned. The unusual **Bridge to Nowhere** remains a haunting relic of this bygone era. It was built in 1936 to service a failed settlement of returned soldiers, but upon completion, only three farmers still remained. Today, it is only accessible

JANETTEASCHE/GETTY IMAGES

via boat, mountain bike or on foot.

Day trips Get a taste for the river by taking a two-hour cruise from Whanganui on a restored riverboat, or by driving the remote Whanganui River Rd to Pipiriki. Pipiriki is the launching point for day tours into the national park incorporating jet-boat rides, short hikes and paddles. It's also possible to take a day paddle from Taumarunui, where tours include a cultural option led by Māori guides.

The Whanganui Journey

Whanganui Journey is one of New Zealand's 11 official Great Walks, despite not involving any actual walking. Rather, it's an epic canoeing or kayaking adventure along an otherwise inaccessible section of the Whanganui River, traversing the heart of Whanganui National Park. This is real wilderness, with very few road access points along the route.

The full five-day journey starts in Taumarunui and heads 145km to Pipiriki at the top of the Whanganui River Rd. Alternatively, you can start at Whakahoro and knock two days and 57km off the trip. Operators at each end provide equipment and guided expeditions.

Above Canoeing, Whanganui River

■ **With input from Jeremy Smith**
Heritage Manager of the Napier Art Deco Trust (artdeconapier.com)

Napier: Art-Deco Capital

HOW AN EARTHQUAKE CAUSED THE CITY'S REBIRTH

Napier's catastrophic 1931 earthquake remains New Zealand's deadliest natural disaster, claiming at least 256 lives. Yet from tragedy, citizens seized the unique opportunity to rebuild with proud, contemporary flourish. The character precinct that literally rose from the ashes remains resplendent today, earning the title 'Art-Deco Capital of the World'.

CHAMELEONSEYE/SHUTTERSTOCK

At 10.47am on 3 February 1931, the clock of Napier's band rotunda stopped forever. Moments later, the ground began to sway, and in just two and a half minutes, the grand seaside town of Napier was in ruins.

The 7.8-magnitude quake left all but a few of Napier's buildings completely destroyed. What the quake didn't flatten was quickly levelled by fires. Attempts to curb the spread of flames were hampered by burst water pipes. The destruction was immense, and few buildings, such as the historic Hawke's Bay Club building, were saved only by the grace of changing winds.

The Arrival of Art Deco

The Napier rebuild was a tonic to local unemployment in the midst of the Great Depression, and authorities issued a clear and simple edict: the new township must be safe, modern and cheap. There was also significant time pressure, with many residents being temporarily housed in government-supplied canvas tents either on their properties or in 'tent towns' at local parks.

Despite not yet bearing its modern name, 'art deco', a prevailing trend that originated in Europe, satisfied many of the above criteria. Heritage Manager of the Napier Art Deco Trust, Jeremy Smith, explains that the art-deco movement 'celebrated the modern age, the machine and synthetic materials', with simple designs that captured an 'optimistic and energetic spirit'. Think basic geometrical motifs (including chevrons and zigzags) and bright, pastel colours. Decorative themes include suns and skyscrapers, as well as symbols of speed, power and flight.

Left Masonic Hotel
Centre National Tobacco Building
Right Art-deco detailing

KAREN LEWIS/GETTY IMAGES

JACQUESVANDINTEREN/GETTY IMAGES

While art deco became the predominant style, the influence of Spanish Mission, Stripped Classical and Classical Moderne styles are also evident. Incredibly, 111 buildings were constructed in Napier's centre between 1931 and 1933. The character revitalisation was accompanied by the establishment of wider streets and the introduction of underground power and telephone lines. The earthquake also uplifted 225 hectares of former seabed into new land able to be developed.

Incredibly, 111 buildings were constructed in Napier's centre between 1931 and 1933.

Art Deco Today

Today, the art-deco precinct is preserved and celebrated by the Art Deco Trust, established in 1985. Notable examples of art-deco architecture include the photographer-friendly National Tobacco Building; the Masonic Hotel, where Queen Elizabeth II once stayed; and the Auckland Savings Bank, where traditional Māori motifs feature prominently. While Napier is the prize showpiece for art-deco buildings, many can also be seen in nearby Hastings.

Though much of the city's art-deco architecture is easily viewed on a casual stroll around Napier's city core, taking a guided tour with a volunteer from the Art Deco Trust (on foot, or in stylish vintage cars) enriches the experience with fascinating historical context and anecdotes. 'Three-hundred and sixty-four days a year, our local volunteers share their love of this great town on walking and vintage-car tours,' says Jeremy. 'Our guides are dedicated, extremely knowledgeable and passionate about Napier's art-deco-era history and present-day stories.'

The Art Deco Festival

Every February, Napier's population practically doubles and the city steps back in time to celebrate the era of art deco.

The lynchpin of the Hawke's Bay social calendar, the festival features over 200 different events, including walking tours, vintage-car parades, fashion shows and concerts. Of course, era-appropriate costume is strongly encouraged.

Jeremy Smith revels in the atmosphere. 'People from across New Zealand flock to Napier to be a part of the festival – their fashion, cars, spirit and style brings magic to the streets. The spectacle is not one to be missed!'

For more information visit artdecofestival.co.nz.

Listings

BEST OF THE REST

Rainy-Day Activities

Govett-Brewster Art Gallery/Len Lye Centre

Behind the mind-bending exterior lies New Plymouth's state-of-the-art contemporary art museum. The adjoining Monica's Eatery is a great spot for breakfast or lunch.

Puke Ariki

A free interactive museum, library and i-SITE information centre makes this complex on the New Plymouth waterfront a one-stop tourism shop.

Tawhiti Museum

An innovative local history museum in Hāwera that feels more like a small theme park. Life-size figures and scale models of battles and colonial life brings history to life.

National Aquarium of New Zealand

Enjoy plenty of close encounters at this family favourite situated on Napier's Marine Parade. The modern complex has a stingray-inspired roof and extremely popular little blue penguins.

New Zealand Rugby Museum

Have a ball at the official museum of the nation's beloved sport in Palmerston North, discovering its history and precious mementos. Kids can test out their skills, too.

Whanganui Essentials

Te Whare o Rehua Sarjeant Gallery

Whanganui's most impressive building reopened in late 2024, fully restored and doubled in size. It's considered one of the country's most important regional galleries.

Rotokawau Virginia Lake

It only takes around 25 minutes to complete the sculpture-filled lakeside circuit but there's also an art-deco winter garden to explore, a playground and an aviary.

Durie Hill Elevator

A unique Whanganui experience, this rattly Edwardian lift links the southeast bank of the river to the top of Durie Hill where there are two viewing towers.

Regional Road-Trip Stops

Tui Brewery

One of the country's ubiquitous beer brands brews in this striking tower overlooking the Mangatainoka River, on SH2 in the Tararua District. Explore the grounds and have a taste.

Manawatū Gorge Track

Stretch your legs mid–road trip and hike a portion of the scenic 11km track, surrounded by native forests, birds and the river far below.

Victoria Esplanade

A pretty public park spread along the banks of the Manawatū River in Palmerston North where you'll find nature trails, rose gardens, aviaries, duck ponds, playgrounds and a miniature railway.

Bell Rock Loop Track

To break up the winding drive from Napier to Gisborne, hike to the Hawke's Bay equivalent of *The Lion King's* Pride Rock. Three hours return, medium intensity.

Pastries & Coffee, Please

BABCO $

A perfect pit stop in Palmerston North, the Brick Artisan Bread Company has a cabinet loaded with fresh breads and pastries to die for. Don't miss the custard-filled beignets.

Knead $

A popular donut shop in New Plymouth's suburbs offering two releases daily to keep up with the demand. With limited hours and a guaranteed queue, plan your visit in advance.

Ozone Coffee Roasters $$

New Plymouth's most famous coffee brand (with branches in Auckland and London) occupies a large central warehouse. Tasty pastries are available at the counter.

Hawthorne Coffee Roasters $

One of Havelock North's most esteemed coffee houses, Hawthorne serves a scone and a brew worth going back for. Plenty of beans and gadgets for sale too.

Ya Bon French Baker $$

This stylish artisan bakery combines pastries, coffee and a fresh deli with goodies such as imported cheeses, chorizo and sourdough.

Cycle the Bridge Pa Wine Triangle

Abbey Cellar

One of the few wineries also housing a brewery, Abbey Cellar is an idyllic weekend spot to enjoy live music and platters in an outdoor picnic area.

Sileni Estate

Prepare to be wowed from the moment you turn into Sileni's long, majestic driveway. Equally impressive is its internationally recognised wine, and its ever-expanding trophy cabinet.

Alpha Domus

A fully certified organic vineyard and winery, Alpha Domus is one of the lynchpins of the triangle. An aeronautical theme pervades the wine names and labels.

Trinity Hill

Live music and food trucks make this winery particularly family-friendly. Its sprawling lawn and outdoor games will keep everyone entertained on a weekend picnic.

Oak Estate

Oak Estate has lovely outdoor seating around a photogenic barn house.

Coastal Swim & Surf

Muriwai Beach

Rural beach settlement on an impressive coastline near Young Nick's Head, south of Gisborne. Arrive in style on the Gisborne City Vintage Railway.

Ōakura Beach

New Plymouth's neighbouring surf-town has cute cafes and a relaxed vibe. Stay over at the Holiday Park right on the beachfront as a relaxed alternative to the city itself.

Mahia Beach

Majestic scenery, prime fishing and small-town vibes await in this small village. Climb to the Mokotahi Lookout at sunset for magical views of the sun across the water.

Waimārama Beach

With the best surf in Hawke's Bay, it is a popular weekend destination for locals due to its good swimming, golden sand and expansive local store. Be mindful of dangerous currents.

Porangahau Beach

With plenty of water-sport hire options, the beach is only a few kilometres from a hill bearing the world's longest place name (85 characters long).

WELLINGTON

CITY LIFE | CULTURE | CRAFT BEER

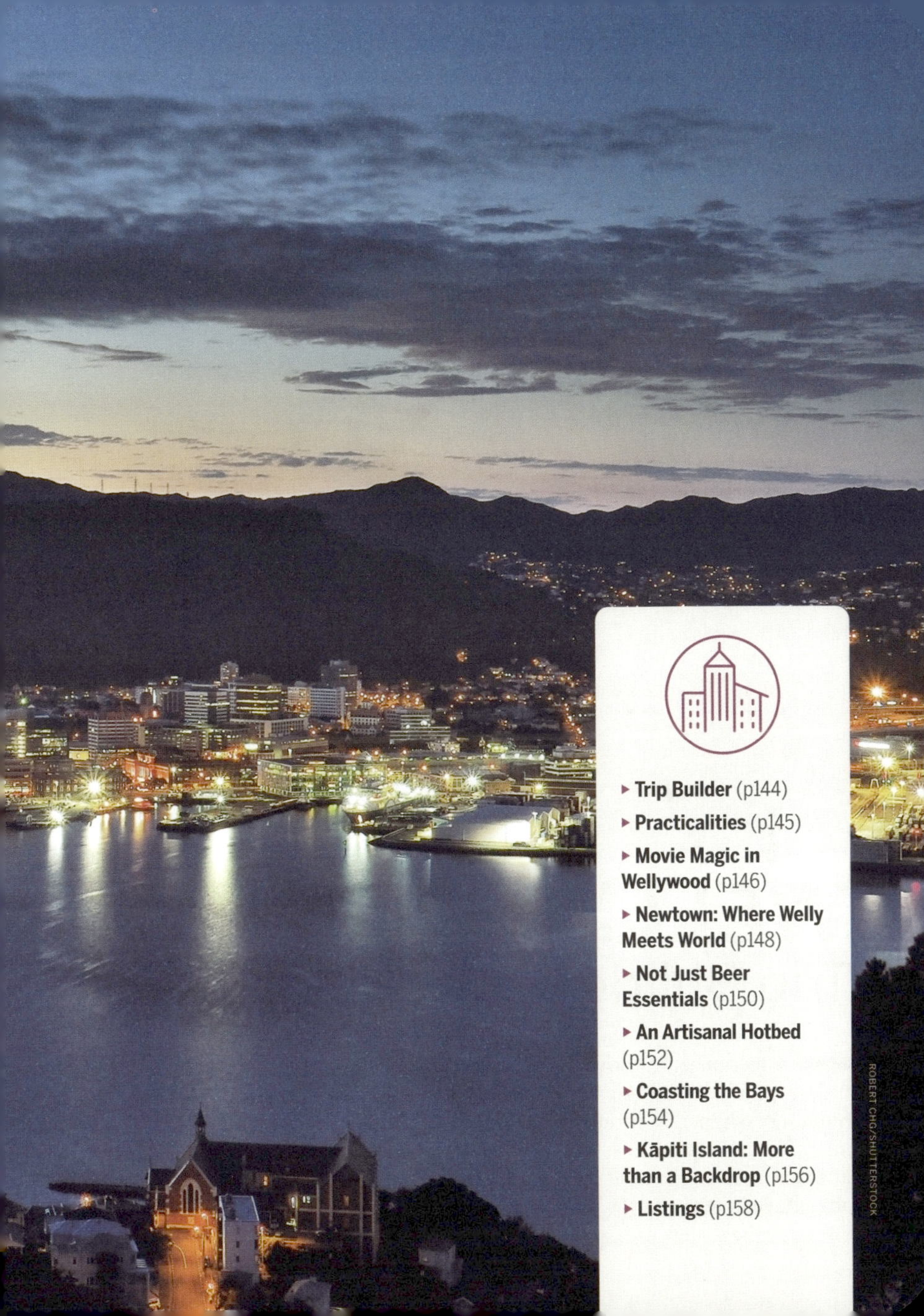

ROBERT CHG/SHUTTERSTOCK

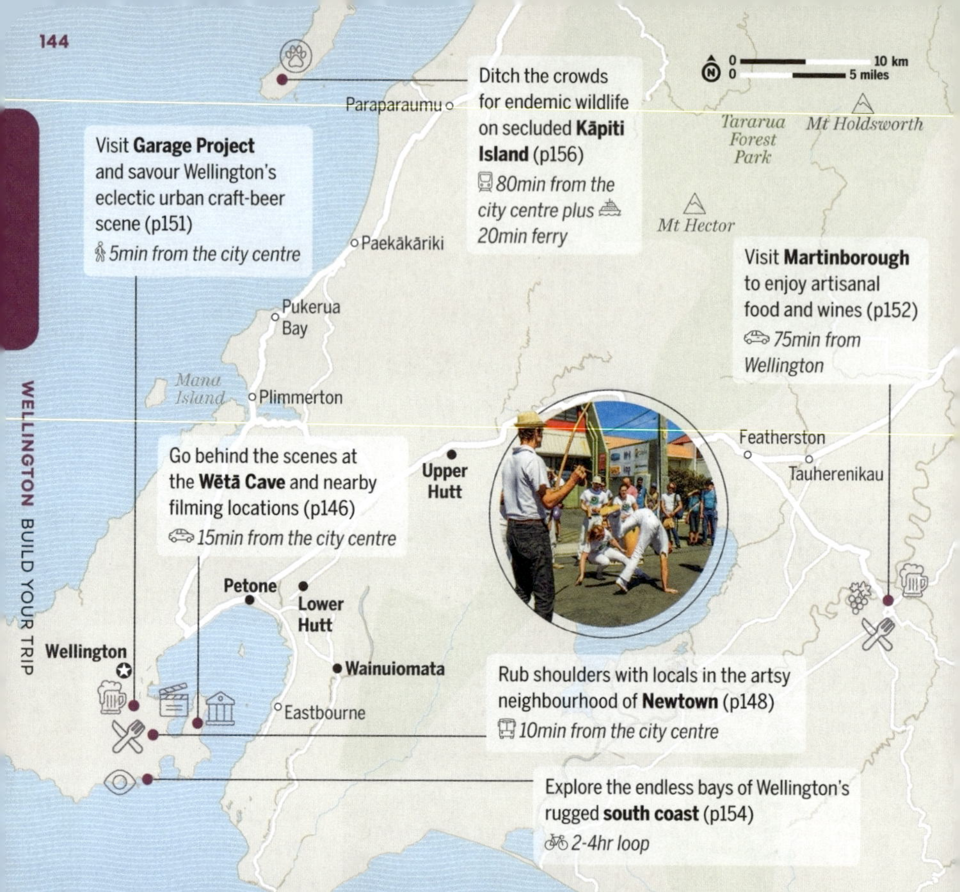

Visit **Garage Project** and savour Wellington's eclectic urban craft-beer scene (p151)
5min from the city centre

Ditch the crowds for endemic wildlife on secluded **Kāpiti Island** (p156)
80min from the city centre plus 20min ferry

Visit **Martinborough** to enjoy artisanal food and wines (p152)
75min from Wellington

Go behind the scenes at the **Wētā Cave** and nearby filming locations (p146)
15min from the city centre

Rub shoulders with locals in the artsy neighbourhood of **Newtown** (p148)
10min from the city centre

Explore the endless bays of Wellington's rugged **south coast** (p154)
2-4hr loop

Paraparaumu
Paekākāriki
Pukerua Bay
Mana Island
Plimmerton
Tararua Forest Park
Mt Holdsworth
Mt Hector
Featherston
Tauherenikau
Upper Hutt
Petone
Lower Hutt
Wellington
Wainuiomata
Eastbourne
South Pacific Ocean
0 10 km
0 5 miles

NATALIACATALINA.COM/SHUTTERSTOCK

WELLINGTON
Trip Builder

Affectionately known as the world's 'coolest little capital', Wellington sits in a wild, windy horseshoe-shaped harbour. The city's beating heart is its compact, cosmopolitan centre, quickly giving way to rugged natural surrounds, meaning adventure is never far away.

Practicalities

ARRIVING

The airport is only 6km from the city, so ride-shares or taxis are most convenient. Cost-conscious travellers can bus but will have to walk the last 700m.

MONEY

Cash is obsolete. Save money by scoping food trucks and catch a local (free) gig or comedy show.

FIND YOUR WAY

Find free wi-fi at the waterfront, Te Papa museum and most cafes. On Cable St, find Wellington's i-SITE visitor information centre.

WHERE TO STAY

Place	Pros/Cons
Thorndon	Lacking charm, but convenient for sightseeing, Parliament, stadium events and transport hubs.
Oriental Bay	Postcard views of Wellington. Close to beaches, cafes and Mt Victoria.
Cuba St	Central to shopping, restaurants, nightlife (loud at night). Ideal without a car.
Newtown	Cheaper prices, neighbourhood feel. Diverse culinary options. Central to airport, city, beaches.

GETTING AROUND

Walking and public transport The city is mostly walkable, and purchasing a pre-paid Snapper card will provide discounted bus and train fares.

Train The train station has connections to the Kāpiti Coast and Wairarapa, and also functions as a bus depot.

TOP: YIUCHEUNG/SHUTTERSTOCK
BOTTOM: ANTHIACUMMING/GETTY IMAGES

EATING & DRINKING

Cuba St and its surrounds is the undisputed centre of Wellington's culinary universe. The laneways are laden with culinary secrets, waiting to be discovered. **Ombra**, in Upper Cuba, and **Highwater Eatery**, in Lower Cuba, are two great options.

Best winery
Poppies in Martinborough (p158)

Must-try salted caramel cookies
Shelly Bay Baker on Leeds Street (p153)

JAN–MAR
Visit artisanal Martinborough or swim in the crisp Pacific Ocean.

APR–JUN
Windy days induce craft-beer tours, shopping and cinema visits.

JUL–SEP
A solid line-up of indoor food, drink and cultural festivals.

OCT–DEC
Warmer, sunnier days pave the way for cycling and hiking.

28 Movie Magic in WELLYWOOD

TOUR | CINEMA | FILM SETS

Home to multiple world-class film studios and a lion's share of talented filmmakers, Wellington was recently named a world Creative City of Film by UNESCO. 'Wellywood' heartily embraces its new cinematic reputation by offering public access to studios, shooting locations and even a homage to Los Angeles' vaunted Hollywood sign (with a characteristically breezy twist).

UMOMOS/SHUTTERSTOCK

How to

Getting around Buses run regularly to Wētā Workshop in Miramar, and organised tours start from the city centre. Having a private car puts a DIY film location tour within easy reach.

Tours Wētā Studio Tours occur onsite, and tour companies such as Wellington Rings Tours organise half- or full-day trips to film locations around greater Wellington.

Timing Consider coinciding your visit with the Māoriland Film Festival, NZ's indigenous film festival held in Ōtaki in March.

Behind the scenes Sleepy Miramar Peninsula is home to Oscar winner Peter Jackson, as well as two globally renowned studios: **Wētā Workshop** (*Avatar, King Kong* and *Lord of the Rings*); and **Park Road Production** (*The Last Samurai, The Adventures of Tintin*). Wētā Workshop offers popular tours, giving behind-the-scenes insight into how props, costumes and miniature effects can create epic fantasy worlds on the silver screen. Don't miss the **Wētā Cave**, a mini museum replete with souvenirs.

On location *LOTR* fans may already know that much of the trilogy was shot in greater Wellington: Rivendell (Kaitoke Regional Park); the Paths of the Dead (Putangirua Pinnacles); Osgiliath Wood (Waitārere Forest); as well as various scenes in the city's parks. But geographic diversity, modern infrastructure and esteemed post-production

ADAM CONSTANZA/SHUTTERSTOCK

resources has made Wellington a stand-in for more than just Middle-earth. Other films shot here include *The Hobbit*, *Skull Island* and *What We Do in the Shadows*.

Popcorn time If you'd prefer not to peek behind the curtain, Wellington boasts many boutique cinemas. The inner city is home to the famous **Embassy Theatre**, which has been screening since 1926 (including the world premiere of *The Hobbit: An Unexpected Journey*). For a more retro movie-going experience, try Miramar's **Roxy Cinema** (and restaurant) – owned by Wētā Workshop's co-founders.

Experience More Film

The iconic **Aro St Video Shop** in the city suburb of Aro Valley is one of the few remaining video stores in the country. It holds an incredible collection of cult and arthouse films and you'd need years to work through its collection.

If you're in Wellington for a few weeks, then I'd recommend buying a three-film sampler pass from the Wellington Film Society. It's a chance to watch eclectic films on the big screen at the Embassy Theatre. Films screen weekly between February and November.

Recommended by Brannavan Gnanalingam *novelist, lawyer, columnist and (former) film reviewer based in Wellington. @Brannavan*

Left Putangirua Pinnacles
Above Wellington Blown Away sign

29 Newtown: Where Welly MEETS WORLD

DIVERSE | VINTAGE | CULTURE

Though renowned for its annual block-party-style festival, the neighbourhood of Newtown is a worthwhile year-round destination. A cultural melting pot, the diverse suburb is dripping with community and humming with life. Escape the city centre and do as the locals do, experiencing the grit, colour and aromas of a community that reflects NZ's unique cultural patchwork.

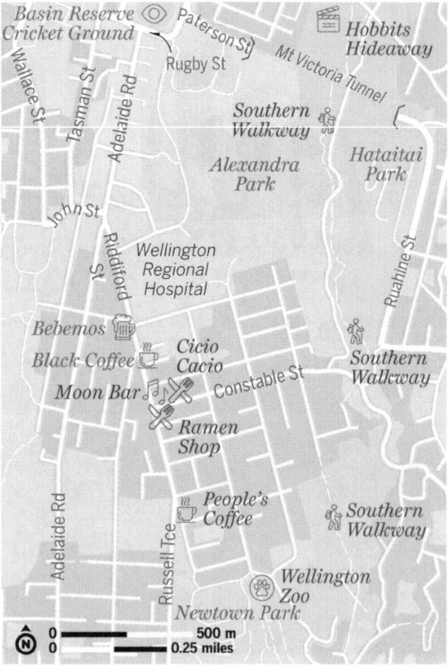

How to

Getting here Most southbound bus routes from the city centre transit through Newtown.

Further exploration Weather permitting, hike the spine of the Southern Walkway from the Mt Victoria Summit to Wellington Hospital for some inner-city tranquility.

Animal lovers Our furry friends at the SPCA (five minutes from the hospital) love cuddles, and also nearby is the Wellington Zoo, although its larger animals are a bit more standoffish.

Adventure on foot Though easily accessed by bus, Newtown is also the endpoint of a particularly scenic section of the Southern Walkway trail. Start at the popular **Mt Victoria summit**, but quickly trade the crowds for quiet solitude. Traversing the wooded ridgeline, the trail provides unbeaten views of the inner harbour and historic **Basin Reserve Cricket Ground**, and can include a short detour to the iconic 'Hobbits Hideaway' *Lord of the Rings* filming location.

Historically a blue-collar landing spot and now home to various diaspora, there's something for everyone in this unpretentious, effortlessly cool neighbourhood. From the vintage racks at Riddiford St's thrift stores to the fresh produce at the Saturday farmers market, there is also plenty to please the cost-conscious.

Fill your belly Naturally, the neighbourhood boasts authentic cuisine from all

corners of the globe. Highlights include the **Ramen Shop**, serving steaming bowls of well-priced goodness; and **Cicio Cacio**, which celebrates seasonal fare on its all-Italian menu.

There's also no shortage of quality vegan and vegetarian options. End the night with local live music at spacey **Moon Bar**, or choose from an extensive beer list at Latin-inspired **Bebemos**.

For the time-conscious, Newtown more than holds its own in Wellington's thriving coffee culture. Try a Double Brown among the work of local artists at **Black Coffee**, or enjoy a socially conscious brew at **People's Coffee**.

Newtown Festival

Every March, 11 blocks of Riddiford St (and numerous side streets) are closed to traffic and instead play home to 12 performance stages and over 400 festival stalls.

More than 80,000 visitors throng the streets each year, from those cloaked in costumes to those with young children in tow.

After its debut more than two decades ago, the event is a lock in every local's calendar, and captures the artistic and community-driven spirit for which the neighbourhood is famed (newtownfestival.org.nz/about-us).

Above Newtown Festival

30 Not Just Beer ESSENTIALS

ARTISANAL | HOPS | CULTURE

Wellington's breweries are like its populace: innovative, fun and quirky. A close-knit brewing community has turned the 'coolest little capital' into the country's craft-beer epicentre. Discerning local clientele now expect quality and inventiveness at a minimum, so brewers increasingly strive to build experiences beyond just another pint to draw in the thirsty masses.

KRISTA ROSSOW/ALAMY

How to

Getting around Wellington's compact hospitality precinct is a pedestrian's paradise – several official taprooms within five minutes of Cuba St! Craftbeercapital.com has a downloadable interactive map.

When to go A truly year-round pastime, with festivals in August (Beervana, the marquee event), November (Beers at the Basin), April (Hopstock – the fresh hop harvest) and May (BrewDay).

Like dogs? Most central breweries are dog-friendly.

KRISTA ROSSOW/ALAMY

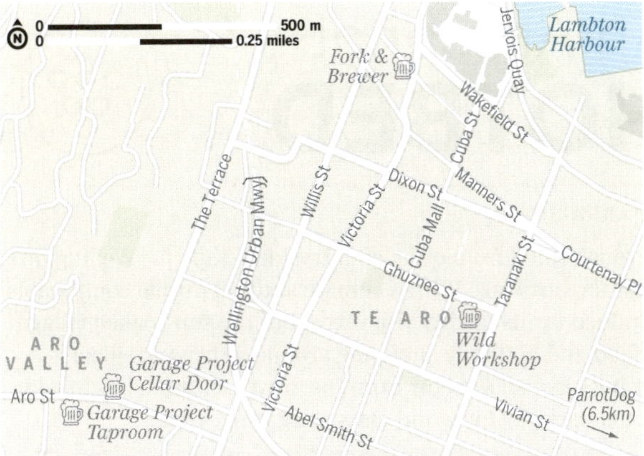

Ringed by hills, Wellington's pedestrian-friendly city centre is its greatest asset. The city's army of urban microbrewers, challenged by limited space, have converted former industrial spaces into suds-producing powerhouses. Taprooms often share space with mash tuns, enabling guests to watch the magic (slowly) happen, final product in hand.

From small things... Excelling in a market that is deliciously saturated, pioneering brewery **Garage Project** was until recently little more than an ambitious upstart, brewing in a 50L kit out of a derelict former gas station. The perennially innovative beer purveyors have since bloated to have multiple taprooms in central Wellington (and one in Auckland), and recently picked up two awards at the prestigious 2024 World Beer Cup.

Big things grow There's always a fresh invention in the Garage Project tanks. A recent venture that has quickly gained traction with Wellington beer-lovers is the **Wild Workshop**: where weird and wacky recipes push the creative limits in Wonka-esque fashion. It's a dedicated space for wild, mixed culture and spontaneous ferments, meaning that unique flavours are quite literally divined from the very air and chattels of the workshop itself.

Even a trip to the washroom is a peek behind the scenes, as you overlook the spontaneous fermentation process. The shapeshifting menu features both beer and natural wine (from another project, 'Crushed'), meaning no two trips will ever be the same.

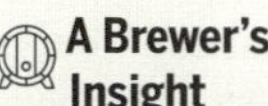

Left Garage Project
Below Craft beer, Garage Project

A Brewer's Insight

Brewers have so many materials to work with: malts, hops, yeast, fruits and ways to age...it's all ripe for play.

We're particularly proud of cult favourite IPA 'Pernicious Weed', recently releasing a 10% imperial edition for our 10-year anniversary. By contrast, we've just released 'Tiny', a non-alcoholic hazy IPA which required plenty of experimentation to perfect the flavour profile.

Further afield, I also recommend Fork and Brewer, an OG brewpub with an eclectic range of batch brews and guest taps, and ParrotDog, a retro brewpub serving tight, concise beers by Lyall Bay beach.

Recommended by Jos Ruffell *passionate dog walker and co-founder of Garage Project* *@garageproject*

31 An Artisanal HOTBED

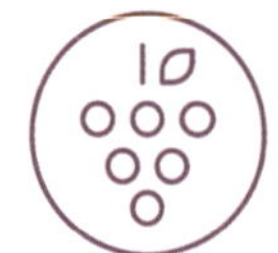

VINEYARDS | TASTINGS | STARGAZING

Martinborough has transformed from quiet countryside escape for Wellington's city-slickers to hotbed for culinary artisans. With a climate and soil profile comparable to Burgundy, it is rightly heralded for its quality vineyards. But the sun-soaked village also boasts award-winning food and boutique shopping around a thriving village square, not to mention gourmet olive oil straight from the grove. All that's left to add is an internationally accredited dark sky for world-class stargazing. Tick.

DAVID WALL/ALAMY

How to

Getting here Drive 70 minutes from Wellington, or take the train from Wellington to Featherston and transfer to the Martinborough bus. The township and vineyards can be navigated on foot, though bike or car is preferable.

When to go Visit during the long, dry summer, and don't miss January's Toast Martinborough festival.

Well travelled? The streets were named for notable cities visited by the village's eponymous founder – how many have you visited?

AGEFOTOSTOCK/ALAMY

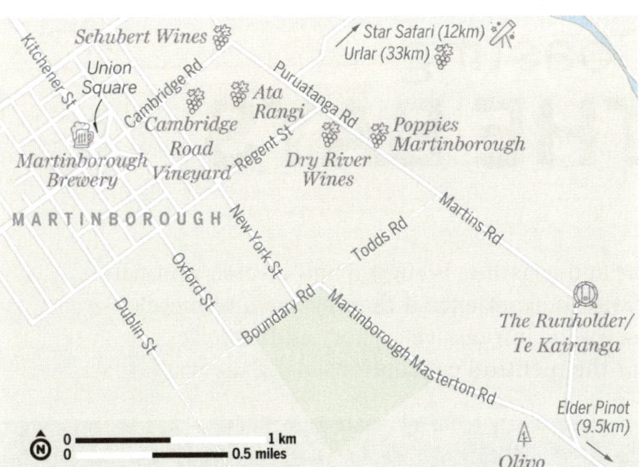

What to taste Martinborough was once a humble service town for local sheep farmers. Over time, the primary industry has shifted from wool to wine, but the emphasis on local persists, attracting a second wave of culinary craftspeople to the village: coffee roasters, olive oil makers, restaurateurs and brewers alike.

Martinborough's trademark drop is a savoury, complex pinot noir, thanks to optimal growing conditions. The towering Tararuas create a dry climate, with free-draining alluvial soil. Hot days and cool nights ensure a lengthy ripening process, and the infamous Wellington wind keeps crop levels low, concentrating the fruit's flavour.

And where to taste it With a high density of small, family-owned wineries, **Puruatanga Road** on the village's north side is a must-visit. **Cambridge Road Vineyard** offers organically produced wine, while close by **The Runholder** showcases **Te Kairanga** and **Martinborough Vineyard** wines at its impressive cellar door and restaurant. Wander a bit further afield to Gladstone to sample wines at Urlar's lakeside cellar door.

Nowadays, Martinborough's artisanal pilgrims need not end their day at the cellar door. Continue the degustation with a tasting tray at **Martinborough Brewery**, or forego alcohol for a tour of **Olivo's** olive groves, studying the varieties and sampling the freshly pressed oils. Round out the day with a meal on picturesque **Union Square** and stargazing and a hot chocolate nearby at **Star Safari** in Carterton.

Left Te Kairanga grape vines
Below Olivo olive oils

Savouring a Pinot Noir

Pinot noir is the local speciality. It is a wine of subtle structure, and should have softness, elegance and a beautiful balance of black fruit with spice and oak. Martinborough's climate provides growing conditions which focus on quality rather than quantity, and flavour rather than power. Don't miss the pinot noir pioneers **Dry River Wines** and **Ata Rangi**, as well as local favourites the **Elder Pinot** and **Schubert Wines**. Visit **Poppies Martinborough** for the best pinot noir and platter pairing!

Recommended by Shayne Hammond
local viticulturist and general manager at Poppies of Martinborough
poppiesmartinborough.co.nz

32 Coasting THE BAYS

VIEWS | CAFES | BEACHES

Wellington's harbour and coastline is rugged and diverse, and with bays for days, what better way to experience it than by *waka* or bicycle? Join *iwi* on the water. Soak up the impressive scenery and historic landmarks, re-energising at the plentiful cafe options along the way.

LIZ RITCHIE/SHUTTERSTOCK

Trip Notes

Getting around E-bike hire is about $90/day, or $40/hour for a rideshare bike.

What to wear Wellington is one of the windiest cities in the world, so it pays to dress warm and bring gloves. Consider bathers on a good day.

Route Using Oriental Bay as a reference point, explore the eastern bays around to the south coast, looping back to the city at Lyall or Island bays.

Paddle Power

A couple of hours on the water with local *iwi* will demonstrate the power (and effort) of a well-coordinated traditional Māori *waka* (canoe). Sign up for a tour with **Te Wharewaka o Pōneke** (wharewaka tours.maori.nz) at the architecturally designed Te Raukura building on the waterfront.

RAYAN AMARASEKARA/SHUTTERSTOCK

■ **With input from Leon Everett,** *a DOC ranger and avid bird photographer @leonberardnz*

Kāpiti Island: More than a Backdrop

REGENERATION IN ACTION

Kāpiti Island is the horizon-defining backdrop for Wellington's coastal traffic, and its iconic outline is instantly recognisable on punnets of New Zealand's treasured Kāpiti Ice Cream. However, the island is more than just a backdrop: it offers visitors a rich history, a neighbouring marine reserve and abundant natural photography opportunities.

Left Kāpiti Island
Centre Kārearea
Right Hihi

SAM LAWRENCE PHOTOGRAPHY/SHUTTERSTOCK

Historic Importance

Kāpiti Island was once the seat of power for expansive empires, strategically prized and fiercely defended. Nowadays the human residents are few, but the island is used for an equally vital purpose – one in which being regarded as a backdrop is not only advantageous, but also intentional. Today, Kāpiti Island is one of NZ's largest offshore predator-free islands and a significant cultural site for local *iwi* Ngāti Toa.

According to Māori *pūrākau* (storytelling), the explorer Kupe created Kāpiti Island with a single stroke of his club. The island has been home to a number of Māori *iwi*, but most recently Ngāti Toa and their notable chief Te Rauparaha, creator of the renowned *haka* 'Ka Mate' of All Blacks fame. A natural fortress, Kāpiti Island was strategically important as a foothold for control of the sea passage between the North and South islands.

The arrival of Europeans saw settlers briefly use the island to rear livestock and hunt whales. Evidence of colonial industry persists, as 'try-pots' used to boil down whale blubber can still be found on shore. Native species on the island soon became threatened by unsustainable resource management, and in 1897 the Crown designated the island a sanctuary. With that, the backdrop was set.

Pioneering naturalist Richard Henry soon took up residence and implemented initiatives that succeeded in stabilising wildlife numbers. The Department of Conservation (DOC) continues this work in partnership with *iwi*, making Kāpiti one of the largest rat-free islands in the world.

ISAAC SPEDDING/SHUTTERSTOCK

BIRD AND SKY/SHUTTERSTOCK

The Marine Reserve & Photography Opportunities

Since 1992 the waters around the island have also been protected. Leon Everett, former DOC Marine Reserve Ranger for Kāpiti, explains the coast is abundant in marine life thanks to nutrient-rich waters coming from the South Island's west coast. 'The marine reserve provides the highest level of protection to a marine area, allowing it to recover without fishing pressure,' says Leon.

As ranger, Leon patrolled for illegal fishing in the reserve and managed ecological monitoring, photographing wildlife in his spare time.

> According to Māori legend, the explorer Kupe created Kāpiti Island with a single stroke of his club.

After a century in the backdrop, Kāpiti Island has become a birder's dream, teeming with endemic species that are rare or extinct outside of protected areas, such as the 1200 little spotted kiwi that call the island home. Other noteworthy locals include the endemic hihi (stitchbird), kōkako, kākā, takahē and tīeke (saddleback).

According to Leon, 'Photographic opportunities start the minute you leave the mainland,' as you may see albatross and other seabirds while crossing through the marine reserve, or dolphins or whales. On the island, the best birding opportunities can be found in the tall forest around Rangatira or on the way to the summit, although the more open North End offers plenty of opportunities for chance sightings, including the kārearea/New Zealand falcon and large flocks of kererū/wood pigeons.

Visit the Island

Kāpiti Island is one of the country's largest offshore eco-sanctuaries. Access is restricted, so book your trip through licensed operator **Kāpiti Island Eco Experience** (kapitiisland.com). Overnight stays and day trips with the whānau (family) who run tours and have cultural ties to the island are possible and begin from $109.

Take a guided walk of the island's natural and cultural history, or be your own guide. The ferry disembarks at centrally located Rangatira or at the North End. The network of bush walks around Rangatira offer some of the island's best bird-watching opportunities, and access to the island's summit (Tuteremoana, 521m).

Listings

BEST OF THE REST

Start the Day Right

Comes & Goes $$

Made famous by its Instagram-worthy chicken Scotch egg, this trendy Petone eatery serves food as aesthetic as it is tasty, so don't forget your camera.

Karaka Café $$

Modern Māori and Pacific cuisine in a harbourfront cafe where the Māori language is proudly reflected in the name of every dish.

Maranui Cafe $$

A tried-and-true Wellington favourite, perched on Lyall Bay beach. Expect a wait – the queue winds down the stairs. Don't miss its thickshakes.

Prefab $$

Buzzy eatery where coffee is made strong, smooth and always fresh. Home-branded ACME bread baked and served on site.

Shelly Bay Baker on Leeds Street $

One of the staple culinary gems making up Hannah's Laneway Precinct; fresh bread, cookies and coffee are the way to go.

Fidel's $$

This Cuba St stalwart serves comforting home-style brunches, all day. The interior is dark, funky and close-quartered, with a more spacious back terrace.

Family Fun in the City

Cable Car

A Wellington icon, this unique transport links Lambton Quay to the hill suburb of Kelburn for easy access to Space Place, the Botanical Gardens and Zealandia (via a free shuttle).

Zealandia

An urban eco-sanctuary seeking to protect and restore native flora and fauna. Take a guided tour or stroll independently, and have fun spotting wildlife in the lush surroundings.

Space Place

Discover space through interactive galleries, exhibits and a historic telescope. Don't miss the planetarium: try to coincide this visit with a talk about New Zealand's night skies.

Botanic Gardens

Explore 25 hectares of sprawling, beautifully curated gardens. With playgrounds, sculptures, lookouts and a duck pond, the tranquil oasis makes for an easy escape from the CBD.

Te Papa Museum

The national museum provides free, interactive and constantly changing exhibits on topics such as Māori history, world wars and nature. Be sure to spot the colossal squid!

Te Wharewaka

Waterfront HQ of a Māori tourism company that runs walking, biking and harbour tours.

Fidel's

Fun way to experience and learn about Wellington's Māori culture from local *iwi*.

Wellington Chocolate Factory

Nestled in the city's core, WCF makes one of the most decadent hot chocolates around. Book a tour to learn the chocolatiers' secrets.

Coastal Day Hikes

Escarpment Track

Climb the 'Stairway to Heaven', traverse 9km from Paekākāriki to Pukerua Bay and be rewarded with sweeping views to Kāpiti Island. Local tip: north to south is easier.

Red Rocks

Explore Wellington's south coast with a 40-minute walk from Ōwhiro Bay to the aptly named Red Rocks. Watch out for seals.

Waterfront Walk

Walk, bike or blade your way around the city's scenic waterfront. Visit the Karaka Cafe to try a traditional *hāngī* meal. Hire a crocodile bike for a group adventure.

Castlepoint Lighthouse

A popular weekend getaway, Castlepoint is a wildly rugged coastal town featuring an easy, scenic walk with magnificent views of unique coastal formations and an iconic lighthouse.

Breweries & Local Drops

Choice Bros $$

Instagram-ready fairy lights line the alleyway to an old boxing gym, gloves and weights discarded in favour of David Bowie–inspired concoctions. Unmissable fried chicken.

Waitoa Social Club $$

Recently expanded from its Hataitai flagship, the CBD location encourages conversation

JIRI FOLTYN/SHUTTERSTOCK

Te Papa Museum

over plates from adjoining Little Penang, combining two of Wellington's favourite institutions.

HeyDay $$

Centrally located, with a pastel aesthetic that stands out on Cuba St, HeyDay offers fun arcade and yard games to keep any beer skeptics in the group occupied.

Fortune Favours $$

Residing in a former dip-strippers', its renovated interior is still heavily influenced by its past life. The upstairs terrace is particularly popular on Wellington's rare windless days.

Brewton $$

Take a train to Upper Hutt and be rewarded with multiple market-leading breweries, a distillery and a plethora of on-site, family-friendly activities.

Puffin $$$

Leading the charge on organic and minimal intervention wines, Puffin's plain facade hides an elegant speakeasy popular with the after-work crowd.

NELSON & MARLBOROUGH

BEACHES | DINING | NATIONAL PARKS

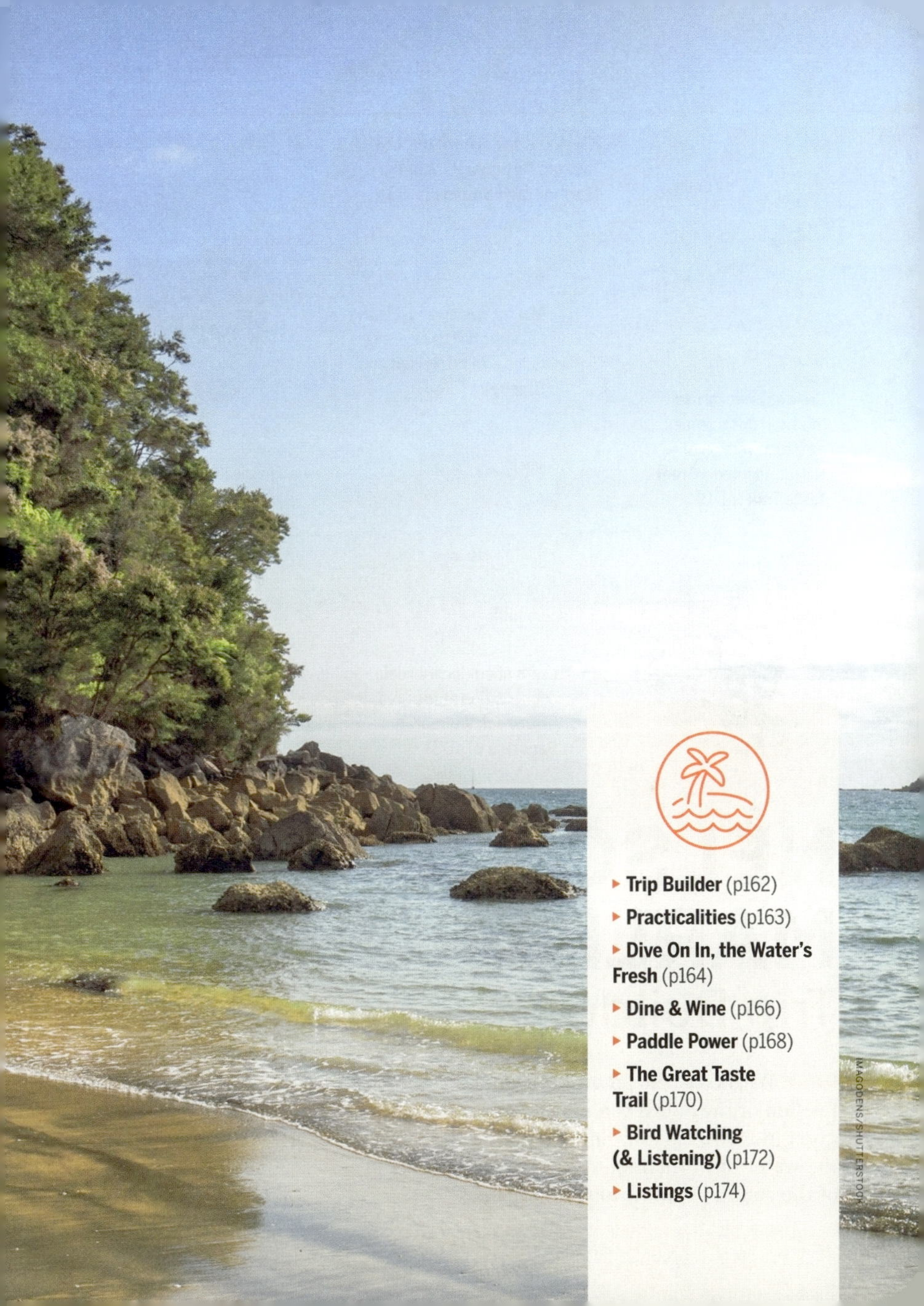

IMAGODENS/SHUTTERSTOCK ©

Kayak the coastline of the **Abel Tasman National Park** or the **Marlborough Sounds** (p168)
1-2hr from Nelson

Make a splash and join the locals at river swimming holes around **Nelson** and **Blenheim** (p164)

Drive between artisan food and drink venues on a road version of Nelson-Tasman's **Great Taste Trail** (p170)

Sample local sav in New Zealand's largest wine-producing region, **Marlborough** (p166)
1-2hr from Nelson

Learn about local wildlife conservation at the predator-free **Brook Waimārama Sanctuary** (p173)
10min from Nelson

NELSON & MARLBOROUGH
Trip Builder

With coastline, mountains and fertile plains, the Top of the South is a microcosm of all that's great in New Zealand. Enjoy outdoor activities on the water or in the mountains and sample some of the country's finest food and drink.

FROM LEFT: GUAXINIM/SHUTTERSTOCK, MARTIN PELANEK/SHUTTERSTOCK

Practicalities

ARRIVING

Nelson Airport is the region's main air hub. There's a smaller airport at Blenheim and an airstrip in Golden Bay. Arrive in Picton from Wellington on a Cook Strait ferry.

MONEY

New Zealand residents enjoy local prices when staying in Department of Conservation huts and campsites in national parks.

CONNECT

Wi-fi is available in main towns and villages but don't count on it inside national parks.

WHERE TO STAY

Place	Pros/Cons
Nelson	A small city with lots of accommodation and food options. Further from some outdoor activities.
Tākaka	Convenient for exploring Golden Bay and the northern Abel Tasman. Only one access road.
Picton	An attractive transport hub that's ideal for exploring Marlborough Sounds. Can get congested.
Blenheim	Wine central, with plenty of accommodation. Further from other activities.

GETTING AROUND

Car Beyond central Nelson you'll need a vehicle to explore very far.

Bus Limited long-distance buses and shuttles connect Nelson with Golden Bay, Murchison, Picton, and Blenheim. Public buses connect Nelson with outer towns.

Train A scenic railway, the Marlborough Flyer, connects Picton and Blenheim.

EATING & DRINKING

Foodies have come to the right place. Nelson has a wide range of locally and internationally inspired restaurants. Blenheim is all about the wineries like Cloudy Bay (pictured left top; p176). Seafood lovers should head for little Havelock, the Greenshell Mussel Capital of the World.

Best seafood
Greenshell Mussel Cruise (p175)

Must-try platters
Tasman's Gravity Winery (p167)

DEC–FEB

Summer brings long days and lots of sunshine, but many tourists and busy campgrounds.

MAR–MAY

Cooler but still pleasant days are ideal for outdoor activities.

JUN–AUG

Low season with cold nights and cool days, but accessible skiing at the Rainbow Ski Area.

SEP–NOV

Wet but increasingly warm, spring welcomes the godwits on their migration south.

33 Dive On In, the WATER'S FRESH

OUTDOORS | ACTIVE | NATURE

The Top of the South has some of New Zealand's clearest, least-polluted rivers. While hitting the beach on a hot summer's day is a favourite pastime throughout coastal New Zealand, locals at the Top of the South are just as likely to head to a river. To enjoy a cooling swim on a hot day without salty seawater residue, make a beeline to a river.

PETER UNGER/GETTY IMAGES

How to

Getting here Rivers snake from mountains to coast throughout the Top of the South. Swimming spots are accessible from main and back roads.

When to go The region's hot, dry summers make this season the ideal time for a swim but waterfalls are most impressive after rain.

Where not to swim Heed local safety warnings and respect Māori requests. The gorgeous Riwaka Resurgence may look inviting but it's disrespectful to swim at the sacred spot.

CSNAFZGER/SHUTTERSTOCK

Life's a River Beach

Make a splash Join the local youths and bomb, dive or (let's be honest) bellyflop from great heights. Jump from rocks at **Pelorus Bridge** (on SH6 between Havelock and Nelson), the **Lee River** (past Richmond), **Paine's Ford** (Tākaka), **Salisbury Falls** on the Aorere River past Bainham in Golden Bay, or swing from ropes above swimming holes in the **Aniseed Valley** (Richmond), **Maitai Valley** (Nelson) and Murchison's **Eel Hole** on the Buller River.

Urban refreshment The Maitai River flows from the mountains east of Nelson, and swimming spots along the river in the Maitai Valley are easy to reach from town.

En route On SH6 between Havelock and Nelson, the **Pelorus Bridge Scenic Reserve** contains a glorious stretch of clean river and wide pebbly beaches. It's a convenient place to take a walk and stretch the legs on a road trip between Blenheim and Nelson, and once you see the water you might be tempted to stay a while.

Family fun The gentle flow and shallow waters at Pelorus Bridge, the Lee River and the Aniseed Valley are ideal for kids and babies to splash about in.

Left Pelorus Bridge Scenic Reserve
Below Cleopatra's Pools

Bathe Like a Queen

A short walk from Anchorage Beach and Torrent Bay in the Abel Tasman National Park is a hidden freshwater swimming spot, **Cleopatra's Pools**.

Here the Torrent River forms a series of rock pools and small waterfalls surrounded by forest. When water levels are suitable, adventurous souls can slip and slide down the wet moss-covered rocks into the pools. Alternatively, lay out a towel and sunbathe on the surrounding rocks, like Cleopatra herself (without the milk).

Whether you plan to hike through the park or visit on a day trip via a water taxi, Cleopatra's Pools are a worthy detour.

34 Dine & WINE

FOOD | DRINK | ENTERTAINMENT

Vineyards with views, restaurants, games and sculpture gardens make winery visits accessible for all. Wine novices, beer drinkers, families and even travellers who prefer a meal *sans* alcohol can experience the Nelson-Tasman-Marlborough region's culinary best by visiting wineries that offer more than typical wine tasting. Wine connoisseurs won't be disappointed by the range of sauvignon blanc available, either.

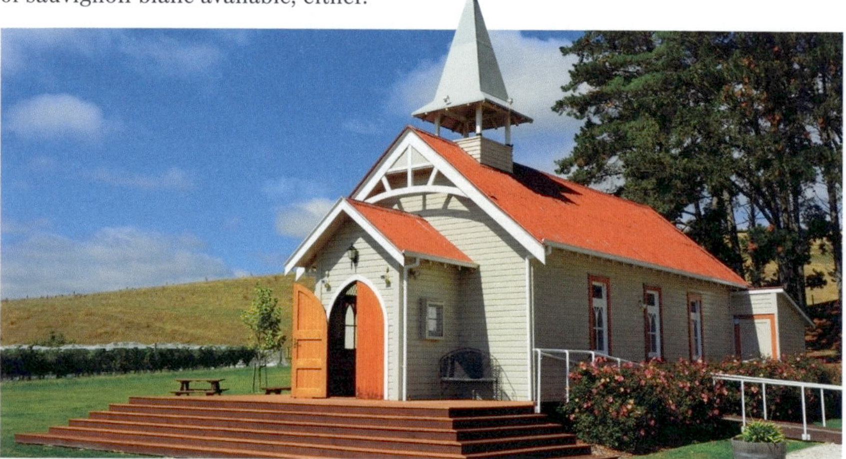

ALIZADA STUDIOS/SHUTTERSTOCK

How to

Getting here The Marlborough region is home to around 30 cellar doors. Winery tour shuttle buses operate around Blenheim so nobody needs to drink and drive.

When to go Many wineries operate year-round, although some restaurants only operate in summer.

Not mad for wine? Swap the cellar door for a winery restaurant. You can order another beverage with your delicious meal.

THE PENANGITE/SHUTTERSTOCK

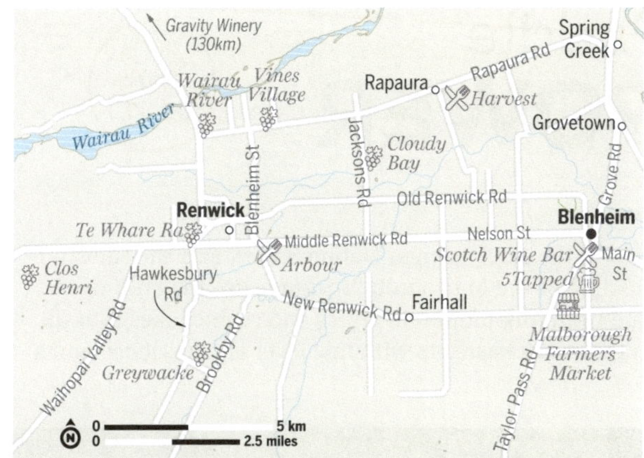

A Foodie's Weekend in Blenheim

Friday night Hang with the locals at **5Tapped**, a coffee and speciality beer bar. Follow with dinner at **Little Amigo's** Mexican food truck and finish at **Scotch Wine Bar**.

Saturday Head to **Vines Village** for breakfast. Then, jump in Explore Marlborough's van to visit some wineries, including **Cloudy Bay**, **Te Whare Ra**, **Clos Henri** (a converted chapel) and **Greywacke** (appointments required). After the tour, have dinner at **Arbour**, a restaurant that does nothing by halves.

Sunday Start with breakfast, coffee and a shop at the **Marlborough Farmers Market**. Visit Hedgerows for fresh strawberry frozen yogurt and a punnet of takeaway strawberries. Stop by the rustic shed at Bush's honey for the most delicate freshly cut honeycomb. End with dinner at **Harvest**, within the sprawling manicured gardens of **The Marlborough**, a luxury country estate.

Blenheim itinerary recommended by Stephanie McIntyre
certified sommelier and food and drink consultant, Blenheim. @outre_nz

Left Clos Henri
Below Cloudy Bay Winery

Grape to Glass & Paddock to Plate

Lawn games For a bit of old-world fun with your Kiwi drop, play a game of *pétanque* at Cloudy Bay Vineyards or Number 11 Restaurant at Wairau River Wines, or croquet at Gravity Winery.

Wine with a side of art Gravity Winery in Mahana runs the Gravity Gallery, showcasing local art. The storytelling sculptures on the lawn at Wairau River Wines are Insta-worthy.

Turn up the temp in the kitchen Wither Hills, Wairau River Wines and Allan Scott Bistro, among others, tell the region's story through seasonally inspired menus and sharing platters.

35 Paddle POWER

OUTDOORS | NATURE | SPORTS

The beautiful beaches of the Abel Tasman National Park and the (mostly) sheltered 1500km-long coastline of the Marlborough Sounds are the stuff of sea kayakers' dreams. Add some tumbling mountain rivers and scenic lakes into the mix and you have a region that suits kayakers with any level of experience and a thirst for adventure.

FRANS LEMMENS/GETTY IMAGES

How to

Getting here Sea kayak rentals and tours of the Abel Tasman coastline operate from access towns south and north of the park. For the Marlborough Sounds, head to Picton or Havelock. Murchison is a white-water kayaking hub.

When to go Conditions are best for water sports in the spring, summer and autumn.

Waka tours Paddle a modernised Māori *waka* (canoe) on a cultural tour of Abel Tasman with Waka Abel Tasman.

JANA SIKOROVA/SHUTTERSTOCK

ANDREW PEACOCK/GETTY IMAGES

Left Mangles River
Far left Kayaking, Abel Tasman National Park
Below Seal, Abel Tasman National Park

This is Where New Zealand Began

The Top of the South is really the best place in New Zealand for kayaking.

Where to go The northern end of the **Abel Tasman National Park** is particularly special because commercial activity is very restricted here. The water taxis that operate in the rest of the park can't go north past Tōtaranui. The area from Tata Beach to Tōtaranui is a snapshot of the best sea kayaking in New Zealand.

What to see These areas of the park are isolated and all these plant species have sprung up that really shouldn't be here, and that wouldn't survive anywhere else. You can see grey spotted shags and reef herons, plenty of seals and kororā (blue penguins), orca and southern right whales.

Layers of history This is where New Zealand began in more ways than one: it's where the land of present-day New Zealand split from Gondwanaland and it's where Māori and Europeans first had contact. The historical human impact here has been small, so it feels special.

Kayaking recommendations by Lisa Savage
Golden Bay Kayaks, Tata Beach
@goldenbaykayaks

Pick Your River, Lake or Bay

Meeting Place The inland Tasman village of Murchison is on the confluence of the Buller and Matakitaki rivers, and is near the Mangles and Matiri rivers. It's an ideal base for white-water kayaking and rafting adventures.

Nelson Lakes In summer, rent kayaks at Lakes Rotoiti and Rotoroa, the two most accessible lakes in the Nelson Lakes National Park. Paddle away from shore to admire the views of forested hills turning to snowcapped mountains.

Spot dolphins There's no need to join a motorised boat tour to get up close to dolphins in the Marlborough Sounds. Dusky, bottlenose and common dolphins might just swim alongside your kayak.

36 Drive the Great TASTE TRAIL

DRIVING | EATING | SCENERY

The Nelson-Tasman region's 174km Great Taste Trail connects some of the area's best food and drink experiences. But if you don't have the time (or, let's face it, the energy) to cycle the route, you can drive it in half a day, stopping to snack at select pit stops along the way. The coastal and mountain scenery is also worth the trip.

ROBERT CHG/SHUTTERSTOCK

Trip Notes

Getting here Nelson is a logical starting point for this driving tour, but it can also be done from other places en route if you're staying there instead, such as Māpua, Motueka or even Kaiteriteri.

When to go Fresh fruit is abundant in this region in spring and summer, and you'll see many roadside stalls. Bring cash.

Stop for a swim If you have plenty of time and the weather's fine, take a detour to Moturoa/Rabbit (pictured above) Island for a swim at the pine-flanked beach.

Which Direction?

You can drive this route in either direction, either heading northwest from Richmond towards Motueka, or continuing southwest through Brightwater, Wakefield and towards Tapawera. Consider how hungry you are before you begin, and whether you want to stop for a full meal or just snacks. There are more sit-down dining options around Māpua and Motueka than elsewhere.

FROM LEFT: MARK DUNN/ALAMY, PHOTOS BRIANSCANTLEBURY/SHUTTERSTOCK

37 BIRD WATCHING (& Listening)

BIRDS | WILDLIFE | NATURE

The birdsong around coastal Nelson-Tasman-Marlborough was once so loud that Captain Cook had to anchor his ship far offshore to hold a conversation. Hike and bird-watch in parks and sanctuaries where efforts are being made to restore New Zealand's birdsong and the habitats native birds need to survive and thrive.

Tasman Sea
Puponga
Farewell Spit
Paturau River
Pakawau
Golden Bay
Mangarakau Swamp
Collingwood
Tākaka
Abel Tasman National Park
Kahurangi National Park
Tasman Bay
Motueka
Mt Arthur
Motuara Island
Māpua
Nelson
Richmond
Brook Waimārama Sanctuary

How to

Getting here Hike, take a bus tour or ride a water taxi to bird conservation areas across the region.

When to go Godwits appear at Farewell Spit, on their round-the-world tour, between September and March.

What to look for Godwits, Mongolian dotterels, gannets, little penguins, oystercatchers, shags, pīwakawaka (fantails), kākāriki, kākā, pāteke (brown teal), titipounamu, tūī, riroriro, kererū (wood pigeons), korimako (bellbirds), ruru (moreporks).

Dawn chorus In the **Abel Tasman National Park**, Project Janszoon and the Birdsong Trust work on pest eradication and to restore and maintain the native forest in which native songbirds thrive. Hikers on the Abel Tasman Coast Track will be woken by the sounds of the toutouwai (robin) and tīeke (saddleback), if they're lucky.

Wonderful waders Not all birds make their homes in the forests. **Farewell Spit** and the **Mangarakau Swamp** are home to wetland and shore birds, some of which fly tens of thousands of kilometres in one stretch. The bar-tailed godwit is a remarkable little bird that flies between China, Alaska and New Zealand every year, and some of them make their seasonal home at Farewell Spit.

CMH IMAGES/ALAMY

An Urban Sanctuary

A purpose-built fence surrounds the **Brook Waimārama Sanctuary**, ensuring the area is free from introduced mammalian pests. This requires 24/7 fence checking and maintenance by staff and volunteers. Endemic populations of birds and wildlife have notably increased. Several 'lost' plants, including fungi, have been discovered in the sanctuary. Among the biggest milestones for bird conservation were the successful translocations of tīeke (South Island saddleback) and kākāriki karaka (orange-fronted parakeet), both of which are critically endangered and were previously absent from the Nelson region. In 2024, 56 tuataras were also translocated to the sanctuary from across the country, to pre-drilled burrows.

Cruise to a kiwi nursery

Motuara Island in Queen Charlotte Sound is used as a nursery for the rare rowi kiwi, who are raised until they're big enough to be returned to their native habitat in southern Westland. It's also home to tīeke, toutouwai and kākāriki. Cruise to the island from Picton and hike the half-hour track to the summit to enjoy views of the Marlborough Sounds.

Above Tīeke, Motuara Island

Listings

BEST OF THE REST

Waterfall Walks

Wainui Falls

Hike through bush on the edge of the Abel Tasman National Park to the impressive 20m-high Wainui Falls. An easy one-hour return walk, but keep kids close.

Salisbury Falls

Towards the start of the Heaphy Track and past Bainham in inland Golden Bay, these small falls on the Aorere River are beside a great swimming hole. A short walk across private land.

Whisky Falls

So-named for the illegal whisky distillery once here, the 40m-high Whisky Falls are a good day-hike adventure from Lake Rotoiti. High-altitude Nelson Lakes National Park is refreshing in summer.

Maruia Falls

Created by the huge Murchison earthquake of 1929, gushing Maruia Falls are a short drive from Murchison. Swing by on the way to the Shenandoah Hwy or the West Coast.

Brook Sanctuary Waterfall

Walk the easy loop track around the Brook Waimārama Sanctuary and find these lovely short waterfalls about halfway. This stream used to provide Nelson's main water supply.

At the Market

Nelson Art Market

Nelsonians' favourite Saturday morning activity, the Art Market in central Montgomery Sq offers local handicrafts, ready-to-eat food and fresh produce.

Isel Park Twilight Market

Historic Isel Park, in the Nelson suburb of Stoke, hosts the chilled-out Twilight Market on Thursdays during the summer, from late afternoon to late evening. Admire the enormous sequoia trees over a picnic dinner.

Nelson Farmers Market

Beside the Elma Turner Library, the Nelson Farmers Market on Wednesday mornings is the best place to get fresh local produce midweek.

Tākaka Village Market

Find fresh food, music, art and crafts in the heart of Golden Bay on Saturday mornings. Small Tākaka is known for its alternative cultural scene and this is an ideal place to see it in action.

Cosmopolitan Dining

Hawker House $$

Street food dishes from around Southeast Asia are served amid an energetic ambience. Team the zesty Vietnamese beef salad with Townshend's Sutton Hoo American Amber Ale from nearby Motueka, but leave room for dessert of cardamon-infused panna cotta.

ERNEST KUNG/GETTY IMAGES

Maruia Falls

Hopgood's & Co $$$

Mediterranean- and Asian-inspired dishes harnessing seasonal ingredients are the focus at this unpretentious restaurant. Relax and enjoy *pāua* (shellfish) dumplings with shiitake and white radish. Five course tasting menus are $95.

Take to the Water

Pelorus Mail Boat

Help deliver the rural mail (which is just as likely to be a live animal than an envelope) on this local-service-meets-tourist-attraction that's been running since 1919.

Greenshell Mussel Cruise

Three-hour cruise to mussel in on Kenepuru's aquaculture. Includes a tasting of steamed mussels and a glass of wine. Bookings essential.

Abel Tasman Water Taxis

Ideal for travellers without the time to hike through the Abel Tasman National Park, water taxis and cruises run up the coast of the park from Kaiteriteri. The cruise to Awaroa's white-sand beach is possibly the best.

Lake Rotoiti Water Taxi

Three-hour cruise to mussel in on Kenepuru's aquaculture. Includes a tasting of steamed mussels and a glass of wine. Bookings essential.

From Dizzy Heights

Centre of New Zealand

Once believed to be the geographical centre of the country, the trig point at the top of Botanical Hill offers sweeping views of Nelson, Tasman Bay and the mountains beyond.

Cullen Point Lookout

Stop on Queen Charlotte Drive to stretch your legs on the short walk to this lookout, overlooking Havelock and Pelorus Sound.

Abel Tasman water taxi

Hawke's Lookout

Take a break from the twists and turns of the Tākaka Hill road at Hawke's Lookout, with the Riwaka Resurgence right below and expansive views of Tasman Bay.

Pupu Hydro Walkway

Follow an old gold-mining-era water race through the hills of Golden Bay, along boardwalks and gravel paths through native forest.

Winery Dining

Gravity Winery $$$

Expansive views of Tasman Bay from a high perch in little Mahana, in the Moutere Hills between Nelson and Motueka. Excellent platters, including an option for kids.

St Clair Family Estate Vineyard Kitchen $$$

Pick more varieties of blueberries than you even knew existed from this farm on the backroads of Hope. Summer only; bring your own containers.

Allan Scott Bistro $$$

Another top spot on Blenheim's Golden Mile. Fine-dining-quality food with a quintessentially Kiwi relaxed atmosphere.

CENTRAL SOUTH ISLAND
ADVENTURE | OUTDOORS | UNSPOILED

CENTRAL SOUTH ISLAND

Trip Builder

Remote and unspoiled, the Central South Island is home to some of New Zealand's most rugged and otherworldly scenery. The Southern Alps dominate the landscape and startlingly blue lakes capture the attention of all who pass. A destination for outdoor enthusiasts and nature lovers.

Cross swing bridges and turquoise water at **Hokitika Gorge** (p194)
4hr from Christchurch

Hike through the majestic **Southern Alps** (p186)
4hr from Christchurch

Kayak with icebergs in the **Tasman Glacier Terminal Lake** (p187)
3½hr from Queenstown

Gaze at the stars at **Lake Tekapo** (p184)
3hr from Christchurch

Mt Ryall
Grey River
Greymouth
Lake Brunner (Moana)
Lake Kaniere
Mt Rolleston
Arthur Pass
Mt Murchison
Craigieburn Forest Park
Mt Bryce
Tasman Sea
Mt Whitcombe
Westland Tai Poutini National Park
Whataroa
Lake Mapourika
Mt Arrowsmith
Lake Coleridge
Franz Josef Glacier
Fox Glacier
Franz Josef Glacier
Fox Glacier
Albert Glacier
Aoraki/Mt Cook National Park
Rangitata River
Mt Hut
Tasman Glacier
Aoraki/ Mt Cook
Methven
Douglas Neve
Mueller Glacier
Lake Tekapo
Lake Pukaki
Burkes Pass

Victoria Forest Park
Nelson Lakes National Park
Mt Haast
Lake Daniell
Faerie Queen
Springs Junction
Lewis Pass
0 50 km
0 25 miles
Observe whales in the wild in **Kaikōura** (p200)
2½hr from Christchurch
Cycle through forests on the **West Coast Wilderness Trail** (p202)
3hr from Christchurch
Hanmer Springs Forest Park
Lewis Pass Scenic Reserve
Lake Sumner Forest Park
Waiau River
Mt Longfellow
Arthur's Pass National Park
Hurunui River
Take an epic train journey through **Arthur's Pass** (p199)
Begins in Christchurch
Lake Pearson
Spend a day discovering local wineries in the **Waipara Valley** (p193)
45min from Christchurch
Ashley River
Porters Pass
Waimakariri River
Pegasus Bay
Christchurch
Eat and drink amid the exciting urban renewal of **Christchurch** (p192)
Lyttelton
Rakaia River
Banks Peninsula
Lake Ellesmere
Akaroa
Learn about Māori and colonial history around **Akaroa and Banks Peninsula** (p182)
1½hr from Christchurch
Canterbury Bight
South Pacific Ocean

Practicalities

UWE ARANAS/SHUTTERSTOCK

ARRIVING

Christchurch International Airport The major transport hub for the region. Route 29 buses ($4) connect the airport with the city centre and it's possible to pay by contactless cards and digital payment apps. Many travellers choose to pick up a rental car from the airport if they intend to travel to more remote areas in the South Island. The airport is approximately 15 minutes' drive from the city centre.

HOW MUCH FOR A

Coffee $5.50

A pint of craft beer $13

Pub meal $30

WHEN TO GO

DEC–FEB
Hot and dry. Best time for hiking, swimming and seeing the lupins bloom.

MAR–MAY
Cooler temperatures are perfect for hiking and outdoor activities.

JUN–AUG
Cold, slightly more rainfall. Best time for skiing and snow-capped-mountain photos.

SEP–NOV
Warm days. Waterfalls are at their best.

GETTING AROUND

Car Long distances with remote areas and mountainous terrain make a car or campervan the best way to get around. This is a region that lends itself to road trips, with many small towns to visit and spectacular scenery along the way. Having your own vehicle is also convenient for visiting Akaroa and Banks Peninsula.

Train Cross from Christchurch to Greymouth through the Southern Alps on the TranzAlpine or journey south from Picton to Christchurch on the Coastal Pacific.

Local buses The best public transport option for getting around Christchurch. For discounted fares, buy a MetroCard ($5) at The Crossing bus exchange and libraries.

EATING & DRINKING

The Central South Island is known for its seafood. Try crayfish in Kaikōura, whitebait fritters on the West Coast, and alpine salmon farmed in glacial rivers around the Mackenzie Country. Some of the country's best salami and sausages come from tiny Blackball on the West Coast, while local drinks include regional craft beers at Christchurch's Canterbury Brewers Collective, Waipara Valley cool-climate wines, and Little Biddy gin at the Reefton Distilling Co.

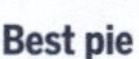

Best pie
(perhaps even in New Zealand)
Fairlie Bakehouse (p205)

Must-try blue cod
Craypot (p205)

CONNECT & FIND YOUR WAY

Wi-fi Free wi-fi is available at libraries and most accommodation, but it's easiest to buy a local SIM card or e-SIM when you first arrive in the country. You may lose data connection and a phone signal when driving on more remote roads.

Navigation Signage is good on most major routes. There is also signage for major attractions and photo stops.

PUBLIC HOLIDAYS

Many cafes and restaurants close on public holidays (especially on the West Coast), so buy groceries or book a table in advance if travelling around Christmas.

WHERE TO STAY

The Central South Island region is relatively sparsely populated, with long distances between major towns. Consider basing yourself in one or more of the towns below, while you explore the surrounding area.

Town	Pros/Cons
Christchurch	One of New Zealand's major cities. Food and accommodation options at all price points. Undergoing a post-earthquake regeneration.
Twizel	Good base for Tekapo and Aoraki/Mt Cook National Park. Good range of affordable accommodation options.
Kaikōura	Coastal town known for marine wildlife and seafood. Accommodation available for all budgets.
Hokitika	Historic town on the West Coast with good food and accommodation options. Carvings crafted from *pounamu* (greenstone or jade) can be purchased here.
Franz Josef	Small village near the glaciers. Very tourist-orientated and busy in summer.

MONEY

Fill up your car in major towns, as petrol can be more expensive in small towns. Buy wine, craft beer and gourmet foods from supermarkets, delis and farmers markets to save money when trying local flavours.

38 Akaroa & Banks PENINSULA

HISTORY | WILDLIFE | ACTIVITIES

Detour from Christchurch to Akaroa, the main town amid Banks Peninsula's spectacular volcanic landscape. It's a fine destination for a concise day trip exploring Akaroa's unique French colonial history, but a longer stay including overnighting in quaint B&B accommodation and getting out on Akaroa Harbour is the best way to experience this destination combining history, wildlife adventures and maritime vistas.

NICSPIXELS/SHUTTERSTOCK

How to

When to go Spring and summer (from October to March) offers the best opportunity for warm and dry weather.

Getting there Akaroa is a 90-minute drive from central Christchurch. By public transport, book a same-day return shuttle with **Akaroa French Connection** (akaroabus.co.nz).

Become a postie for a day Explore Banks Peninsula with postman Jeff on his **Akaroa Eastern Bays Scenic Mail Run** (akaroamailrun.com) departing Akaroa at 9am Monday to Friday.

IMAGEBROKER.COM/SHUTTERSTOCK

La France en Nouvelle-Zélande Established as a French colony in 1840, a Gallic South Pacific enterprise which lasted until 1849, the charming harbour town of Akaroa still features memories of its colonial past. Street names include Rue Balguerie and Rue Lavaud, there's a French tinge to local cafes, and descendants of 1840s settlers still live in the settlement.

Echoes of history Located in Langlois-Éteveneaux Cottage, the only original structure from colonial times, **Akaroa Museum** (akaroamuseum.org.nz) is a fascinating showcase of historical times from local Māori *iwi* to the French. Don't miss the 20-minute historical film screening in the adjacent restored courthouse. For the ultimate French experience, including historical re-enactments and markets, visit for the biennial **Akaroa French Festival** (akaroafrenchfest.co.nz), held in October in odd-numbered years.

Important Māori heritage Located 20km northeast of Akaroa, the **Okains Bay Māori & Colonial Museum** (okainsbaymuseum.co.nz) features a nationally significant collection of historical Māori artefacts. Highlights include a replica *wharenui* (meeting house), *waka* (canoes) and stone tools. Opening hours vary seasonally so check online before setting off.

Sky-high and on the water views For the best perspective of Banks Peninsula and Akaroa Harbour, known as 'Long Harbour' in the local Kāi Tahu Māori dialect, join a boat trip, or drive the vertiginous Summit Rd for views of a spectacular volcanic landscape formed eight to 12 million years ago.

Left Akaroa
Below Banks Peninsula

Best Outdoor Adventures

Akaroa Dolphins Hook up with dolphin-spotting dogs on boat trips that also include Akaroa's Māori heritage and natural history.

Black Cat Cruises Nature and wildlife experiences around Akaroa Harbour and also on Quail Harbour near Lyttelton.

Fox II Sailing Wildlife cruises on a 1922 gaff rigged ketch. Regular sightings include Akaroa's endangered Hector's dolphins and *kekeno* (NZ fur seals).

Pohatu Penguins Conservation-focused tours of mainland New Zealand's largest colony of *kororā* (little penguins). Includes a 4WD journey to isolated areas of Banks Peninsula.

Akaroa Guided Sea Kayak Safaris Expertly guided kayaking trips, including a sunrise tour, Akaroa's Māori history and seabirds aplenty.

39 Dazzling Stars & DARK SKIES

STARGAZING | NIGHT ACTIVITY | FAMILY-FRIENDLY

Discover stars and constellations unique to the southern hemisphere in one of the largest Dark Sky Reserves in the world. On the shores of Lake Tekapo, you can wonder at faraway planets and galaxies while learning about the local Māori connection to the night sky. The surrounding mountains and lakes also provide the perfect setting for trying your hand at astrophotography.

How to

Getting here Lake Tekapo is about three hours' drive from Christchurch and the same from Queenstown.

Expect to pay $210 for an observatory tour.

Weather Stars are visible all year round; however, winter is best for cloudless skies. Spend a few days in the region to increase your chances of a clear sky.

What to wear The wind can be cold on the summit so wear warm clothes, even in summer.

Dark skies for miles Tekapo is situated in the heart of the **Aoraki Mackenzie International Dark Sky Reserve**, the largest dark sky reserve in the southern hemisphere. Stretching for almost 4400 sq km, there is minimal light pollution in the area, meaning that the stars look incredibly bright and you can easily see the Milky Way, Magellanic Clouds and the Southern Cross on a clear night. On rare occasions you can even see the Aurora Australis (Southern Lights).

Reaching for the stars
To get as close as you can to the stars, head up the summit of **Mt John**. The hill rises above Lake Tekapo and is home to New Zealand's premier astronomical research centre, the **Mt John Observatory**. This is one of the few observatories located in a dark sky reserve in the world, and the views through the telescopes are spectacular.

Hot Springs & Stargazing

For an indulgent take on stargazing, marvel at the night sky from a hot spring. Bathe yourself in the hot waters at **Tekapo Springs**, while staring at the heavens and learning about the constellations overhead.

This is a particularly special experience in winter, when you'll be greeted with a hot chocolate at the dimly lit Tekapo Springs complex. Rather than shiver in the cold, submerge yourself in an underwater hammock, with the best of the night sky on display above you. It's a relaxing way to see the stars, in complete comfort, with next to no light pollution.

Soak-and-stars experiences are available at **Tekapo Star Gazing** (tekapostargazing.co.nz).

Through the telescope Gaze through powerful telescopes and see the marvels of space up close. Depending on the time of year, you can see various planets and distant star systems including Alpha Centauri and the Globular Star Cluster.

Capturing the experience If you want to learn more about astrophotography, there are several tours dedicated to photographing the night sky – just remember to bring your camera and a tripod. A photo of the **Church of the Good Shepherd** with the Milky Way shimmering overhead is a particularly beautiful way to remember your trip.

Above Aoraki Mackenzie International Dark Sky Reserve

40 Taking the Mountains TO THEIR LIMIT

HIKING | SKIING | MOUNTAINEERING

Explore glaciers, turquoise lakes and sheer mountain peaks in some of New Zealand's most photogenic countryside. Make your way through tracks bordered by alpine forest and past fields of colourful wildflowers as you head into the heart of the Southern Alps.

CHARNCHAI WASINANONT/SHUTTERSTOCK

How to

Getting here Aoraki/Mt Cook National Park is four hours from Christchurch by car.

When to go November to May for hiking and July to October for skiing. Scenic flights and day walks are accessible year round. January and February is tourist season. Lupins are at their best from November to early January.

Getting around Hire a car for a stellar road trip or travel from Lake Tekapo with Tekapo Shuttle.

NANOSTOCKK/GETTY IMAGES

Walks Beneath Soaring Peaks

Exploring **Aoraki/Mt Cook National Park** is possible for all ages, with trails of varying lengths and options suitable for different levels of ability. Take a flat trail past colourful lakes, or opt for a short yet strenuous climb up multiple stairs which culminate on the edge of the **Tasman Glacier Terminal Lake**. You can do a short walk to a lookout over Tasman Glacier and/or try the very popular half-day **Hooker Valley Track**, which meanders through alpine streams, past glaciers and over swing bridges. Start early in the day or later in the afternoon to avoid the crowds.

For those after more of a challenge, consider an overnight hike instead, staying in one of the DOC huts in the national park. The **Mueller Track** is a popular overnight hike, while the three- to four-day **Ball Pass**

I VIEWFINDER/SHUTTERSTOCK

Flower Fields

For photos of blue and pink lupin flowers on the shores of the blue lakes of the Mackenzie Country, visit between November and early January. Technically, lupins are an invasive species, and efforts are underway to control their spread, but bordering the shores of **Lake Tekapo** they are undeniably photogenic.

Above left Tasman Glacier Terminal Lake
Above Tourist helicopter, Aoraki/Mt Cook National Park
Left Hooker Valley Track

Crossing is a demanding alpine trail best suited to experienced hikers.

Those looking for more relaxing options should consider a lakeside walk at the foot of the mountain along the shores of **Lake Pukaki**. The **Pukaki Boulders** and **Pukaki Kettle Hole Track** (4km return) are popular choices. See doc.govt.nz for track notes and more detailed information.

Ski from Great Heights

For a unique experience, try heliskiing in the Aoraki/Mt Cook ranges, home to New Zealand's highest peak and exciting skiing and snowboarding terrain. Helicopter up and ski among glaciers and alpine lakes with runs across six mountain ranges. Best for experienced skiers and snowboarders.

Fly over a Glacier

Take flight and see Aoraki/Mt Cook National Park from its best vantage point, with the glaciers and snowfields spread out below you. Fly between mountain peaks and along the length of the Tasman Glacier, before seeing Mt Cook up close. Many flights include a snow

Why Are Glacial Lakes So Blue?

As you travel through Mackenzie Country, you'll quickly notice that the water in the lakes and rivers is a remarkable turquoise colour. When you see Lake Tekapo and Lake Pukaki, it can be hard to believe that the lakes are naturally this colour.

The turquoise hue is caused by fine silt particles (or glacial flour) in the water. The silt is so fine, it remains suspended in the water and when the particles catch the light, the water appears an intense blue-green colour. The turquoise lakes and rivers contain a large amount of water from melting glaciers.

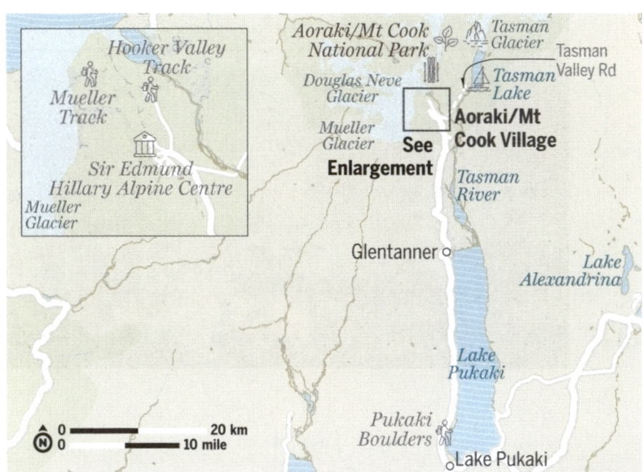

landing and it's also possible to fly to the West Coast and Westland National Park to see the impressive Franz Josef and Fox Glaciers too.

Discover New Zealand's Greatest Explorer

Learn about Sir Edmund Hillary at the **Sir Edmund Hillary Alpine Centre**, at the Hermitage Hotel. The museum pays tribute to the great explorer and showcases the Aoraki/ Mt Cook National Park region. If you can't get out into the mountains, the 3D film is the next best thing to flying through the mountain range, hiking up the peaks or skiing between the glaciers. There is also a planetarium on site.

Explore a Glacial Lake

Book an excursion with **Glacier Explorers** (hermitage.co.nz) to get out on the Tasman Glacier Terminal Lake by inflatable boat and also enjoy remarkable mountain views. The lake is growing as the glacier melts and there are frequently icebergs floating on the lake, which have torn from the glacier. As you drift past, it's possible to touch and even taste the glacial crystals. If you have some kayaking experience, it's also possible to kayak on the lake and get even closer to the icebergs. Contact **Southern Alps Guiding** (mtcook.com).

Left Lake Tekapo (p187)
Below Statue of Sir Edmund Hillary by Bryn Jones

MICHAL TESAR/SHUTTERSTOCK

Maramataka: The Māori Lunar Calendar

THE TURNING OF THE MOON

Traditionally, the Maramataka was an integral part of Māori life, signalling the best times to go fishing, plant crops or gather food. Working with the rhythms of nature was vital to the survival of early Māori in New Zealand, and this ancient knowledge still has relevance today.

Left Fireworks to celebrate Matariki
Centre Full moon, Kaikōura
Right Matariki star cluster (the Pleiades)

Like many seafaring societies, Māori have traditionally lived their lives by the cycle of the moon and its influence on the tides and land. The Māori lunar calendar is called the Maramataka, which literally means the turning of the moon.

In June, the Matariki star cluster (the Pleiades) first appears in the sky, signalling the New Year and the start of the Maramataka. Throughout the year, the Maramataka gives people guidance on the best time for gathering food and whether the next season will be an abundant one. Included in the lunar calendar are the most appropriate and inappropriate times for gathering food, planting and harvesting crops and catching seafood *(kai moana)*.

Months of the Maramataka

Each month begins on the night of the new moon and has a star or constellation associated with it.

The months of the Maramataka:

Pipiri (May–June) All things on earth are contracted because of the cold; likewise man.

Hongonui (or Hōngongoi; June–July) Man is now extremely cold and kindles fires before which he basks.

Here-turi-kōkā (July–August) The scorching effect of fire is seen on the knees of man.

Mahuru (August–September) The earth has now acquired warmth, as have vegetation and trees.

Whiringa-ā-nuku (September–October) The earth has now become quite warm.

MATTHEW MICAH WRIGHT/GETTY IMAGES

MANFRED_KONRAD/GETTY IMAGES

Whiringa-ā-rangi (October–November) It has now become summer, and the sun has acquired strength.

Hakihea (November–December) Birds are now sitting in their nests.

Kohi-tātea (December–January) Fruits are now ripe, and man eats the new food of the season.

Hui-tanguru (January–February) The foot of Rūhī (a summer star) now rests upon the earth.

Poutū-te-rangi (February–March) The crops are now harvested.

Paenga-whāwhā (March–April) All straw is now stacked at the borders of the plantations.

Haratua (April–May) Crops are now stored in pits. The tasks of man are finished.

Do People Still Use the Maramataka Today?

Fishing and planting food in accordance with the moon, the tides and the elements is still common today and so the Maramataka still plays an important part in many people's lifestyles.

> The Maramataka gives people guidance on the best time to gather food.

For example, eel fishing during a full moon often results in a smaller catch, as eels generally avoid brighter light. Shellfish are also more common after a low tide. Some of the months also coincide with the seasons for planting or fishing.

There are still many different types of Maramataka in use across Aotearoa New Zealand.

The Stars Marking the New Year

Matariki is a star cluster which appears in the sky in June (midwinter), marking the start of the Māori New Year.

The Matariki star cluster (the Pleiades) brings the old lunar year to an end and marks the beginning of the new Maramataka. Matariki takes place after the traditional harvest, which meant people had more time for family and festivities.

This was traditionally a time of renewal and new beginnings with festivities and celebrations including lighting ritual fires, making offerings to god and honouring ancestors while celebrating life.

Nowadays, Matariki is celebrated with community events often involving light shows and fireworks.

41 An Exciting FOOD SCENE

FOOD | VINEYARDS | BREWERIES

Christchurch has re-emerged from the devastating earthquakes of 2010 and 2011 with a creative and exciting food scene. Changes in the city layout and a wealth of non-traditional spaces have created new dining destinations. Experience Christchurch's gastronomic revolution in new eateries around the city, sample local craft beer, and venture further afield for the best of North Canterbury wine in the Waipara Valley.

TRAVELLIGHT/SHUTTERSTOCK

How to

Where to go Central Christchurch has the highest concentration of good restaurants and bars. The nearby harbour suburb of Lyttelton also has good eating and drinking.

Expect to pay Around $20 for a cheap lunch. Fine-dining restaurants charge more than $40 for a main dish.

Local favourites Savoury treats from the **Butcher's Pie Shop** in Riverside Market.

TRABANTOS/SHUTTERSTOCK

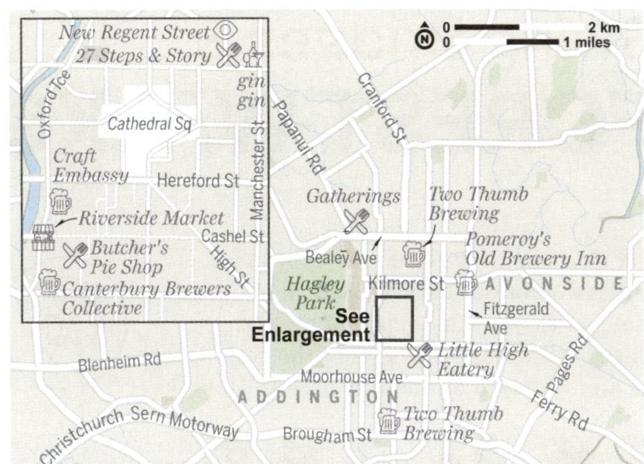

Left New Regent St
Below Riverside Market

Quick eats For a quick meal or to cater to a diverse group of eaters, head to either **Riverside Market** or **Little High Eatery**. Open all day, Riverside Market has a global array of food stalls and restaurants, often featuring culinary contributions from recent arrivals to the city. Further from the river, Little High Eatery offers a range of food including sushi, burgers, barbecue and noodles, and has a fun, informal and unpretentious atmosphere. It can get busy around the dinner rush.

Cocktails and dinner Walk along the Spanish Mission cityscape of **New Regent St** for delicious food options in a charming setting. Grab a pre-dinner cocktail at **gin gin** before heading to a nearby restaurant for dinner – both **Story** restaurant and **Twenty Seven Steps** are excellent choices. If you have the time, venture slightly north of the city centre to try **Gatherings** restaurant, a local favourite and one of Christchurch's top-rated restaurants.

Sample local craft beer Craft breweries are thriving in Christchurch. In the city, order a tasting flight of local brews at the **Canterbury Brewers Collective** at Riverside Market, or take in Avon River views nearby at **Craft Embassy**. On the city fringe, try **Pomeroy's Old Brewery Inn**, and the **Manchester St** or **Colombo St** locations of **Two Thumb Brewing**.

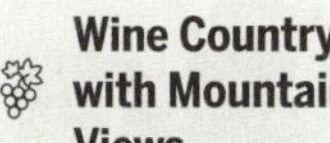

Wine Country with Mountain Views

Take a drive out of Christchurch and explore the North Canterbury wine region. Waipara Valley, on the road to Lewis Pass, has excellent wine, locally grown food and relatively few visitors.

An up-and-coming wine region, North Canterbury is known for its aromatic, cool-climate whites, particularly pinot gris, riesling and gewürztraminer, and is building a reputation for its pinot noir too. There are over 90 vineyards in the region, and **Waipara Springs Winery and Restaurant** makes an excellent destination to stop for lunch and taste some of the region's produce.

42 Swing Bridges & FOREST WALKS

WALKS | DAY TRIP | SWIMMING

Pick your path to the Hokitika Gorge and marvel at the turquoise waters and dense native forest. Stop for a quick photo at the first lookout, or negotiate an easy 2.4km loop trail through the bush and over a swing bridge with wonderful views of the gorge. Stop for a swim at a glacial lake and waterfall on the way back to Hokitika.

RAIMUND LINKE/GETTY IMAGES

How to

Getting here Hokitika Gorge is about half an hour's drive from Hokitika.

When to go There are fewer visitors early in the day or late in the afternoon, although the colour of the water tends to be more intense around midday. Avoid visiting after heavy rain, as the water looks grey rather than deep blue.

Top tip Take insect repellent as there are mosquitos and sandflies in the gorge.

SHAUN JEFFERS/SHUTTERSTOCK

An accessible path to the first lookout Sweeping views of the Hokitika Gorge are visible from a **viewing platform** just a five-minute stroll from the car park. This part of the track is accessible for wheelchairs and prams, and the viewpoint over the gorge and a **suspension bridge** is a great photo stop.

Enjoy a longer detour Traditionally, the path from this first lookout continued across the suspension bridge to a second lookout, and then followed a one-hour loop path back to the car park. At the time of writing, however, the bridge was closed due to flood damage. Instead, make a return 2.4km walk (one hour to 90 minutes) from the carpark via the equally spectacular **upper gorge suspension bridge** to the **second lookout**. Check online at doc.govt.nz to see if the one-hour loop path has reopened for your visit. Onsite signage will also make this clear.

Relax at the second lookout Take a detour through a small gate to the rocks and a small beach at the river below. Take note of the warning signs, as swimming in the river can be dangerous. With pristine waters cascading over the rocks, it's a peaceful and reflective spot.

Take the scenic route back Head back to Hokitika via Lake Kaniere, a half-hour drive from the gorge. Take a picnic and relax by the water. Then head around the lake, back to Hokitika, stopping at **Dorothy Falls**, a cascading waterfall, on the way.

Left Hokitika Gorge suspension bridge
Below Dorothy Falls

Things to do in Hokitika

- Visit the **Glow Worm Dell** after dark to see the glowworms lighting up the trees and the forest.
- Watch the sunset on **Hokitika Beach**.
- Feed the eels and see kiwi at the **National Kiwi Centre**.
- Take a walk along **Lake Mahinapua**, just 10km south of Hokitika. This is particularly good for children, with safe swimming.
- Follow the **Hokitika Heritage Walk** for interesting insights into local history.
- Take a ride on the **West Coast Wilderness Trail** as a day trip or longer.

Recommended by Sharyn & Butch Symons
Hokitika locals and owners of Amberlea Cottages

43 A Family-Friendly ADVENTURE

FAMILY-FRIENDLY | HIKING | SWIMMING

Walk through the forest, alongside a blue, glacial river to a lake with mirror-like reflections of mountains and sky. Camp at the lakeside or stay in a modern hut and spend your time swimming, fishing or simply marvelling at the stars. The track to Lake Daniell is accessible for all ages – you can walk it, run it, stay overnight or just visit for the day.

STEVE TODD/SHUTTERSTOCK

How to

Getting here Lake Daniell is signposted off SH7 near Lewis Pass. It's a 2½- to 3-hour drive from Christchurch, or just over an hour from Hanmer Springs.

When to go Go in summer if you want to swim. During winter, you'll have snow on all the peaks around you – just remember to check for avalanche risks.

What to bring Layers, a swimsuit, sunblock, insect repellent and a raincoat, just in case.

NICKSPLACE/GETTY IMAGES

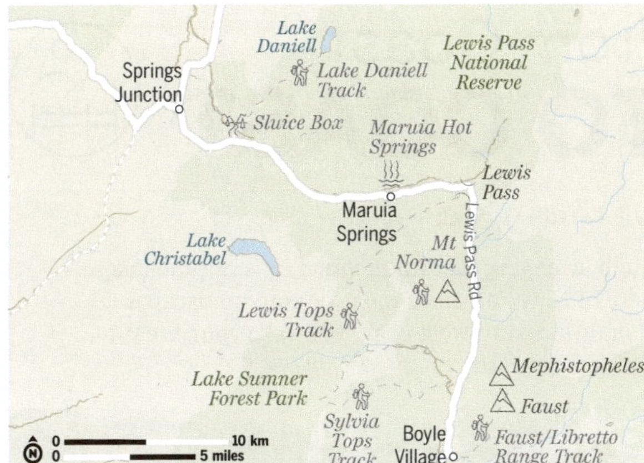

Left Lake Daniell Track
Below Tomtit

A hike for the whole family A great trail for beginners or families, the **Lake Daniell Track** is reasonably flat and takes around two to three hours one way. The route takes you through forests and over bridges with views of the surrounding mountains.

A highlight on the walk is the **Sluice Box**, a narrow channel cut into the rock by the Maruia River. The water is a deep blue and the bridge over the small gorge makes for gorgeous photos.

Relax at the lake The hike culminates at **Lake Daniell**, a clear, shallow lake tucked into mountains. On a still day, the reflections of the nearby peaks in the water make for remarkable photos. Stay overnight to give little legs a rest and make the most of the safe swimming and good fishing.

The DOC hut at the lake has double glazing and a fire, and is very spacious and modern. You do need to book in advance, but that guarantees your bed, which gives you peace of mind when travelling with little ones. There is also a cooking shelter for campers.

Feathered companions The track to Lake Daniell is part of a special biodiversity area, meaning the area is predator-free. As a result, you're likely to see some of New Zealand's favourite birds on the walk, with tomtit, rifleman, tūī, fernbird, silvereye, grey warbler, bellbird, and even kākā living in the area.

Looking for More of a Challenge?

Try one of the several tracks that take you up on one of the peaks, also known as the Tops. There are four to choose from: Sylvia Tops, Mt Faust/Libretto Range, Lewis Tops and Mt Norma.

Go running or hiking, savour the forest, camp by tarns and enjoy the stars.

Then soak it all away at **Maruia Hot Springs**, natural hot pools overlooking rugged, mountainous landscapes. They are geothermally heated and all electricity is hydro generated. The pools are in a stunning location and they have a number of accommodation options.

■ **Recommended by Aaron & Mariska Penman**
Canterbury locals and outdoor enthusiasts

44 From Coast TO COAST

MOUNTAINS | SCENIC TRAIN | NATIONAL PARK

Make your way through sweeping mountain views, past alpine lakes and rivers, and through some of New Zealand's most remote landscapes. The route from the South Island's east to west coast will take your breath away, and fill your camera's memory card.

STEVE HEAP/SHUTTERSTOCK

An Alpine Railway

The TranzAlpine railway connects Christchurch and the West Coast via the spectacular Arthur's Pass. The journey takes just under five hours and meanders through some of New Zealand's most beautiful scenery, including over the Waimakariri River gorge (pictured).

How to

When to go Visit all year round. The pass is especially beautiful between June and October, when the mountains are covered in snow. Use chains in June and July as there can be ice on the roads.

Stop for photos Take your camera and allow extra time for the trip. There are many beautiful viewpoints on the route which are well-signposted.

Top tip Stop in Arthur's Pass village to see the kea, a native mountain parrot.

FROM LEFT: NONTHACHAI SAKSRI/SHUTTERSTOCK, TRAVELFACE/GETTY IMAGES

45 Whales in THE WILD

WILDLIFE | MARINE LIFE | NATURE

See the giant sperm whale up close in the waters of Kaikōura, on the east coast of the South Island. Search for whales by boat or in the air and take in your beautiful surroundings with dramatic mountain landscapes in the distance. If you're lucky, you'll also see a variety of other marine animals including orca, dolphins, humpback whales, seals and sea birds.

WINTAWATWINWIN/SHUTTERSTOCK

How to

Getting here Kaikōura is under 2½ hours' drive from Christchurch. You can also take the scenic Coastal Pacific train from Christchurch or Picton.

When to go Sperm whales are resident in Kaikōura all year round.

Expect to pay \$175 to \$255 per adult. Tours start at \$60 for children.

What to wear Prepare for all weather conditions and bring rain jackets, hats, wind breakers, extra layers, sunblock, glasses etc.

NATALIA KHALAMAN/SHUTTERSTOCK

FELICITY MEADE/SHUTTERSTOCK

Left Dusky dolphin
Far left Sperm whale
Below Yellow-eyed penguin

Getting out on the ocean Spend a day in a boat searching the seas for whales. The giant sperm whale is visible all year round and watching one in the water is a magical experience. There is a high chance of seeing a whale on boat tours (there's even a partial refund if you don't) and on clear days, you can even catch a glimpse of these majestic creatures from shore.

Whale-watching from the sky If you're after an extra special whale-watching experience, head to the skies. Take a helicopter ride over the ocean and mountains and spot the whales from the air. In winter, you can also land on a snowy mountain top, and the scenery is breathtaking all year round.

Meet the other marine visitors There is more than sperm whales to see in Kaikōura. Visit in January, February or March to see the wide variety of species visible off the coast, including dolphins, orca, penguins, seals and albatross. From June to August there is also an opportunity to see other migrating whales, including humpback whales, pilot whales and even blue whales.

The ultimate memento If you are in search of the ultimate scenic photograph, go whale-watching between May and August. The air is clear and the mountains are covered in snow, providing the ultimate back drop.

Tips for Whale-Watching

The weather and sea conditions are very unpredictable – we suggest you prepare for all weather conditions.

Make sure you have plenty of space on your phones or cameras for footage and images. Both the scenery and the marine life you will encounter are worthy of capturing for lasting memories.

If your sea legs aren't great and you tend to get a wee bit queasy on the sea, the local pharmacy has created a lifesaver for sea sickness. Just ask for the 'Kaikōura Cracker' at the pharmacy in town.

Recommended by Abba Kahu
Whale Watch Kaikoura
@whalewatchkaikoura

46 Cycle the Wild WEST COAST

CYCLING | FOREST | HISTORY

Cycle along historic bush tram lines past alpine lakes and through shady forests and wetlands to the rugged coast. Follow the tracks made by pioneering miners and discover historic gold-mining towns and old bridges, with views of the snow-capped Southern Alps in the distance.

ANDREW BAIN/ALAMY

Trip Notes

Getting around The full cycle trail takes four days; however, you can pick a section of the trail for a day trip. It's also possible to drive between the towns and explore your surroundings by foot.

Bike hire There are bike hire and repair shops in the nearby towns of Greymouth and Hokitika.

Luggage transfers You can do a cycle tour which includes shuttles and luggage transfers, or book as a single service.

Sustenance on the trail

Fuel up at these stops along the West Coast Wilderness Trail.

Superior pies, savouries and sweet treats from **Blanchfield's Bakery** in Greymouth.

Pub dining and a locals' welcome at the **Theatre Royal Hotel** in Kumara.

Pizza, wine and craft beer at **Fat Pipi Pizza** near the beach in Hokitika.

FROM LEFT: SIMONBRADFIELD/GETTY IMAGES, HUGH MITTON/ALAMY

Listings

BEST OF THE REST

Meals Worth Lingering Over

Blue Lake Eatery, Tekapo $$

Beautifully presented food in an attractive setting in the heart of Tekapo. Be sure to try the local craft beers from Burke's Brewing Co.

Inati, Christchurch $$$

Innovative fine dining showcasing the best of local and seasonal Canterbury produce. Six- to eight-course menus are a worthwhile investment.

Manu, Christchurch $$$

Pacific and Southeast Asian flavours feature at this recent Christchurch opening. Manu's cocktails are as colourful and vibrant as the Pasifika decor.

Odeon, Christchurch $$$

Versatile dining destination including leisurely Mediterranean-inspired brunches and Middle Eastern shared plates for lunch and dinner.

Great Drinks, Excellent Food

Greedy Cow, Tekapo $$

Go for breakfast or lunch or get a pastry or sandwich on the go and enjoy arguably the best coffee in Tekapo. Located in the centre of town, so grab a snack and eat it by the lake.

Barker's Foodstore & Eatery, Geraldine $$

Stop in for brunch and coffee and enjoy good-sized portions and hearty food. Lots of free samples of chutneys and condiments.

The Welder, Christchurch $$

Superlative baked treats from Grizzly Baked Goods, relaxed Japanese izakaya dining at Bar Yoku, and Mexican flavours at Xolo.

Noki, Christchurch $$

Korean and Vietnamese flavours enliven excellent brunch dishes at this popular cafe worth the short journey from central Christchurch.

Betsy Jane Eatery & Bar, Fox Glacier $$

The best burgers in glacier country. A great option for a filling meal after a long day exploring the national park. The steak and blue cod are also worth a try.

Quick & Affordable Eats

Sheffield Pie Shop $

Stop for a quick bite with some of the most popular pies in New Zealand. Filling, simple fare that's sure to keep you going during your outdoor adventures.

Lyttelton Farmers Market $

Saturday morning music, entertainment and damn fine coffee and eating in the shade of Lyttelton's heritage townscape.

FREEDOMKIM/SHUTTERSTOCK

Pork Belly and Apple Pie, Fairlie Bakehouse

Hokitika Sandwich Shop $

If the bottomless coffee isn't enough to attract you, the substantial sandwiches definitely will be: freshly baked bread piled with local ingredients. Order ahead if you're in a rush as there's often a queue.

Fairlie Bakehouse $

Serving award-winning pies in New Zealand, a must-try if you're in the area. Pies are freshly baked daily, using local ingredients. The salmon pie is especially popular.

West Coast Pie Co, Westport $

World-famous-in-Westport pies crammed with game meat including hare, venison and tahr (mountain goat). Meat is both wild-caught and sustainable.

Craypot, Jackson Bay $

One of the best fish and chip shops on the West Coast, and renowned for its blue cod, whitebait fritters and crayfish. Definitely worth the coastal detour south from Haast.

Spirits, Wines & Beer

Terrace Edge, Waipara $$

Award-winning, organic winery offering aromatic white wine and a small selection of light reds. Opt for the food pairing with your wine tasting to sample carefully prepared local foods.

Reefton Distilling Co $$

A gin-lover's paradise, perfect for long afternoons sipping gin flavoured with local botanicals. Learn about the gin-making process on a distillery tour and also sample the recently released Moonlight Creek whisky.

Shortjaw Brewing, Westport $$

New Zealand malts and hops are used to craft approachable and refreshing brews at this favourite of Westport locals. Try the robust Kiwi Dark lager.

Sir Edmund Hillary Alpine Centre

Heritage, Nature & Hot Springs

Sir Edmund Hillary Alpine Centre

Learn about the life of Sir Edmund Hillary at this fascinating museum. There's a range of memorabilia on display and documentaries to view. Situated in the Aoraki/Mt Cook National Park.

Tekapo Springs

A perfect place for families to stop after a long drive, right in the middle of Tekapo. Relaxing hot pools, offering ice skating in winter, and a fascinating stargazing night-time experience.

Dark Sky Project, Tekapo

Located in the Aoraki Mackenzie International Dark Sky Reserve, this is a wonderful place to see some of the brightest stars in the world. Learn about the southern skies and Māori astronomy or go on a guided tour to Mt John Observatory.

Maruia Hot Springs

A great place to relax tired muscles after a hike, especially in winter. Soak in quiet, peaceful surroundings with expansive bush views. Situated in the Lewis Pass Scenic Reserve.

West Coast Tree Top Walk

Stroll above rimu and kamahi trees for views of Lake Mahinapua and the Southern Alps.

Suitable for all ages and also includes an optional zipline.

Ōpuke Thermal Hot Springs & Spa

In the shadow of Mt Hutt on the outskirts of Methven with family-friendly pools and more private options for adults keen on secluded relaxation.

Punakaiki

Negotiate an accessible and well-formed path for views of the Pancake Rocks, a highlight of driving the spectacular Great Coast Road.

Glacier Adventures & Mountain Expeditions

Franz Josef Wilderness Tours

Go kayaking or fishing or take a cruise in lakes with a mirror-like reflection among the Southern Alps and glaciers. Or challenge yourself by exploring glaciers on foot, by helicopter or on a quad bike.

Mt Cook Ski Planes & Helicopters, Mt Cook

Fly through the Southern Alps, see the lakes and Hochstetter Icefall from the air, and land on New Zealand's longest glacier, Tasman Glacier. Walk along the glacier and explore ice caves if the weather allows.

Mt Cook Heliskiing

Head to the largest heliski area in New Zealand, with alpine guides taking you on the most exciting trails in Aoraki/Mt Cook National Park. Explore the incredible terrain through New Zealand's highest peaks.

Alpine Guides, Mt Cook

Your go-to for guided climbing, mountaineering and glacier hikes. New Zealand's longest established mountain-guiding company can take you on the hidden tracks to make the most of your South Island adventure.

Getting Close to Wildlife

Whale Watch Kaikoura

Gaze at sperm whales, dolphins and seals in their natural environment from an excellent vantage point on the water. A unique opportunity to learn about marine mammals and seabirds in an extraordinary setting.

South Pacific Helicopters NZ, Kaikōura

Head into the sky and see whales, dolphins and fur seals from above. Take a scenic flight over Kaikōura's dramatic landscape and look down on the stunning coast. An exhilarating experience.

Willowbank Wildlife Reserve

A must for learning about New Zealand birds and wildlife and a wonderful opportunity to see a kiwi up close. Wander through the trails and learn about Māori culture and native birds.

Scenic Journeys

TranzAlpine Railway, Christchurch

Take one of the world's greatest scenic train journeys from Christchurch to the West Coast. Admire the remarkable scenery from the viewing carriage or stop along the way to explore the mountains and countryside.

NARUEDOM YAEMPONGSA/SHUTTERSTOCK

Maruia Hot Springs

Kiwi Journeys

Hokitika-based and arranging everything you need to cycle the West Coast Wilderness Trail, including bike hire, shuttle pick-up and advice. Challenge yourself on the four-day ride, or opt for day adventures in stunning natural surroundings.

Underworld Adventures, Charleston

Explore caves adorned with glowworms, try underwater rafting or take a scenic train ride through peaceful rainforest with views of huge karsts. Good for families with older kids and outdoor enthusiasts of all ages.

Local Delicacies

Mt Cook Alpine Salmon, Pukaki

High-quality salmon, sustainably farmed in the glacial waters of the Mackenzie Country. Fresh and smoked options available at the shop, as well as sashimi, which can be eaten on-site with stunning lake views.

Blackball Salami Co

Award-winning producers of excellent salami, black pudding, bacon and sausages. High-quality products with tastings available in store. A great option if you're self-catering during your trip.

Exploring Māori Culture

Āmiki Tours

Culinary walking tours of Christchurch infused with a Māori cultural perspective. Definitely come along with a good appetite.

Te Rua & Sons

Join a guided cultural *hikoi* (walk) along the Arahura River near Hokitika to source

ALISHA NEWTON/SHUTTERSTOCK

Takahe, Willowbank Wildlife Reserve

pounamu, the sacred stone of spiritual importance to Māori.

Pounamu Pathway

Galleries and exhibitions stretching from Westport to Franz Josef via Greymouth and Punakaiki, and telling the story of *pounamu* on the West Coast.

Carefully Crafted Treasures

Bonz n Stonz, Hokitika

Join with the experienced Steve Gwaliasi to spend a day carving *pounamu* or bone into interesting and culturally significant designs.

Hokitika Glass Studio

Beautiful, unique pieces of handblown glass in a variety of colours, including bowls, vases and tiny figurines. Watch the fascinating process of glassblowing and pick a treasure to keep.

Traditional Jade Hokitika

Handmade New Zealand *pounamu* designs, perfect to give as gifts (traditionally greenstone is given, not bought). Learn the meanings behind the Māori symbols or choose a more contemporary piece.

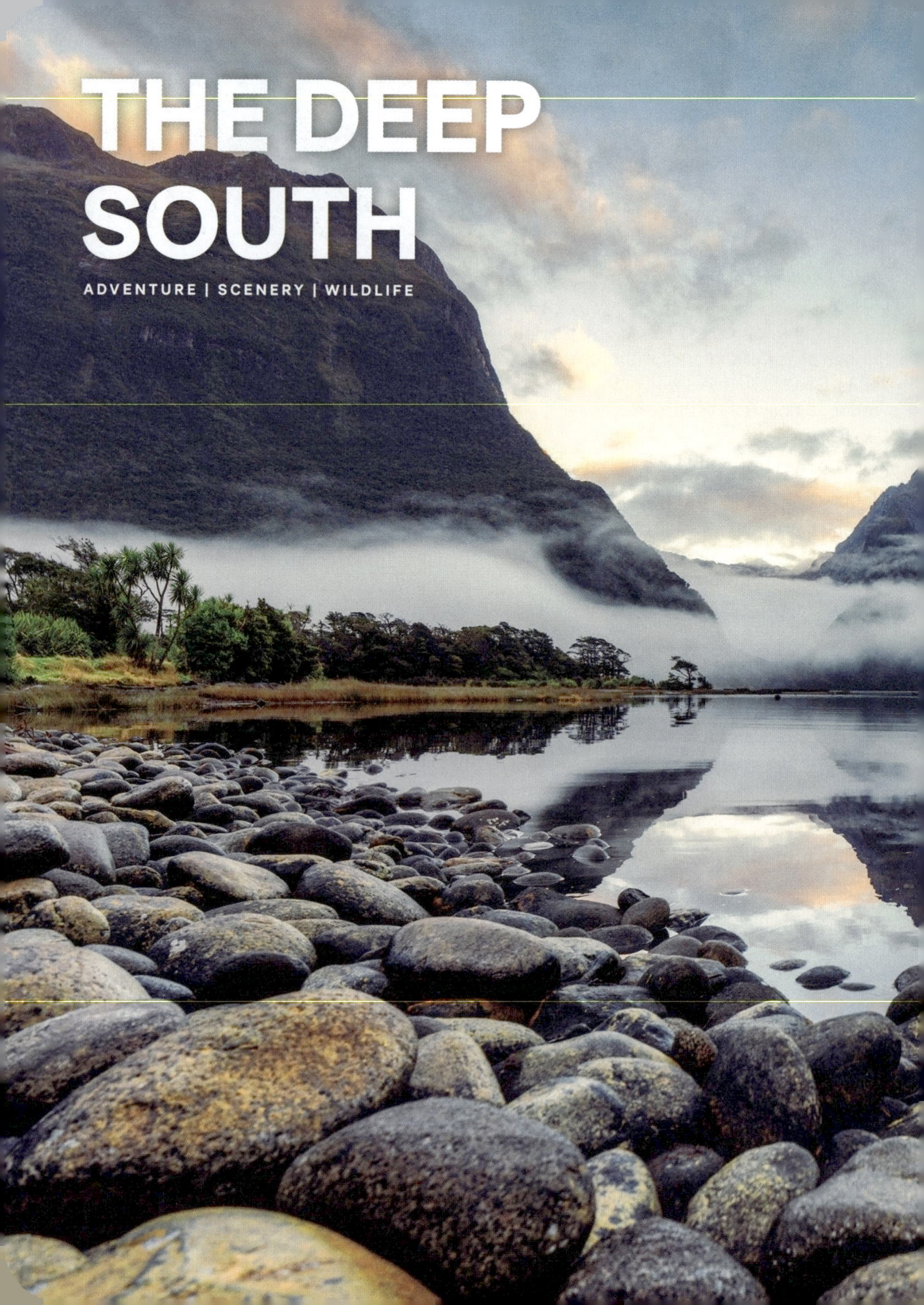
THE DEEP SOUTH
ADVENTURE | SCENERY | WILDLIFE

MUMEMORIES/SHUTTERSTOCK

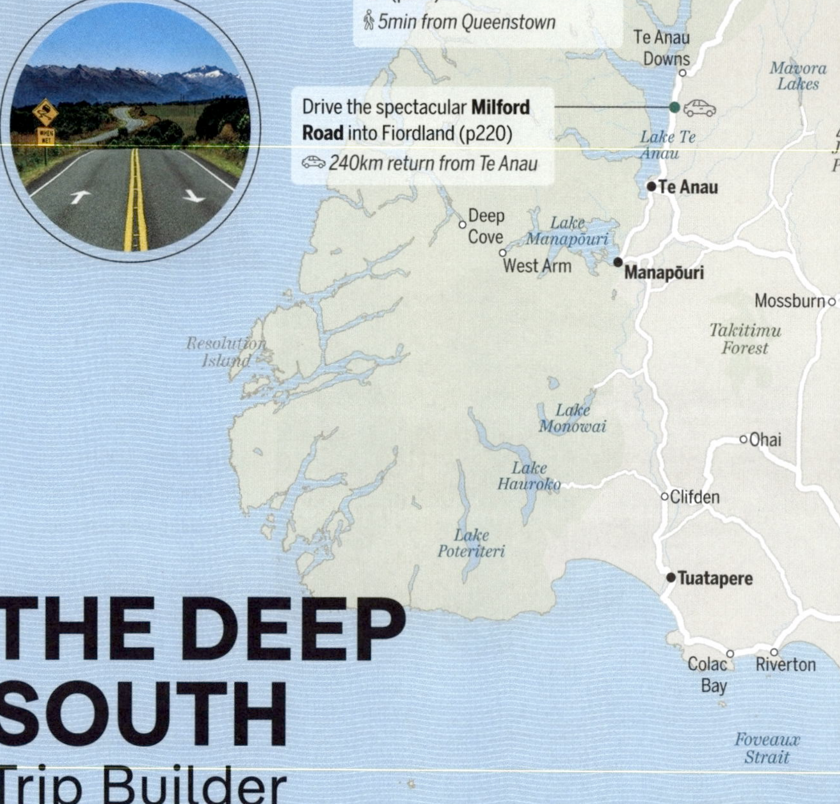

THE DEEP SOUTH

Trip Builder

Think of the Deep South as being a tad like the Wild West. Almost anything goes here, with adventurous mountain resorts, remote fiords and islands, weird and wonderful wildlife, plus historic goldfields and world-famous wineries.

CLOCKWISE: FROM LEFT: ERIK_V/GETTY IMAGES, CUHRIG/GETTY IMAGES, STEVE FLEMING/GETTY IMAGES, PETER KOLEJAK/GETTY IMAGES

Enjoy steampunk and penguins in **Ōamaru** (p228)

5min from Ōamaru

Get on your bike on the **Otago Central Rail Trail** (p230)

1hr from Queenstown

Watch albatrosses soar over the **Otago Peninsula** (p232)

45min from Dunedin

Explore the stunning **Southern Lakes** region, taking in a flash down the slopes at Cardrona Alpine Resort (p218)

day trip from Queenstown

Try legendary local brews at **Emerson's** in Dunedin (p235)

5min from Dunedin

Meet the bird life on predator-free **Ulva Island** (p224)

15min from Oban

Practicalities

STOCKPHOTO MANIA/SHUTTERSTOCK

ARRIVING

Queenstown Airport Located 7km east of the town centre, this is the region's busiest airport and fourth busiest in the country. International flights wing in from Australia. Orbus Queenstown (orc.govt.nz) runs buses into town and around the Lake Wakatipu Basin.

Dunedin Airport Located 22km southwest of the city centre. Shuttles and taxis run into the city.

Invercargill Airport Located 2km west of the city. There are flights from here to Stewart Island/Rakiura (stewartislandflights.co.nz).

HOW MUCH FOR A

Bungy jump $320

Daily lift pass $160

Milford Sound cruise $150

WHEN TO GO

DEC–JAN
The height of summer; expect crowds of Kiwi families.

MAR–APR
Golden autumn leaves; temperatures starting to cool.

JUN–OCT
Snow time at the Queenstown and Wānaka resort ski areas.

NOV–APR
Hiking season on tracks throughout the south.

GETTING AROUND

Your Own Wheels This is a big region with far-flung attractions. Your own wheels provide flexibility and the chance to stop whenever you please. Rental cars, 4WDs and campervans are readily available at major airports and towns. Rental bicycles are all over.

Buses & Shuttles InterCity (intercity.co.nz) operates buses between the region's cities, while shuttle companies run to smaller towns and hiking trailheads. Buses depart daily to the ski areas from the resort towns in winter.

Ferry Hop on the ferry at Bluff for the one-hour crossing of Foveaux Strait to Stewart Island/Rakiura.

EATING & DRINKING

For craft beer, try Altitude (p235) in Queenstown, Emerson's (p235) in Dunedin and Scotts Brewing (p235) in Ōamaru. Central Otago wineries are renowned for their pinot noir, while the Cardrona Distillery crafts fine spirits. Cafes abound, none better than Queenstown's Bespoke Kitchen (p215).

The resorts boast an abundance of eateries. Try venison at Redcliffs (p237) in Te Anau, legendary Bluff oysters (pictured bottom right; season March to August), and don't pass on seafood at the South Sea Hotel (p236) on Stewart Island/Rakiura.

Best bar
Blue Door (p235), Arrowtown

Must-try burgers
Fergburger (pictured top right; p236), Queenstown

TOP: I VIEWFINDER/SHUTTERSTOCK
BOTTOM: MO CHEN/SHUTTERSTOCK

CONNECT & FIND YOUR WAY

Mobile Networks & Wi-fi There is good coverage in the cities and resort towns, but limited coverage in remote mountain areas.

DOC There are DOC visitor centres (doc.govt.nz) in Queenstown, Wānaka, Te Anau, Dunedin and in Oban on Stewart Island/Rakiura.

DRIVING ROUTES SOUTH

State Hwy 1 (SH1) runs down the east coast from Christchurch to Dunedin; SH8 goes through the middle to Central Otago; and SH6 runs between the west coast and Wānaka.

WHERE TO STAY

Visitor hotspots offer good accommodation options; most have places to suit all budgets. Book early for the summer season (November to March) and the winter sports season in the resorts (June to September).

City/Town	Pros/Cons
Queenstown	Plenty of options but can get busy in Aotearoa's top resort town.
Wānaka	Popular mountain and lakeside resort with lots of places to stay and play.
Te Anau	Caters for all budgets as the gateway to Fiordland National Park.
Dunedin	The South Island's second-biggest city is a good base for exploring Otago Peninsula.
Ōamaru	Stay to see the penguins in the evening, but options are limited.
Oban	Book before you go as accommodation is limited on Stewart Island/Rakiura.

MONEY

Check out Queenstown start-up company **First Table** (firsttable.co.nz) for 50% off your food bill when you book the 'first table' for breakfast, lunch or dinner at participating restaurants (rapidly expanding throughout the country).

Climbing Ben LOMOND

HIKING | SCENERY | ADVENTURE

Queenstown may be known as 'the adventure capital of the world', but you don't have to jump in a jetboat or throw yourself off a bridge with a rubber band tied to your ankles to have an exciting outdoor experience.

PETER UNGER/GETTY IMAGES

How to

Getting here Walk up to the Skyline Gondola from central Queenstown.

When to go Best hiking is from November to April; visit Queenstown's DOC office (doc.govt.nz) for track conditions.

Best advice Shorten the day with a gondola ticket (skyline.co.nz), taking two hours and 500 vertical metres off the climb and descent; allow five to six hours for the return hike from Skyline.

Be prepared Ben Lomond's summit is nearly 1500 vertical metres above Queenstown; take warm clothing, sunscreen, and plenty of liquids and snacks.

ANDREW PEACOCK/GETTY IMAGES

Skyline Views

Named after Ben Lomond in the Scottish Highlands, Queenstown's Ben Lomond is the massive mountain that towers almost directly behind town. At 1748m, it provides a spectacular alpine backdrop for Lake Wakatipu and the country's best-known resort.

Thanks to **Skyline Gondola**, however, the peak is surprisingly accessible. The gondola whisks visitors up from town to 800m above sea level at Skyline in five minutes – leaving less than 1000 vertical metres of climbing to the summit. You'll recognise the stunning vista from Skyline's viewing deck from all those iconic images that enticed you to come to Queenstown in the first place. While the township sits far below, **Lake Wakatipu** is a mesmerising deep blue and the rugged Remarkables mountain range dominates

DANNY YE/SHUTTERSTOCK

Bespoke Kitchen

Named NZ's Cafe of the Year only six months after opening, **Bespoke Kitchen** (bespokekitchen.nz) isn't far from the Skyline Gondola's bottom station. Either fuel up for the hike in the morning, or recover here later with tasty delicacies off the menu or from the enticing cabinet choices.

Above left Queenstown views from the Skyline Gondola
Above View from Ben Lomond Saddle
Left Skyline Gondola

to the east. Taking endless photos is as far as most visitors get though.

Climbing to the Peak

Get mentally prepared to go higher. Head out the back of the Skyline building and follow signage for Ben Lomond, initially through and over Skyline's luge tracks, then into the dark Douglas fir forest. By this stage you'll have left the populated world behind. Within 10 minutes, your first views of the peak of Ben Lomond from the track unfold before you, dead ahead. It's a magnificent mountain, if a somewhat daunting-looking climb.

After passing through a patch of native beech forest, you'll be above the treeline and climbing steadily towards Ben Lomond Saddle on a well-formed track, fringed with low-growing tussock. Views to the south and east out over glacial-carved Lake Wakatipu and its surrounding mountains just get better and better as you climb. Once you hit **Ben**

Ben Lomond Tips

Climbing Ben Lomond is a highlight of any trip to Queenstown, but shouldn't be taken lightly. It's a big climb, especially if you walk the whole way to the summit from the bottom of the gondola. I highly recommend using the gondola, at least on the way up, for a more enjoyable day. Don't forget to head out to the Skyline viewing deck for spectacular views before you start walking. The weather can change very quickly up in the mountains. Check forecasts before you go and be adequately prepared.

Recommended by Henare Dewes
mountain and fishing guide
@exploremaorisamurai

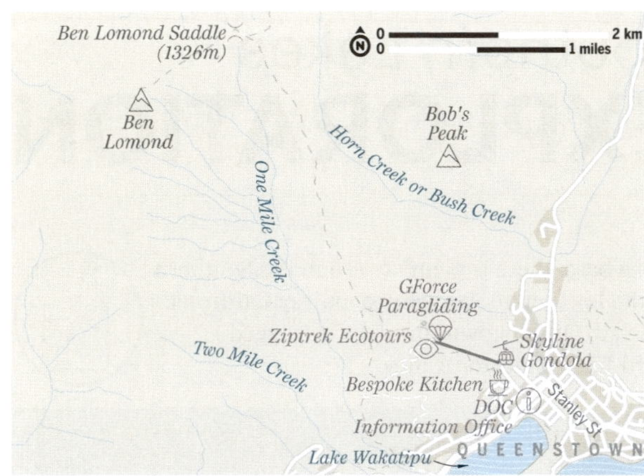

Left Hiking, Ben Lomond
Below Paragliding from Skyline

Lomond Saddle at 1326m, snowcapped distant peaks pop into view to the north, and it's time for a break.

There's still a 420m climb to the imposing peak though, high to the southwest. As you ascend up the ridgeline, the track you walked up from Skyline sits far below, then as the trail curls around near the peak, horseshoe-shaped Moke Lake appears below to the west. After a final push you'll be at the top, with a 360-degree panorama of mountains and lakes. It feels strange to be so high above and looking down on aircraft approaching to land at Queenstown Airport. It's kind of like sitting on top of the world. If you're lucky, kea (alpine parrots) will soar in to see what they can steal from your picnic lunch. They've done this before and work in teams, so don't fall for any of their tricks!

A Quick Descent from Skyline

From the peak, you'll be walking back down to Skyline on the same track you climbed on. Should you be looking for more excitement, a couple of gravity-fuelled opportunities await for the final descent into Queenstown: tandem paragliding (nzgforce.com) down to land on Queenstown School's sports ground, or zipping down through the forest on one of the world's steepest ziplines (ziptrek.co.nz).

48 Southern Lakes EXPLORATION

CULTURE | WINE | HISTORY

With Queenstown as a base, there is plenty to see in the Southern Lakes region. Head out on the big loop to Arrowtown, quirky Cardrona, Wānaka, Cromwell, then back to Queenstown through the rugged Kawarau Gorge and vineyard-filled Gibbston Valley.

JOHN A DAVIS/SHUTTERSTOCK

Trip notes

Getting around Make the most of the day with your own wheels (but you'll need a designated driver).

When to go Year-round. The golden leaves of autumn are gorgeous; the Crown Range Rd can get icy in winter.

Best advice Leave the wineries until later in the day. Do the loop clockwise, heading to Arrowtown first, then over the Crown Range Rd to Cardrona.

Don't miss The Cardrona Bra Fence, opposite the Cardrona Alpine Resort entrance.

My Favourite Wineries

Rippon Vineyard (pictured above; rippon.co.nz) Stunning Lake Wānaka scenery.

Mt Difficulty Wines (mtdifficulty.nz) Winery restaurant in Bannockburn.

Te Kano Estate (tekanoestate.com) Wine, architecture and art.

Mt Rosa Wines (mtrosa.co.nz) Rustic cellar door in the vineyards.

Recommended by Heidi Farren *co-founder of Altitude Tours*

@altitudetoursnz

03 Wander the waterfront and town centre of popular lakeside resort town **Wānaka**. It's hard to beat the backdrop, especially at Rippon Vineyard and Glendhu Bay.

02 At the alpine village of **Cardrona**, drop into the rustic 1863 Cardrona Hotel (cardronahotel.co.nz) for a coffee or Cardrona Ale, visit the Cardrona Distillery, and make a donation to the attention-grabbing Bra Fence.

01 In picturesque **Arrowtown**, walk historical Buckingham St, visit the Lakes District Museum and stroll by the Arrow River in this 1860s gold-rush town. April's Autumn Festival is a highlight.

04 The orchards and vineyards around **Cromwell** beckon with seasonal stone fruits and world-renowned pinot noir. Stroll the historic precinct, pick your own cherries in summer and revel in the countless wineries.

05 **Gibbston Valley** is home to wineries galore and the infamous bungy bridge (if wine has fortified your courage!). The drive to Chard Farm winery is an adventure in itself.

49 DRIVE TO Milford Sound

SCENERY | WILDLIFE | ADVENTURE

With rugged snowcapped mountains, steep-sided, glacial-carved valleys and few roads, Ata Whenua/Fiordland is not the easiest to explore. But, the Milford Rd is, without doubt, one of the most spectacular drives in the world. While many race on through to meet a cruise departure point, it is worth taking your time for fascinating scenic stops and short walks along the way.

How to

Getting here Te Anau is the gateway to Fiordland National Park.

When to go Year-round, though winter driving conditions can be hazardous; occasionally closed due to avalanche danger in winter.

Recommendation Visit Fiordland National Park Visitor Centre and check weather forecasts in Te Anau before you go.

Important There are no petrol stations after Te Anau and limited mobile-phone coverage after Te Anau Downs (28km from Te Anau).

Tasman Sea
Milford Foreshore Walk
Milford Sound
The Chasm
Mt Talbot
Homer Tunnel
Hollyford
Gertrude Valley
Kaka Creek Lookout
Mt Anau (1956m)
David Peak
Fiordland National Park
Lake Gunn Nature Walk
Knobs Flat
Eglinton Valley
Te Anau Downs
Lake Te Anau
Mt Lyall
Mavora Lakes
Fiordland National Park Visitor Centre
Te Anau
0 20 km
0 10 miles

Engineering marvel Before the Milford Rd was completed, the only way to get to Milford Sound/Piopiotahi was to walk on the Milford Track or to sail into the fiord from the Tasman Sea. But since the completion of the **Homer Tunnel**, visitors can drive the 120km to Milford from Te Anau. The 1.2km tunnel is an engineering marvel, a civil works project started in Depression-era 1935, but not completed until 1953.

The high point Jumping out of your car at the tunnel's eastern portal: the road's highest point, 945m above sea level and 99km from Te Anau, is an experience in itself. Sheer granite walls tower above, topped by ice and snow. Mangled steel and concrete by the tunnel entrance and melting piles of ice beside the road pay testimony to violent avalanches that have crashed down the precipitous walls. There's also a boulder-strewn valley, and a thunderous waterfall that drops off the side of 2105m Mt Talbot. Below Talbot's eastern face is aptly named **Psychopath Wall**. The sheer steepness of the valley walls is breathtaking.

Don't be fooled! Adding to the alpine atmosphere, cheeky kea – super-intelligent mountain parrots – emit raucous 'kiyaaaa' calls as they glide in to land on car roofs to see what they can steal or cadge from gullible visitors. This unbelievably rugged setting is Fiordland at its best. Savour it before driving through the tunnel and dropping down into Milford Sound.

Best Stops on the Milford Road

Eglinton Valley (53km from Te Anau) Mind-blowing views of this massive glacial-carved valley.

Lake Gunn Nature Walk (75km) A 45-minute loop walk through ancient beech forest; a top spot to see native birds.

Kaka Creek Lookout (88km) Glorious views into the Darran Mountains and of the Routeburn Track traverse.

Gertrude Valley (97km) A short walk into the valley to a proliferation of native flowering plants in summer.

The Chasm (110km) Short walk through beech forest to dramatic waterfalls.

Milford Foreshore Walk (119km) An enjoyable 20-minute walk with magnificent views out to Milford Sound.

Recommended by Steve Norris *owner of Trips & Tramps, Te Anau* *@tripsandtramps*

Above Approaching the Homer Tunnel, Milford Rd

What's in a Name?

IS IT TIME FOR A FEW CHANGES?

There are some weird and wonderful names in New Zealand. Milford Sound is actually a fiord and the Mt Cook lily is really the world's largest buttercup. Nobody knows who bestowed the name New Zealand on these islands and there's increasing interest in the use of te reo Māori as a language of public life.

Left Milford Sound/Piopiotahi
Centre James Cook
Right Former Prime Minister Jacinda Ardern

SOUTHERN LIGHTSCAPES-AUSTRALIA/GETTY IMAGES

As you drive to magnificent Milford Sound/Piopiotahi, consider this: Milford Sound is not actually a sound, but a fiord. A sound is a river valley flooded by the sea, while a fiord is carved by glacial action. The fiords of Fiordland were misnamed by early European explorers. In 1952, the new national park, highlighting the inconsistencies, became Fiordland National Park, but the individual fiords kept their names as sounds. Confused? Should such historical inconsistencies be corrected?

Who Named New Zealand?

Ask Kiwis who named New Zealand and you'll be surprised at the variety of answers. Many think that it was Dutchman Abel Tasman, the first European to turn up in 1642, but Tasman mistakenly named his discovery Staten Landt, thinking it was part of a land already called that by other Dutch explorers. When Dutch map-makers recognised Tasman's mistake, they needed a new name for his discovery. It's thought that as they already had a New Holland (later to become Australia) on the western side of what is now the Tasman Sea on their map, they labelled their name-needing landmass Nova Zeelandia after the Dutch maritime state of Zeeland.

It took 126 years for the next Europeans to show up. Captain James Cook dropped by in 1769, using a Dutch map, and as the land was labelled Nova Zeelandia on his map, he anglicised that to New Zealand. While New Holland became Australia in 1824, New Zealand didn't have any form of government at that time to consider such a change.

GEORGIOSART/GETTY IMAGES

HAGEN HOPKINS/GETTY IMAGES

Despite few Kiwis knowing where *old* Zealand is, and *new* Zealand having no relationship whatsoever with *old* Zealand, the name has stuck. Between 1840 and 1852, the North Island, South Island and Stewart Island were known as New Ulster, New Munster and New Leinster. Most breathe a sigh of relief on hearing that these names were scrapped.

> Is it time for New Zealand to become Aotearoa New Zealand?

These days, the North Island is also officially named Te Ika-a-Māui (the Fish of Māui), the South Island is Te Waipounamu (the Waters of Greenstone) and Stewart Island is Rakiura (Glowing Skies).

Time for a Rethink?

It's more than 200 years since New Holland became Australia in 1824. Is it time for New Zealand to become Aotearoa? Or Aotearoa New Zealand? There are growing calls for recognition of Māori place names throughout the country, names that fit with an island nation in the South Pacific. Auckland is increasingly becoming known as Tāmaki Makaurau/Auckland – Tāmaki Makaurau meaning 'Tāmaki desired by many', in reference to its abundance of natural resources. Mt Cook has officially been known as Aoraki/Mt Cook since 1998, and the volcano that Captain Cook called Mt Egmont in 1770 is now known as Mt Taranaki.

Polls suggest that Kiwis like the name Aotearoa New Zealand. The practice of performing the national anthem in Māori, then in English, has been in place since the 1990s and, in a similar fashion, it may not be long before the country's name becomes Aotearoa New Zealand.

Road to a Republic?

The British monarch is head of state of New Zealand, presenting an interesting set of conundrums for a modern, egalitarian, immigrant country. A New Zealander cannot become head of state of New Zealand, as the head of state is chosen by birth, and as the British monarch is also the head of the Church of England, New Zealand's head of state can only be of one religion.

A number of former prime ministers, including David Lange, Jim Bolger and Helen Clark, have expressed support for a republic, while recent prime minister Jacinda Ardern believes the country will become a republic 'in her lifetime'. In early 2022, the Māori party called for a 'divorce' from Britain's royal family.

50 Bird Life on ULVA ISLAND

ADVENTURE | WALKING | WILDLIFE

Discover wonderful bird life on the predator-free sanctuary of Ulva Island/Te Wharawhara, a short boat ride from the township of Oban on Stewart Island/Rakiura. Ulva is bristling with birds, including the flightless kiwi and weka, plus species such as the tīeke (saddleback) and mōhua (yellowhead), reintroduced to the island as part of conservation efforts to ensure their survival.

CHRISTIAN HANDL/GETTY IMAGES

How to

Getting here You'll need to get to Stewart Island/ Rakiura first. For Ulva Island, take a guided tour, or for a self-guided visit, take a water taxi from Golden Bay Wharf, just over the hill from Oban.

When to go Best between October and April.

How much? **Ulva's Guided Walks** (ulva.co.nz) $194; **Rakiura Charters & Water Taxi** (rakiuracharters.co.nz) $30 return.

What to take Sturdy footwear, refreshments, wet-weather gear, warm clothing.

DAVID C TOMLINSON/GETTY IMAGES

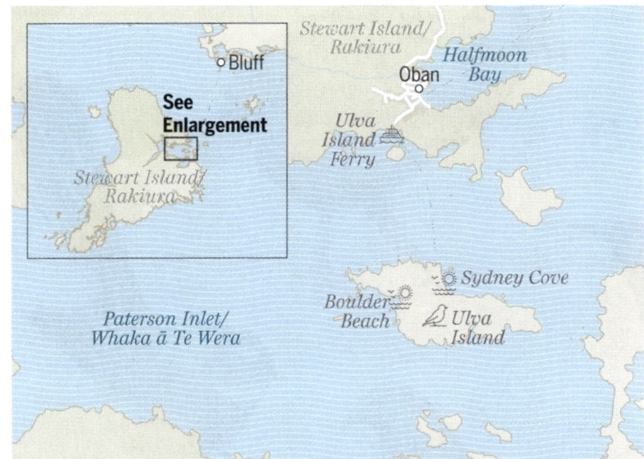

Ulva history This half-day adventure starts with a 10-minute boat ride across Paterson Inlet from Golden Bay Wharf to Post Office Bay on Ulva Island. The post office was a focal point for locals living around the inlet from 1872 to 1923, when the postmaster would raise a flag to alert them that the mail boat had been by. In the 1880s the Tourist Department provided funding for the island's walking tracks, and in 1922 Ulva Island became the first scenic reserve in the country.

Boulder Beach walk Pick up an *Ulva: Self-guided Tour* pamphlet at the jetty and start by walking the track to Boulder Beach (45 minutes). The tracks are in great shape, well signposted and easy to follow. You'll hear myriad calls, similar to the choruses that enthralled early European settlers before the introduction of predators such as rats, stoats and possums that have decimated the country's native bird life. Never milled, Ulva Island has been pest-free since 1997. If you hear scratching in bushes by the track, it's likely to be a flightless weka.

The west end From Boulder Beach, take the track to West End Beach (45 minutes). The stunning native podocarp forest is dominated by rimu, southern rātā and kāmahi, with stands of tōtara and miro. Allow an hour to walk back across to Sydney Cove, then 20 minutes to get back to Post Office Bay to meet your boat.

Left West End Beach
Below Toutouwai

Ulva's Top Tips

If you want to see lots of birds on Ulva Island, the key is to take your time. Don't rush along the trails. Make as little noise as possible and when you come across a bench to sit on by the track, take a seat, watch and listen. If birds come close by, avoid making fast movements. Stay as still as possible. A toutouwai (robin) may even come and stand on your shoe.

You'll be walking under the native forest canopy most of the time, so an umbrella isn't a bad option in rain.

To learn more about Aotearoa's birds and the country's conservation efforts, take a guided tour.

Recommended by Ulva Goodwillie *author of Ulva Island: A Visitor's Guide* *@ulvasguidedwalks*

BIRDS
of Aotearoa

01 Tīeke (saddleback)
A conservation success story, the tīeke takes its name from its call (ti-e-ke-ke-ke-ke) and is better at hopping than flying.

02 Takahē
Thought extinct for 50 years, the flightless takahē has made a comeback after being rediscovered in remote Fiordland in 1948.

03 Pīwakawaka (fantail)
The much-loved fan-tail flits through the forest catching flying insects, enthralling hikers with its incessant chattering.

04 Weka
With a reputation as being curious, cheeky and feisty, the flightless weka is considered a vulnerable species.

05 Kererū
This plump native pigeon was once a major food source in Māori culture, but protection now ensures its survival.

06 Korimako (bellbird)
Surviving well, the korimako's distinctive calls featured in the dawn chorus of birdsong noted by early European settlers.

07 Kea
The world's only alpine parrot, the

endangered kea is intelligent, curious and cheeky, much loved by international visitors.

08 Kākā

The lowland cousin of the kea, the kākā is a large parrot found in native forests and even in urban areas such as Wellington.

09 Kiwi

The flightless kiwi has become so iconic that its name is used worldwide as a colloquial term for New Zealanders.

10 Kōkako

While the blue-wattled North Island kōkako struggles to survive, the orange-wattled South Island kōkako is believed extinct.

11 Ruru (morepork)

A small, mainly nocturnal owl, the ruru gets its more common name from its two-tone call: 'more-pork'.

12 Kākāpō

This large, flightless, nocturnal parrot, rescued from the brink of extinction, survives only on predator-free islands.

13 Tūī

The boisterous tūī, with its distinctive white throat tuft, boasts a noisy, complex song and is flourishing, even in urban areas.

01, 04 IMOGEN WARREN/SHUTTERSTOCK, **02, 05, 07, 09** LILIYA BUTENKO/SHUTTERSTOCK, **03** RON KOLET/SHUTTERSTOCK, **06** DAN WILSON/500PX/GETTY IMAGES, **08** ANDREY OLEYNIK/SHUTTERSTOCK, **10** XAMYAK/SHUTTERSTOCK, **11** TOGLENN/GETTY IMAGES, **12** NAOKI NISHIO/SHUTTERSTOCK, **13** CAROLYN SMITH1/SHUTTERSTOCK

51 Town of CONTRASTS

STEAMPUNK | PENGUINS | CULTURE

The largest town in North Otago, Ōamaru has a couple of fascinating, if contrasting, attractions. It's hard to go past its Victorian precinct, highlighted by Steampunk HQ and the town's claim to be the 'steampunk capital of the world', but it's a totally different ballgame along the waterfront with the nightly return of the penguins at the Ōamaru Blue Penguin Colony.

LUPENGYU/GETTY IMAGES

How to

Getting here Ōamaru (pop 14,000) is 247km south of Christchurch and 113km north of Dunedin. You'll want your own wheels to make the most of the place.

When to go September to February is the best viewing season for penguins; winter numbers may drop to below 20.

Enjoy the penguins Plan your day around the estimated daily returning time of the blue penguins (penguins.co.nz). Take warm clothing; no cameras. Adult/child from $45/28; it's all over in 60 to 90 minutes.

MARTIN PELANEK/SHUTTERSTOCK

RUSLANKALN/GETTY IMAGES

Left Steampunk HQ
Far left Ōamaru
Below Blue penguin

Quacking penguins This surprisingly interesting town deserves at least one night on your journey so you can watch the return of the blue penguins (kororā) around dusk. Almost right in town, at the end of Waterfront Rd, the tiny penguins turn up in groups of 30 to 50 (safety in numbers!), after a day of fishing out at sea. Announcing their impending arrival by quacking like ducks, they make alarmingly inelegant beach landings, waddle tentatively up the rocky beach, avoiding pesky basking seals, then lean forward and start running for home when they hit flat land.

Noisy socialising As they've been feeding all day and have big bellies, there are inevitable balance issues, including the occasional face-plant. When the penguins have found a safe spot, they dry off and preen while socialising, before disappearing into their nests to feed chicks or chatter noisily with their mate. If you want to see what they get up to in their nests, check out the online Nest Cam. Up to 400 penguins return each evening, depending on the season.

The scenic route If you've got kids in tow, the tiny penguins, the world's smallest, are a source of great excitement, especially if they take the scenic route home by jumping some tiny steps and waddling right through the middle of your viewing grandstand, so close that you're bound to get a whiff of their somewhat fishy body odour. It's all part of the fun.

Steampunk Capital

Ōamaru claims to be the steampunk capital of the world.

Steampunk is a quirky genre of science fiction that features steam-powered technology. It's set in an alternate, futuristic version of 19th-century Victorian England – the 'world gone mad' as Victorian people may have imagined it.

Steampunk HQ (steampunkoamaru.co.nz) features an intriguing collection of retro-futuristic, sci-fi art, movies, sculpture and sound in the 'Grain Elevator', an 1883 building at the entrance of the Victorian precinct. Upstairs in the Woolstore Complex, the **Gadgetorium** is a science fiction inventors' emporium showcasing alternate gadgetry, props, curios and collectables of merchant time travellers.

Recommended by Merchant Lucretia
owner, Gadgetorium
@merchantlucretia

52 Ride the Central RAIL TRAIL

BIKING | ADVENTURE | HISTORY

Take three days to ride the 152km gravel trail linking Clyde with Middlemarch, the route of the former Central Otago Railway (1892–1990). The rails and sleepers have been pulled up to produce a popular, family-friendly 'rail trail' for cyclists and walkers.

TRABANTOS/SHUTTERSTOCK

How to

Getting here Clyde is a one-hour drive east of Queenstown; drive yourself or hop on a Trail Journeys shuttle (trailjourneys.co.nz).

When to go October to April.

Practicalities Rent a bike or e-bike, and arrange luggage transfers, vehicle relocation or transport back to Clyde or on to Dunedin with Trail Journeys.

Best direction Allow three days to ride from Clyde to Middlemarch, with prevailing winds behind you.

Accommodation See otagocentralrailtrail.co.nz for options along the trail.

On Your Bike!

If you haven't been on a bike for a while, do a bit of cycling before you come to avoid a saddle-weary backside! Don't rush.

Take plenty of time to see the quaint little towns, meet friendly locals and enjoy the unique Central Otago scenery along the way, including the Poolburn Viaduct (pictured above).

Recommended by Stu Duncan *owner, Wedderburn Cottages* *wedderburncottages.co.nz*

0 10 km
0 5 miles

02 From **Omakau**, you'll pass old station sites, cross rail bridges and pass through dark tunnels on the 30km ride to Oturehua; after a break, there's still 25km to ride to Ranfurly.

03 It's a long last day of 60km from **Ranfurly** to Middlemarch, but the gentle 1:50 gradient required by the steam trains of old is ideal for recreational cyclists and walkers.

Becks
Oturehua
Lauder
Wedderburn
Naseby
Chatto Creek
Ophir
Kyeburn
Waipiata
Kokonga
Daisybank
Tiroiti
Alexandra

04 Thirty-three kilometres into the last day you'll hit **Hyde**; check out the refurbished old railway station and a stone cairn memorial to 21 people who died in a tragic train crash in 1943.

01 Get organised at Trail Journeys at the **Clyde** trailhead. It's 25km to the welcoming Chatto Creek pub (chattocreektavern.co.nz), then 12km to Omakau, target for your first day.

Rock & Pillar

05 Expect to be weary at the end of the trail at **Middlemarch**; from the old Middlemarch Station transport options can take you back to Clyde or on to Dunedin.

Sutton

FROM LEFT: JANICE CHEN/SHUTTERSTOCK, TRABANTOS/SHUTTERSTOCK

53 MEETING the Albatross

WILDLIFE | CRUISE | HISTORY

The world's only mainland breeding colony of the northern royal albatross is only 30km away from Dunedin. Visit Taiaroa Head/Pukekura, first by sea on a Monarch Wildlife Cruise, then on land at the Royal Albatross Centre. Viewing the giant albatrosses with their massive wingspans soaring overhead and nesting at the tip of the rugged Otago Peninsula is positively breathtaking.

IHLOW/ULLSTEIN BILD VIA GETTY IMAGES

How to

Getting around You'll want your own wheels to fully explore the peninsula.

When to go Albatrosses are here year-round, but the best viewing is from December to March.

Best advice Head out along waterfront Portobello Rd to Portobello; make the return trip to Dunedin via Highcliff Rd.

Bookings Book the Double Albatross Combo at albatross.org.nz. Adult/child $114/40; self-drive with 60-minute cruise and 60-minute colony tour included.

SANKA VIDANAGAMA/NURPHOTO VIA GETTY IMAGES

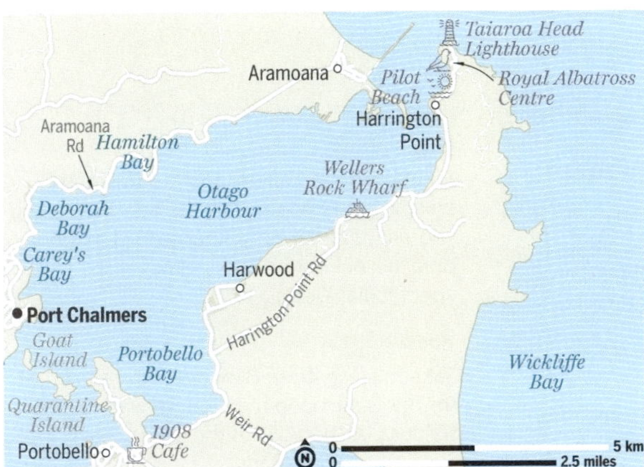

Out at sea Drive out to Wellers Rock Wharf for the cruise part of your combo, with scenic waterfront views over Dunedin, Port Chalmers and the protected inner harbour along the way. The Monarch Wildlife Cruise's sturdy little boat then putters out to Taiaroa Head and the open Pacific Ocean, searching out marine mammals such as blue penguins, dusky and Hector's dolphins, and seals, and keeping an eye out for soaring albatrosses and other seabirds. Over 10,000 seabirds live at Taiaroa Head, many nesting in large numbers on cliff ledges, so spotting birds won't be a problem. The historic 1865 **Taiaroa Head Lighthouse** is high above and it's easy to understand why it was needed to keep approaching ships off the rugged rocks below.

Back on land Back at Wellers Rock Wharf, it's an action-packed short drive to the **Royal Albatross Centre**. Keep your eye out for sea lions (rāpoka) lazing away on **Harrington Point Beach**, while fur seals (kekeno) are regulars at **Pilots Beach**, just below Taiaroa Head. At the centre, the 60-minute guided tour part of the combo includes a fascinating film on the albatross breeding cycle, then a walk to a glassed observatory to view the albatrosses soaring and nesting. Royal Cam is a 24-hour live stream of an albatross nest in breeding season, while a tracking map follows the incredible routes taken around the southern hemisphere by albatrosses hatched at Taiaroa Head.

Left Taiaroa Head Lighthouse
Below Northern Royal Albatross

The Giants at Taiaroa Head

At the tip of the Otago Peninsula lies Taiaroa Head, home to a rather famous seabird with a 3m wingspan: the northern royal albatross.

Guided tours offer an exclusive look into this unique breeding colony. These large seabirds have a long breeding cycle of 11 months, which is great for visitors as there is nearly always something to see.

These giants are a sight to behold when flying by on the breeze over Taiaroa Head, best seen on windy days, with the wind often picking up in the afternoon. Allow plenty of time to enjoy all the centre has to offer.

Recommended by Hoani Langsbury *Ecotourism Manager, Royal Albatross Centre @albatrosscentre*

Listings

BEST OF THE REST

White-Knuckle Adventures

AJ Hackett Bungy

What could be more Queenstown than jumping off the original, 43m-high Kawarau Bridge, with a thick rubber band tied to your ankles?

NZone Skydive

Tandem skydiving with up to 45 seconds of free fall with the Remarkables and Lake Wakatipu as the backdrop. As NZone says, 'embrace the fear!'

Ziptrek Ecotours

Zip down through the forest from Queenstown's Skyline on one of the world's steepest ziplines (they just keep getting steeper!).

Hydro Attack

No sharks in a lake, right? Wrong! Queenstown Hydro Attack's unique submersible 'sharks' dive into and leap from the water at blood-curdling speeds.

Epic MultiDay Hikes

Milford Track

This 54km classic, labelled 'the finest walk in the world' by the *London Spectator* in 1908, leads from the northern end of Lake Te Anau out to Milford Sound.

Routeburn Track

Thirty-three-kilometre alpine adventure over the South Island's water divide in Fiordland and Mt Aspiring National Parks, that can be walked in either direction.

Kepler Track

Sixty-kilometre alpine loop starting and finishing in Te Anau. Walk the beech-forested shorelines of Lakes Te Anau and Manapōuri, plus tussock-covered ridgelines with spectacular views.

Rakiura Track

Take the ferry from Bluff over Foveaux Strait for this 32km loop track on Stewart Island/Rakiura, where 85% of the island makes up Rakiura National Park.

Historic Pubs & Bars

Danseys Pass Hotel $$

It's tough to get more remote than here in the Kakanui Hills between Central Otago and Ōamaru. Drop in for lunch or stay while driving over legendary Danseys Pass.

Chatto Creek Tavern $$

This 1886 classic is a sight for sore eyes and saddle-weary bottoms on day one for those riding the Otago Central Rail Trail. It's 10km to Omakau after a cold beer here!

ROBERT CHG/SHUTTERSTOCK

Skydiving over Queenstown

The Church Manapōuri $$

This Presbyterian church built in the 1880s is now a rollicking restaurant and bar in Manapōuri, 21km south of Te Anau. The fireplace is always blazing in winter.

Blue Door $$

Arrowtown's classic venue for 'tiny room concerts' is loved by everyone. Wander down the side alley to find...a blue door with peeling paint in an ancient stone building.

Vulcan Hotel $$

You can stay at the iconic 1882 Vulcan in St Bathans, Central Otago, but it's rumoured to be haunted. Better to just drop in for a drink!

Best Craft Breweries

Emerson's $$

Born and bred in Dunedin (established in 1992), Emerson's has shiny new premises with brewery, taproom and restaurant on Anzac Ave. The Bookbinder Session Ale is legendary.

Scotts Brewing $$

Down in an old railway building near the waterfront in Ōamaru, Scotts is a popular locals' hang-out, brewing classics like the Harbourmaster IPA and Smokey Joe Smoked Red Ale.

Canyon Brewing $$

Popular Queenstown microbrewery and restaurant based in the Shotover Canyon at Arthur's Point. Innovative stuff going on here, including the Zenkuro Dry, a yuzu rice lager.

Altitude Brewing $$

Award-winning Queenstown craft brewery with changing visiting food trucks at Frankton Marina. Get its brews, including the Mischievous Kea IPA, all over the south.

CHRIS MILLER/GETTY IMAGES

Chatto Creek Tavern

Cafes & Cheap Eats

Bespoke Kitchen $

Queenstown's top spot to prepare for or recover from some major adventuring, with huge choices in enticing cabinet food.

Kai Whakapai $

'Kai corner' in Wānaka is the place to go for the town's best coffee by day. It's a relaxed bar by night; act fast to get a seat outside on sunny evenings.

Sandfly Cafe $

This is one Fiordland sandfly you'll be keen to lay eyes on in Te Anau; jump in here to fuel up before heading out into the wilds.

Ironic Cafe & Bar $

A former NZ Cafe of the Year, Ironic is an innovative Dunedin institution, focusing on seasonal local ingredients and products.

Remote Places to Stay

Kinloch Lodge

At the northwest corner of Lake Wakatipu, fully 70km from Queenstown, this is a remote, historic lakeside beauty, operating since 1868. Enjoy the peace, nature and exquisite cuisine.

Cardrona Hotel

Between Queenstown and Wānaka on the Crown Range Rd, the Cardrona Hotel is an ageless, iconic spot operating since 1863. Rumoured to be the most photographed building in the country.

South Sea Hotel

Remote in that it's on Stewart Island/ Rakiura. This is Oban's one-stop shop with rooms, restaurant, public bar and a legendary pub quiz on Sunday nights that's not to be missed.

Larnach Castle

Built in the 1870s high on Otago Peninsula, this mock castle may be the biggest surprise of your visit to the Deep South. Unique accommodation and dining.

Winter Ski Areas

Coronet Peak

As the closest ski area to Queenstown, just a 25-minute drive from the resort, Coronet is the busiest, with wide open pistes, well-groomed trails and unbelievable views.

The Remarkables

A 45-minute drive from Queenstown, high up in the Remarkables range, this family-orientated ski resort has a good range of runs and an excellent terrain park.

Cardrona Alpine Resort

High above the Cardrona Valley, an hour from Queenstown and 30 minutes from Wānaka, Cardrona has it all, from family-friendly runs to extreme snowboard terrain.

Treble Cone

A 30-minute drive west of Wānaka, this is the highest and largest ski area in the region, with long, uncrowded, groomed runs and gorgeous views out over Lake Wānaka.

Iconic Southern Foods

Jimmy's Pies

A Central Otago classic with its tiny shop in Roxburgh and an unchanged family recipe for five decades. Munch on a Jimmy's all around the south.

Fergburger

You can gauge how busy Queenstown is by the length of the line outside Fergburger, snaking up Shotover St. Known as the best burgers in the world.

Bluff Oysters

Hauled out of the Foveaux Strait each year between March and August, these fleshy delicacies have put the Aotearoa mainland's most southern town on world maps.

Mutton Bird

The sooty shearwater (tītī, aka the mutton bird) was said by one early commentator to taste remarkably like sheep meat. We think more like anchovies... A Deep South delicacy.

Cheese Rolls

A real local experience, sometimes cheekily known as 'southern sushi', these are a slice of bread smothered in grated cheese, rolled into a tube, then toasted.

Fergburger

Galleries & Museums

Lakes District Museum

Built around three historic buildings in Arrowtown's main street, here you'll find Lakes District history, including the gold rushes, plus a top art gallery.

Toitū Otago Settlers Museum

This regional history museum in Dunedin covers the territory of old Otago Province, though its main focus is on the very Scottish city of Dunedin.

Rakiura Museum Te Puka O Te Waka

Home to an extensive collection of historic items, artefacts and photographs, this is the story of Stewart Island/Rakiura; established and run by local volunteers.

Steampunk HQ

Intriguing stuff going on in Ōamaru's Victorian precinct with this fascinating collection of retro-futuristic, sci-fi art, movies, sculpture and sound in the 'Grain Elevator'.

Quality Dining Experiences

Botswana Butchery $$$

On Queenstown's waterfront in historic Archer's cottage, award-winning Botswana's menu has an extensive range of premium meat and seafood options.

Redcliff Restaurant & Bar $$

Te Anau's top restaurant, Redcliff has a reputation for great food, wine and friendly service. Try local hare and venison, straight from the hills.

Muttonbird $$$

Exceptional dining in Wanaka with a changing seasonal menu and an extensive wine list. Try the Muttonbird Mix.

Curio Bay Petrified Forest

Bacchus Wine Bar & Restaurant $$

Award-winning Bacchus, on the lively Octagon in central Dunedin, offers a popular three-course menu, plus extensive cocktail, wine and whisky options.

Weird Geographic Phenoms

Moeraki Boulders

While some believe that these unusually spherical boulders on the beach south of Ōamaru are just balls of mudstone, others think they are alien eggs ready to hatch.

Elephant Rocks

These large weathered limestone rocks in a farm paddock inland from Ōamaru come in a fascinating range of shapes and sizes and are featured in the *Chronicles of Narnia*.

Curio Bay Petrified Forest

Wander out on the fossilised remains of an ancient Jurassic (yes...Jurassic!) forest that is exposed at Curio Bay in the Catlins on the south coast during low tide.

Tunnel Beach

South of Dunedin, take a walk to check out the amazing sea-carved sandstone cliffs, rock arches and caves – and even a man-made tunnel to the beach.

Practicalities

Hiking the Mueller Track (p187), Aoraki/Mt Cook National Park

EASY STEPS FROM THE AIRPORT TO THE CITY CENTRE

Auckland is the primary point of entry for most visitors to New Zealand. Combining adjacent international and domestic terminals, the airport is 21km south of the city centre. Facilities include cafes, restaurants, ATMs and car-rental desks. Christchurch, Queenstown and Wellington also receive occasional international flights (mainly from Australia). Cruise ships are regular visitors, especially from December to March. Popular ports include Auckland, Napier, Lyttelton (near Christchurch) and Port Chalmers (near Dunedin).

AT THE AIRPORT

SIM CARDS
SIM cards for unlocked phones can be purchased from One NZ or Spark. Both have stores in the international arrivals area and branches in central Auckland and main shopping malls. Costs range from $29 (one month) to $49 (two months). NZ E-sims are available online prior to travel.

TRAVELEX
There is has a currency exchange booth (4am–11pm) near the check-in area on the ground floor of the international terminal in Auckland. It also has booths on Queen St, central Auckland's main thoroughfare. There's also a Travelex booth at Christchurch Airport near check-in.

PHOTOS BRIANSCANTLEBURY/SHUTTERSTOCK

WI-FI Free and unlimited in the international and domestic terminals. Select the Auckland Airport network.

ATMS Machines linked to global networks are available in the arrivals hall of the international terminal, and also in the domestic terminal.

CHARGING STATIONS Upstairs, landside near the international departure gate – there are a few seats with adjacent wall sockets using NZ's three-point plugs.

BIOSECURITY IN NEW ZEALAND

As an island nation, New Zealand enforces strict biosecurity rules. Upon arrival, visitors must declare items including food, plants, animal products, and camping and outdoor gear. Check the guidelines online at mpi.govt.nz, and consult border staff when you arrive to ensure smooth entry and protect the country's environment. Fines for failing to declare potentially harmful items can lead to significant fines.

GETTING TO THE CITY CENTRE

SkyDrive ($20) links the airport to Sky City in Auckland's city centre. Buy tickets online at skydrive.co.nz or from the driver.

Super Shuttle (supershuttle.co.nz) provides a convenient minibus service from the airport to city hotels. Book online (per person $35). Shuttles depart from the airport's specialist Transport Pick-Up Zone outside door 11 of the international arrivals area. SkyDrive's departure point is also nearby. Look for signage.

Ride-share services operating from Auckland airport are limited to Uber. The pick-up location is within wi-fi coverage.

Taxis (and Uber) also depart from the Transport Pick-Up Zone outside door 11 of the Arrivals Hall. Depending on traffic, the journey to central Auckland can take up to one hour.

AT HOP Card
Available at Take Home Convenience in the international terminal, this card ($10) can be used for discounted bus and ferry transport around Auckland. Search AT HOP on at.govt.nz.

i-SITE
Source transport information and maps at this visitor information centre in the arrivals hall of the international terminal.

Bus & Train The AirportLink bus travels to the Puhinui train station every 10 minutes from 4.30am to 12.40am. From Puhinui, trains travel on the Eastern or Southern lines to the Britomart station in central Auckland. Total cost is $5.40 and overall travel time is approximately one hour. Credit cards and contactless digital payment methods can be used.

OTHER POINTS OF ENTRY

Wellington airport is located 6km southeast of the city centre. As New Zealand's capital city, it's an important domestic hub, and has direct flights to Australian cities including Sydney, Melbourne and Brisbane. Taxis to the city centre cost around $45 and take from 15 to 25 minutes. Ride-share services are around $40 and transfers with SuperShuttle are from $20. The Airport Express bus is $11.

Christchurch airport is the South Island's main gateway, located 12km northwest of the city. International destinations include major Australian cities, Singapore and Guangzhou. Taxis to the central city take around 25 minutes and cost around $60. Ride-share services are around $40 to $45. For bus transport, take route 29 ($4) to the Christchurch Bus Interchange (30 minutes).

Queenstown airport is 7km east of the town centre. Taxis charge around $55 to the lakefront and ride-share services around $40 (around 20 minutes). SuperShuttle is $30. By bus, catch number 1 ($10, around 30 minutes). Flights to Queenstown from Australian cities increase in frequency during winter.

Auckland is a popular stop for **cruise ships**, with vessels docking at Princes Wharf in downtown. Spring and summer are the busiest times.

TRANSPORT TIPS TO HELP YOU GET AROUND

New Zealand is ideal for road-tripping, and many visitors harness the independence and flexibility afforded by having their own rental car or campervan. Crossing Cook Strait by ferry is a classic Kiwi travel experience, while a trio of tourism-oriented train services showcase some of NZ's finest coastal and mountain scenery. Use frequent domestic flights to get around NZ efficiently.

CAR & CAMPERVAN HIRE

Both can be hired from main cities, airports and tourist towns. Locally owned companies usually offer better rates; vehicles may be slightly older but still in good condition. Unlimited kilometre contracts are recommended and the minimum age to rent is usually 25.

ON-THE-ROAD INFORMATION

The NZ Automobile Association (aa.co.nz/travel) offers destination information and accommodation listings. Emergency assistance is provided for members of affiliated overseas organisations. Visitor information centres are helpful locations to source maps.

Some rental companies are OK with travellers taking their cars with them on the Cook Strait ferry, while others prefer to have renters pick up/drop off different vehicles in either Wellington and Picton. Check specific conditions when you book, including the opportunity to take advantage of special deals the rental car companies often have with the ferry operators, Interislander and Bluebridge. Campervan rentals almost always allow their vehicles to be taken on the ferry.

FERRY Interislander and Bluebridge offer competing services linking the North and South islands across Cook Strait. Sailings can be booked a few days in advance, but school holidays and Easter may require more lead time. A daytime crossing taking in the Marlborough Sounds is recommended.

FLYING Air New Zealand's domestic network of 20 destinations provides the opportunity to fast-track your trip with fast and frequent internal flights. Airfares linking main cities are good value, but can become more expensive for secondary regional cities. Check online with **Grabaseat** (grabaseat.co.nz) for last-minute discounts.

DRIVING ESSENTIALS

Drive on the left: NZ steering wheels are on the right.

.05 Blood alcohol limit is 0.05% (0% for drivers under 20).

One-way bridges are common in NZ. Give way if the smaller red arrow is pointing in the direction of your travel.

Roads in NZ are often narrow and winding.

Fuel prices are cheaper in bigger cities than regional areas.

JAMES HARRISON/SHUTTERSTOCK

ROAD CONDITIONS NZ's weather, particularly in alpine regions, can change from sunny to stormy in a matter of minutes, and washouts and road closures are not uncommon. Check road conditions at journeys.nzta.govt.nz/highway-conditions. In rural areas, a common road hazard is farmers moving cows or sheep. Slow to a crawl, or stop your vehicle altogether, and let the animals move unrestricted. It's a classic Kiwi photo opportunity.

BUSES & SHUTTLES Intercity buses are a reliable and relatively frequent option for linking major cities; in regional areas, locally owned shuttles providing transport for hikers often offer a similar service. Without your own transport, you'll need to join tours to experience nearby attractions and destinations.

TRAINS Great Journeys of New Zealand (greatjourneysofnz.co.nz) offers three scenic train services. The spectacular TranzAlpine runs right through the Southern Alps from Christchurch to Greymouth, while the Northern Explorer links Auckland with Wellington through the sub-alpine expanses of Tongariro National Park. Also in the South Island, the Coastal Pacific runs from Picton to Christchurch, and includes a stop at Kaikōura, a coastal town with excellent marine wildlife watching.

ROAD DISTANCE CHART (KMS)

	Auckland	Christchurch	Dunedin	Invercargill	Napier	Nelson	Queenstown	Wellington
Christchurch	980							
Dunedin	1427	360						
Invercargill	1631	570	210					
Napier	420	760	1104	1307				
Nelson	875	425	775	990	551			
Queenstown	1455	480	285	190	1235	820		
Wellington	640	340	791	995	320	238	815	
Whangārei	160	1230	1584	1788	580	1032	1707	790

KNOW YOUR CARBON FOOTPRINT

Flying from Auckland to Wellington would emit around 120kg of carbon dioxide per passenger. For road journeys, the corresponding emittance per person is 23kg in a bus and 127kg when travelling by car. By train would emit around 18kg per person. To calculate the impact of your own travel, see sustainabletravel.org/our-work/carbon-offsets/calculate-footprint.

SAFE TRAVEL

New Zealand's scenery includes beaches, forests and mountains, and it's important to follow guidelines to safely enjoy getting active in the outdoors. Violent crime is unlikely to impact visitors, but theft from vehicles is an ongoing issue.

SWIMMING SAFETY As an island nation, NZ unfortunately records around 40 deaths by drowning each year. At surf beaches, beware of rips and undertows, which can drag swimmers out to sea, and always swim between the flags where surf lifeguards are on patrol. Extra care should also be taken around lakes, rivers and waterfalls.

ROAD SAFETY NZ's roads are often winding and narrow, and driving is on a different side of the road for visitors from many countries. Take extra care when driving, and if you've arrived after a long-haul flight from North America or Europe, spend a night in your city of arrival and recharge before getting behind the wheel. See drivesafe.org.nz.

OPPORTUNISTIC THEFT Unfortunately it's not unknown for rental cars and campervans to be targeted by opportunistic thieves, especially at unattended car parks at beaches, remote trailhead locations and also some popular tourist areas. It's worth considering taking passports, money and any valuable items with you when you leave your vehicle.

Hiking safety in NZ's great outdoors includes the following guidelines. Log your walk intentions online with **Adventure Smart** (adventuresmart.org.nz) and hire a PLB (personal locator beacon) from local DOC offices for more challenging experiences. See mountainsafety.org.nz.

Krazy Kea Expect the attention of kea, NZ's alpine parrots, in Arthur's Pass or outside the Homer Tunnel. They'll probably have a go at your windscreen wipers, and it's essential not to feed the inquisitive birds.

DRESS FOR SAFETY

NZ's weather is very changeable, especially in mountain areas. Being equipped for 'four seasons in one day' is always a wise idea. Carry waterproof gear and dress in layers to reduce the chance of getting exposure.

RĀHUI

Sometimes visitors will see a beach or other swimming place that has had a *rāhui* (temporary ban) placed on it by local Māori for conservation or cultural reasons. It's important to respect these directives.

QUICK TIPS TO HELP YOU MANAGE YOUR MONEY

CREDIT CARDS (Visa, Mastercard) are widely accepted for accomodation, activities, cafes, restaurants and bars, and are also essential when renting a car. Contactless payment is increasingly the norm, and Apple Pay and Google Pay are widely accepted. Credit cards can be used for cash advances at ATMs and banks, but transaction charges apply. Diners Club and American Express are not widely accepted in NZ.

PAYING THE BILL
While cafes and restaurants may have table service, it's often normal to pay your bill at the counter when you leave.

BARGAINING
Haggling isn't part of NZ's commercial culture. One exception could be purchasing fresh produce at a farmers market at the end of the day.

CURRENCY

NZ dollar

HOW MUCH FOR A

Flat white coffee
$6

Pint of craft beer
$14

Brunch for two
$60

DISCOUNTS & SAVINGS

Most sights, activities and public transport services offer reduced rates for children and senior travellers. Family deals are also commonplace. When booking adventure activities, check websites for combo deals and online booking discounts. Booking direct with accommodation is sometimes cheaper than booking through a third-party website. For occasional discounts on regional flights with Air New Zealand, check grabaseat.co.nz.

TAXES & REFUNDS New Zealand's Goods & Services Tax (GST) is a flat 15% tax on purchases of all domestic goods and services. No GST refund is available to travellers when they leave the country.

ATMS & EFTPOS
ATMs are widespread around the country, including in smaller rural and regional towns. Eftpos terminals – increasingly offering contactless transactions – are ubiquitous for retailers and hospitality venues.

MONEY CHANGERS
Foreign currency can be changed at most NZ banks and licensed money changers like Travelex, but the exchange rate for cash withdrawals at an ATM from your own bank will always be superior.

Tipping is completely optional in NZ and restaurants do not usually add a service charge.

Restaurants The total on the bill is all you need to pay. For excellent service, an additional tip of 5% to 10% can be added. Cafes often have cash tip jars at the counter.

Taxis It's common practice to round fares up to the nearest dollar.

Guides Kayaking and adventure sports guides are happy to accept tips; $10 per person would be appropriate.

RESPONSIBLE TRAVEL

Tips to leave a lighter footprint, support local and have a positive impact on local communities.

ON THE ROAD

Calculate your carbon emissions at sustainabletravel.org/our-work/carbon-offsets/calculate-footprint.

Consider renting an electric vehicle. Car rental companies including Avis, Budget and Go Rentals all offer EVs. Availability is limited so booking well ahead is recommended.

Reduce fuel consumption by regularly emptying your grey-water tanks if you're travelling in a campervan.

Take the Tiaki Promise. Based on the Māori ethos of *kaitiakitanga* (guardianship/protection), Tourism NZ's Tiaki Promise outlines ways for travellers to care for the country's natural landscapes and respect NZ's cultural diversity. See tiakinewzealand.com for videos and information on acknowledging the travellers' promise of 'guardianship' of Aotearoa.

Kauri dieback disease is a significant threat to NZ's iconic kauri forests. Adhere to shoe-cleaning protocols at trailheads, and see kauriprotection.co.nz for more guidelines and advice on track closures.

BIRD AND SKY/SHUTTERSTOCK

GIVE BACK

Support wildlife biodiversity by visiting sanctuaries and protected reserves. Excellent projects across Aotearoa include Sanctuary Mountain Maungatautari and Zealandia.

Eat out for a good cause Active in both Auckland and Wellington, **Everybody Eats** (everybodyeats.nz) is a not-for-profit community-focused organisation providing meals to both drop-in diners and socially disadvantaged people. Shared-table meals are made from produce and ingredients that would normally go to waste.

Contribute to a greener Aotearoa Opportunities to facilitate tree planting, clean up waterways and inspire NZ's drive to offset climate change include the **Million Metres Project** (millionmetres.org.nz) and **Trees That Count** (treesthatcount.co.nz).

Clean up the coastline Join a regular volunteer event with **Sustainable Coastlines** (sustainablecoastlines.org).

DOS & DONTS

Do learn a few phrases in NZ's indigenous language, te reo Māori. Download the interactive Kupu app (kupu.maori.nz) to get started.

Do experience a Māori perspective by seeking out Māori-owned tours and cultural experiences.

Don't enter a Māori *marae* (traditional meeting house) before being invited, and respect the *pōwhiri* (welcoming ceremony).

LEAVE A SMALL FOOTPRINT

Go bush Explore the best of NZ's national parks, Great Walks, campsites and nature reserves with comprehensive and authoritative information from the **Department of Conservation** (doc.govt.nz).

Two-wheeled adventures Set out on NZ's network of scenic cycle trails (nzcycletrail.com). Standout experiences include the Hauraki Rail Trail, the Otago Central Rail Trail and the West Coast Wilderness Trail.

Collect those tote bags New Zealand banned single-use plastic bags in 2023. Tote bags are definitely your friend when shopping at supermarkets and farmers' markets. Pretty handy for a trip to the beach, too.

HAM PHITCHAYA/SHUTTERSTOCK

SUPPORT LOCAL

Eat locally Buy fresh ingredients, artisan gourmet products and good-value food truck surprises at farmers markets around NZ. See farmersmarkets.org.nz.

Make a big impact on small towns Search 'Shop Local' on Facebook for various destinations, including Queenstown and Tauranga, promoting local retailers.

Support tangata whenua Literally 'people of the land', and the name given to Māori. See maoritourism.co.nz for listings of Māori-owned tourism experiences.

CLIMATE CHANGE & TRAVEL

It's impossible to ignore the impact we have when travelling, and the importance of making changes where we can. Lonely Planet urges all travellers to engage with their travel carbon footprint. There are many carbon calculators online that allow travellers to estimate the carbon emissions generated by their journey; try resurgence.org/resources/carbon-calculator.html. Many airlines and booking sites offer travellers the option of offsetting the impact of greenhouse gas emissions by contributing to climate-friendly initiatives around the world. We continue to offset the carbon footprint of all Lonely Planet staff travel, while recognising this is a mitigation more than a solution.

RESOURCES

doc.govt.nz

nzcycletrail.com

sustainabletourism.nz

qualmark.co.nz

maoritourism.co.nz

UNIQUE & LOCAL WAYS TO STAY

New Zealand's accommodation ranges from simple hostel dormitory rooms through to self-contained motels and hip design hotels in the main cities. The country's luxury lodges are among the world's best, while good-value and flexible campervans are a great way to experience NZ's stellar scenery. Beachside cottages – known as 'baches' – are a popular self-catering option for NZ families.

HOW MUCH FOR A

DOC campsite
$20–23/night

Beachside bach
$200–300/night

Luxury lodge
from $400/night

MAXSON_DESIGN/GETTY IMAGES

DOC CAMPSITES

Often in national parks and near the country's Great Walks, campsites run by NZ's **Department of Conservation** (DOC; doc.govt.nz) are usually located in tranquil, secluded and scenic spots. Facilities can include kitchens, showers and toilets. Booking ahead online is recommended for the most popular locations. Note: some more basic sites cannot be pre-booked and only operate on a first-come, first-served basis. It's around $23 per adult/night for a powered site.

Spectacular locations include White Horse Hill in Aoraki/Mt Cook National Park and Fletcher Bay on the Coromandel Peninsula.

HOLIDAY PARKS

A convenient and versatile option for visitors, NZ's holiday parks offer unpowered and powered sites for tenters and campervan travellers, good-value cabins and self-contained units. Well-equipped shared kitchens, playgrounds and games rooms tick all the boxes for travelling families, and in regional NZ, holiday parks are often located near lakes, beaches or rivers.

NIGELSPIERS/SHUTTERSTOCK

LUXURY LODGES

Combining mountain, lake or coastal scenery with excellent food and outdoor adventure, New Zealand's luxury lodges rate among the world's best. Even if you're staying in motels most nights, splurge-worthy luxury options worth considering include the following:

Te Arai Lodge, Mangawhai (tearailodge.co.nz)

Hapuku Lodge + Tree Houses, Kaikōura (pictured; hapukulodge.com)

Lakestone Lodge, Lake Pukaki (lakestonelodge.co.nz)

JUSTIN FOULKES/LONELY PLANET

FREEDOM CAMPING Don't assume it's OK to park up and stay overnight anywhere. It's a significant area of debate in NZ, and freedom camping regulations vary by region, with some local councils providing secure park-up spaces. See camping.org for pre-trip planning and on-the-road information, and download the CamperMate and Camping NZ apps listing council-approved campsites around the country. Nationwide freedom camping legislation finalised in 2024 strictly limits freedom camping to vehicles with onboard toilet facilities and wastewater disposal systems.

CAMPERVAN CAPERS

Offering both independence and flexibility, hiring a campervan is a popular way for visitors to explore New Zealand. Holiday parks feature around the country, most with family-friendly facilities including swimming pools and playgrounds, and the Department of Conservation (DOC) also offers many places to park up overnight in remote and scenic locations.

Another option is **Okay2Stay** (okay2stay.co.nz) 100-plus locations around NZ where program members can park campervans overnight for free for one night if they purchase local products from their hosts.

Members of some overseas travel clubs can also apply to become interim members of the New Zealand Motor Caravan Association (nzmca.org.nz), and stay at their own parks.

BOOKING

Local visitor information centres (i-SITES) are an excellent destination when researching local accommodation options, and can usually make bookings on behalf of travellers.

Booking accommodation in advance is recommended, especially for beach destinations during summer, school holidays and long weekends. Easter is also busy, and booking ahead is recommended during winter in snow-sports hubs, including Queenstown, Wānaka, Methven and Tongariro National Park.

Lonely Planet (lonelyplanet.com/new-zealand/hotels) Find independent reviews and recommendations on the best places to stay, and book them online.

Airbnb (airbnb.com) Wide range of options including city apartments.

Automobile Association (aa.co.nz/travel) Online bookings with a good selection of motels, B&Bs and holiday parks.

Bach Care (bachcare.co.nz) Listings for rentals with many beachfront options.

Bed & Breakfast Association (bedandbreakfastnz.co.nz) B&B and hosted accommodation.

Book a Bach (bookabach.co.nz) Holiday home rentals.

Holiday Houses (holidayhouses.co.nz) Self-contained holiday rentals.

Luxury Lodges (luxurylodgesofnz.co.nz) High-end accommodation.

Rural Holidays NZ (ruralholidays.co.nz) Farmstay and homestay options in rural NZ.

CHOOSE THE BACH LIFE

Renting a bach near the beach is a favourite summertime escape for Kiwi families. Places usually include a barbecue, and maybe bikes, kayaks and fishing gear to make the most of a stay.

ESSENTIAL NUTS & BOLTS

WAITANGI DAY
Commemorating the signing of 1840s Treaty of Waitangi between the British Crown and Māori tribal chiefs, 6 February is NZ's national day.

CHRISTMAS CLOSEDOWN
Many businesses close from just before Christmas to a week after New Year's Eve. Restaurants in Auckland, Wellington and Christchurch often also take a break at this time.

KEEPING FLEXIBLE
Changeable weather can see outdoor activities postponed at the last moment. Build flexibility into your travelling schedule.

FAST FACTS

Time Zone
GMT+12 hrs

Country Code
64

Electricity
230V/50Hz

GOOD TO KNOW

The legal drinking age is 18. Drinking is not allowed near some beaches and in some parks.

Duty-free shopping is available at airports on arrival and departure and at selected retailers.

If you're invited for a barbecue or dinner at someone's house, it's customary to bring along wine, beer or a nonalcoholic beverage.

'Bring a plate' means bring along a dish to be shared with everyone at a dinner party or barbecue.

ACCESSIBLE TRAVEL

NZ accommodation caters relatively well for travellers with mobility issues, and most hostels, hotels and motels are equipped with ramps and one or two wheelchair-accessible rooms.

Wheelchair access is becoming more common at tourist attractions. For advice on local attractions with good accessibility, ask at the local i-SITE visitor information centre.

Tour operators with accessible vehicles operate in most major destinations, and key cities offer 'kneeling buses' and wheelchair-accessible taxis. Rental car companies usually offer vehicles with hand controls, but booking well ahead is necessary.

For active travellers, NZ's Department of Conservation (DOC) has improved wheelchair access to a range of shorter walks. They are categorised as 'easy access short walks' on the DOC website. For winter activities, check out the 'Adaptive' section on snowsports.co.nz.

Firstport (firstport.co.nz) offers guidance on transport for mobility-restricted travellers, while **Ability Adventures** (abilityadventures.co.nz) arranges bespoke NZ tours.

ONLINE AT THE LIBRARY

Public libraries almost always have free wi-fi hotspots, usually also available outside of opening hours.

SMOKING

Smoking is banned in restaurants, cafes and all retailers. Bars may have an outside area where it's allowed.

KEEP CUPS

Most cafes will fill customers' keep cups for takeaway coffee to reduce the use of packaging.

FAMILY TRAVEL

Family discounts Many attractions offer reduced rates for family groups.

Children's menus Midrange cafes, restaurants and pubs often offer a children's menu.

Seat belts Mandatory in all vehicles, including appropriately secured capsules and booster seats for the youngest travellers.

Changing rooms Many shopping malls and some cafes have dedicated rooms for changing nappies.

LetsGoKids (letsgokids.co.nz) Plenty of ideas for family adventures throughout New Zealand.

Kidspot (kidspot.co.nz) Check out the 'Family Fun' section.

MĀORI LANGUAGE

The use of te reo Māori, NZ's indigenous language, is fast becoming more accepted. On road signs, Māori place names are spelled correctly with macrons – indicating an elongated vowel – and don't be surprised if you're greeted with a cheery *kia ora* (hello).

CHRISTMAS AT THE BEACH

It may seem obvious, but some travellers overlook the fact that southern hemisphere seasons are opposite to the north. Look forward to a beach picnic or barbecue if you're visiting for Christmas, and wrap up warmly in July and August.

CREATIVE PHOTO CORNER/SHUTTERSTOCK

LGBTIQ+ TRAVELLERS

Kiwis are generally accepting of same-sex relations and gender fluidity, and laws protecting marriage, adoption and other human rights for same-sex couples were adopted in 2013, ahead of anywhere else in the Asia-Pacific region.

Auckland and Wellington have the most prominent LGBTIQ+ communities, and you're unlikely to experience overt homophobia and transphobia anywhere in an increasingly liberal and tolerant country.

See Gay Stay NZ (gaystaynewzealand.com) for links to many LGBTIQ-hosted accomodation options around the country.

Winter Pride (winterpride.co.nz) makes Queenstown party central in August. **Auckland Pride** (aucklandpride.org.nz) is in February.

Index

000 Map pages

C

D

E

F

G

000 Map pages

H

I

K

L

M

T

U

V

W

Z

"Tough to beat the thrill of a skinny-legged toutouwai (bush robin) jumping on your boot looking for insects to eat on Ulva Island."

CRAIG MCLACHLAN

"The flax outside my office window was flowering as I wrote my chapters, so I was constantly visited by colourful native birds (pictured left). Even in the suburbs, nature brings its 'A' game here."

PETER DRAGICEVICH

"If you're planning on driving the windy, gravel road to Russell instead of taking the car ferry, don't repeat my mistake by ensuring you hire a 4WD."

TOMMY DE SILVA

"After a long drive to the Salisbury Falls on the Aorere River in Golden Bay, my seven-year-old daughter ran with her arms out through a meadow of long, green grass towards the river, shouting 'I'm in my element!' So was I."

ELEN TURNER

"A snow-line helicopter landing high above the glacial expanse of Tasman Lake (pictured above right) is easily one of my top three travel experiences."

BRETT ATKINSON

FROM LEFT: DON HOGBEN/SHUTTERSTOCK, JACKSO0999/SHUTTERSTOCK

THIS BOOK

Commissioning Editor
Jessica Lockhart

Production Editor
Kathryn Rowan

Cartographer
Vojta Bartos

Image Editor
Compton Sheldon

Assisting editors
Melanie Dankel, Kate Mathews, Saralinda Turner, Maja Vatrić

Cover researcher
Daisy Korpics